THE COMPLETE PRACTICAL BOOK OF
—COUNTRYCRAFTS—

THE
COMPLETE PRACTICAL BOOK OF
COUNTRY CRAFTS
Jack Hill

With line drawings by the author

DAVID & CHARLES
Newton Abbot   London   North Pomfret (Vt)

British Library Cataloguing in Publication Data

Hill, Jack
    Complete practical book of country crafts.
    1. Handicraft – Great Britain   2. Country life
    – Great Britain
    I. Title
    680   TT57

ISBN 0-7153-7706-X

Library of Congress Catalog Card Number: 79–51091

Photoset and printed in Great Britain
by Redwood Burn Limited, Trowbridge & Esher
for David & Charles (Publishers) Limited
Brunel House Newton Abbot Devon

Published in the United States of America
by David & Charles Inc
North Pomfret Vermont 05053 USA

CONTENTS

ACKNOWLEDGEMENTS

In compiling this book, the author has been privileged to meet a number of practising craftsmen and women, and is grateful for the willing assistance which they have given. Thanks are due also to a number of individuals and organisations who made available their time, knowledge and facilities, notably Mr Fred Lambert of Worcester, for inspiration; the Museum of English Rural Life, Reading, for the provision of research facilities and for supplying many of the photographs; the Council for Small Industries in Rural Areas, Salisbury, for providing photographs; Frances Head of the publishers, David & Charles, for giving guidance; and a number of colleagues in the teaching profession, for their help and constructive criticism. The writings of an earlier generation of authors on rural matters provided fascinating reading, and many proved to be valuable sources of information — for the reader's benefit, these are listed in the bibliography. Finally, a debt of gratitude is owed to my family, who have had to endure this, my first venture into the world of books, and in particular to my wife, who also typed the manuscript.

Acknowledgements are due to the following for permission to reproduce photographs:

British Industrial Plastics 36, 37
Council for Small Industries in Rural Areas (CoSIRA) 15, 27, 47; and pp 138 (top and bottom), 139, 192 (top and bottom)
Russell Edwards 43
Halifax Museum p 60 (left)
Jaycee Furniture Ltd, Brighton 14
M.C. Photos 46
Museum of English Rural Life, University of Reading 5, 6, 7, 8, 10, 12, 16, 17, 18, 19, 21, 22, 23, 24, 25, 26, 28 (Eric Guy Collection), 29 (Miss Wight Collection), 30, 33, 35, 39, 40, 41, 45, 51, 53
Radio Times Hulton Picture Library 31, 32, 34, 38, 50
C. F. F. Snow 1, 4, 9, 20, 42, 44, 48, 49
Miss M. Wight 13

The remaining photographs are by the author.

INTRODUCTION

There is currently a growing reappraisal of, and interest in, both the countryside and hand-made goods. The products and way of life of our rural past, when the pace was much more leisurely, have taken on a new significance in our busy, industrial present. The idea of the simple country life appeals to many people – a trait which radio and television and the advertising business exploit fully, with village greens and rustic atmosphere as regular features of the popular media. In a society geared to the elaborate technology of mass-production, to population centralisation and the mistaken philosophy that more is better, this step back in time and consciousness is a pleasing sign, attributable, it seems, to dissatisfaction with sameness and the monotony of urban living and to the age-old need to express one's individuality.

That many people of all ages want this self-expression to be of an active, practical nature – want actually to make something with their own hands which is satisfying to creator and observer alike – is manifest in the continuing interest in practical craft subjects of pupils in many schools who are otherwise disenchanted with their secondary, second-hand or second-rate education, and in the increasing demand by adults for part-time day and evening classes in creative crafts of all kinds. The growth of 'do-it-yourself' has been part of this movement too, although, unfortunately, this aspect of self-help has been cheapened by more imitation than imagination and by the too frequent use of unsuitable materials.

This book is concerned with some of the crafts and trades, known generally now as country or rural crafts, which were once an essential part of rural life throughout the whole of Britain. The work was largely of a functional nature, carried out by hand with simple tools, and while it flourished it was respected but rarely extolled. With the coming of the industrial revolution and the increased demand for cheap manufactured goods of all kinds, together with the greater mobility of those goods and of the people who bought them, these village crafts declined. Machines replaced the men and women who had practised them – machines which all too often produced goods in quantity only at the expense of what William Morris has described as fitness for purpose and honesty in design. Many crafts virtually died out, and their few remaining true exponents are extremely difficult to find. Some survived as leisure activities or as folk art – pottery and weaving are two examples – and have attained high status as contemporary creative crafts. Now, with increased awareness of the high level of sound craftsmanship inherent in so many of the crafts of the countryside, more of them have been, and are being, revived.

7

The book's main purpose is to play a contributory role in this revival by acting as a stimulus and as a source of ideas and information, mainly of a practical nature. Coupled with this, it is hoped that the descriptions and illustrations of the old craftsmen and women will help towards a better understanding of their work and their way of life.

Some of the crafts included here were traditionally cottage crafts and can be practised quite easily in the home with the simplest of tools. Others, it is true, require some special pieces of equipment, and details of where these can be obtained or how they can be made are included in the book, together with sources of the materials best suited to the work. For school and college use, the work is suitable for a wide range of abilities and ages from Middle School upwards, and experience has shown that a wide variety of adult recreation groups enjoy these activities and find the work of interest too.

Within these pages every reader will find something of interest to him or her as an individual, whether he or she is a skilled craft worker with a well-equipped workshop, a beginner with little more than the kitchen table, a sharp penknife and a lot of enthusiasm, or even an 'armchair' reader wishing only to learn about the history of these ancient crafts.

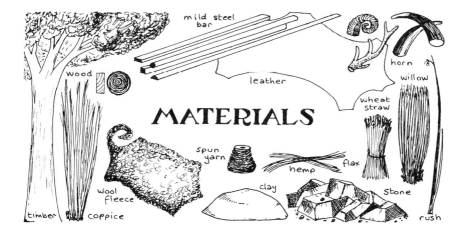

MATERIALS

With few exceptions, the materials used in rural craftwork are all natural materials, i.e. not manufactured. The craftworker handling these basic raw materials is the manufacturer in this sense, and without a knowledge of their properties and capabilities and, above all, their limitations, he is unable to do his work satisfactorily or satisfyingly.

A brief description of all the materials necessary for the craftwork covered in this book is given here, together with sources of supply, including the addresses of some specialist suppliers. Further information about the materials themselves will be found in the various publications recommended for further reading under the appropriate subject title.

Some readers will perhaps already know how to obtain supplies from natural sources; others might like to try, and for this reason brief details of where to look and how to recognise suitable materials are also included where appropriate. Remember that almost all our countryside belongs to someone and permission should be obtained before taking anything from it, however 'wild' it may appear. Bear in mind also the need for conservation.

Wood

Trees, and the woods which come from them, are divided into two botanical groups: broadleaved (or hardwood) and coniferous (or softwood). From a workability point of view, however, all hardwoods are not hard, nor are all softwoods soft.

Only those hardwood species which have been traditionally used in rural crafts are discussed here; the numerous imported hardwoods with strange-sounding names were never used and seem out of place in this work. Softwoods are discussed only briefly as these too are largely imported and, with the exception of pine, were little used in British crafts. All softwoods and most hardwoods are available through good timber merchants (see list of addresses, p 246). Some woods (e.g. apple) are not cut in commercial quantities and so are rarely available from these sources; these are marked with an asterisk.

9

Hardwoods

ALDER *Alnus . . .* *

One of the softer hardwoods, alder grows best close to water. It is frequently seen coppiced or pollarded. Its wood is light in weight and colour; it is resistant to water and is easy to work. Its uses include broom heads and soles for wooden footwear.

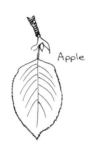

APPLE *Malus . . .* *

One of several 'fruit woods' (another is pear, *Pyrus . . .*) useful in craftwork, apple is a warm brown, even-textured wood. Mainly used in fine carving, it is easily worked yet durable. Common in orchards and gardens. **CRAB APPLE** (*Malus sylvestris*) also grows wild in many places.

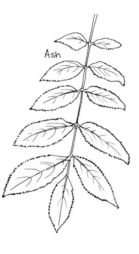

ASH *Fraxinus . . .* *

Sometimes called the toughest timber, ash is notable for its combination of strength and resilience. It grows almost everywhere, but best on limestone. Frequently coppiced; large trees in woods and hedgerows. Readily cleft and easily bent; used in coach building, furniture making, and handles of all kinds – axes, garden tools, sports equipment.

BEECH *Fagus . . .*

Beech is a moderately hard, close-grained wood of even texture. Pale pinkish brown in colour, it keeps its shape well after seasoning. Can be cleft when green, bends easily and is much used in furniture making, toy making and turnery. Used for chisel handles, plane blocks etc. Beech woods common, especially on chalk; old pollarded trees in many areas.

BIRCH *Betula* . . .*

One of the first trees to colonise bare ground, birch is common throughout northern temperate regions and was formerly used for many purposes requiring a close, even-grained wood. Now mainly seen as plywood veneer. Good for turnery and carving, replacing sycamore and beech in Scandinavia and Canada where it is also used in furniture making.

CHERRY *Prunus* . . .

Wild cherry is common in many parts; cultivated species in parks and gardens. Its wood is a warm reddish brown in colour and it is fine-grained and easy to work. Used in furniture making, especially fine cabinet work, and turnery. Musical instruments and smokers' pipes also made from it.

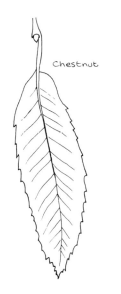

CHESTNUT *Castanea* . . .

The sweet chestnut (not to be confused with horse chestnut, *Aesculus hippocastanum*), is hard and durable and cleaves easily. It is used extensively to make fence palings and as a cheaper alternative to oak in some types of furniture, where it is easily distinguished by its lighter weight. Bends readily and is used 'in the round' to make walking sticks. Found mainly as coppice in southern England; elsewhere as large ornamental trees.

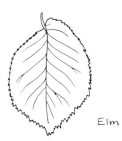

ELM *Ulmus* . . .

Elms of one kind or another are common in many places, predominantly as tall trees in hedgerows. Resistance to splitting is the wood's greatest asset, its interlocking grain and tough texture making it ideal for the seats of stools and chairs, wheel hubs and mallet heads. These same properties make it almost impossible to cleave. Available in wide, sawn boards, suitable for furniture making if well seasoned. Can be steam-bent in small sections. The wood, which has rich grain markings, is not spoiled by Dutch elm disease.

11

Hawthorn

HAWTHORN *Crataegus* . . .*
Common thorn-hedge shrub of agricultural land. Also in woodland clearings and as isolated trees in open situations. The stem is fluted and irregular, but its hard, fine-grained wood, pinkish brown in colour, is useful for small decorative work, turnery, carving etc. Used also for rake tines, tool handles and knobbly walking sticks.

Hazel

HAZEL *Corylus* . . .*
Rarely attaining tree stature, hazel remains shrub-like and coppices readily. Cultivated as an annual coppice crop for hundreds of years, its pliant poles provided material for wattle fencing, hurdles and large baskets. It cleaves easily, but is frequently used in the round, and bends readily when green or after seasoning. Used also for walking sticks and shepherds' crooks.

Holly

HOLLY *Ilex* . . .*
Native evergreen shrub found in woodland and also planted as hedges. Its heavy, white wood, close-grained and hard, is useful for fine carving and turnery: as in the making of chessmen (black pieces are dyed to resemble ebony).

Laburnum

LABURNUM *Laburnum* . . .*
Bright yellow sapwood and dark chocolate brown at the heart makes this a beautiful, lustrous 'two-tone' wood of rare quality. Good for small decorative work, carving spoons etc., and turnery. A common tree in gardens and parks. Poisonous.

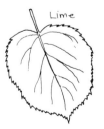

Lime

LIME *Tilia* . . .
Most commonly seen as a street or avenue tree and in parks, the lime or linden yields a soft-textured, even-grained, pale-coloured wood. Excellent for carving, especially fine, delicate work.

12

Oak

OAK *Quercus* . . .

For strength and durability oak is unsurpassed. Its wood is close-grained and hard, yet it cleaves quite readily when green and can be steam-bent. It is used in constructional work of all kinds and also in furniture making, where its attractive 'figure' (grain markings) is used to advantage. Also for carving and turned work. Oak, the dominant native tree, is found throughout the British Isles, from large woodland trees, many of which have been pollarded, to coppiced scrub.

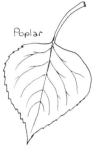
Poplar

POPLAR *Populus* . . .*

A member of the willow family; some poplars have similar properties to willow wood, but were little used in craftwork. The wood of most commonly grown varieties is frequently irregular and knotty, but new hybrids are being grown now for matches, baskets and box making.

Sycamore

SYCAMORE *Acer* . . .

A member of the maple family, known as the plane in Scotland, sycamore is common everywhere. Its wood is moderately hard and close-grained, rather like beech, but its colour is pale creamy white. Its clean appearance and hard-wearing qualities make it very suitable for table tops, bread boards, chopping blocks, spoons and turnery, e.g. rolling pins. It can be cleft and carves easily, especially when green.

Willow

WILLOW *Salix* . . .*

Numerous species and hybrids, usually, but not always, close to water. Many are pollarded. Another 'soft' hardwood, light in colour and weight, willow is strong and quite resilient. It cleaves readily and wood from larger species is used in some coachwork and for tool handles (as a substitute for ash), rake making and, of course, cricket bats. Material from smaller species is used in basket making (see p 17).

13

YEW *Taxus . . .**
A coniferous tree which, strictly speaking, should be in the next section, yew produces a 'hard' softwood. Its russet colours – ivory white sapwood, red-brown heart – and interesting grain markings are much prized for decorative work. It bends well and is used in furniture making and also for carving. Traditionally planted in churchyards and gardens, it grows wild in isolated places.

Softwoods

Formerly used in craftwork in most European countries, though not so much in England, softwoods are mainly imported in large quantities as sawn timbers under a variety of trade names. These including RED DEAL, YELLOW DEAL, REDWOOD (Scots pine, *Pinus sylvestris*) and WHITEWOOD (Norway spruce, *Picea abies*). Also obtainable under certain varietal names such as COLUMBIAN PINE (*Pseudotsuga menzisii*), WESTERN RED CEDAR (*Thuja plicata*), LARCH (*Larix decidia*), etc. Used mostly in construction and joinery work, softwoods are readily available from timber merchants in a range of stock sizes. Selected qualities are used for a variety of other purposes including boat building and furniture making (the now popular 'pine' kitchen furniture, for example). Several species of softwood conifer are grown in British forests. Thinnings from these forests are often available and are sold as 'rustic' poles. These may be used in the round for garden furniture, fencing etc.

14

Seasoning wood

Small and sometimes large pieces of wood useful in much of the work described here may be obtained when suitable trees are being pruned or trimmed back or perhaps removed altogether from gardens, parks, roadsides etc. In some areas it may also be possible to obtain locally cut coppice or to obtain permission to cut it yourself. All such material, newly cut, is referred to as 'green'. It contains a great deal of moisture in the form of sap, even when cut in the winter time, and this must be reduced by the process known as seasoning. As the moisture content of wood is reduced, shrinking takes place, and uneven or too rapid shrinkage can lead to warping (twisting) and the formation of shakes (splitting). To minimise this problem the following points should be observed:

1. Do not try to hurry the seasoning process. Initially, leave the material outdoors in good air circulation but protected from rain and direct sun. If the wood is to be used indoors it should be moved first into an unheated workshop or shed before going into a heated room.

2. A year for each inch of thickness is the period often recommended for natural seasoning. This applies to wide sawn boards and varies in any case from one wood to another and according to the time of year. For green branch or coppice material of up to 2in (50mm) in diameter two to three months outdoors followed by the same amount of time indoors is usually all that is needed. Larger material will need proportionally longer.

3. Long straight branches or coppice poles should be stacked on end, butt down.

4. Seasoning time is reduced if bark is removed, but seasoning with it left on seems more satisfactory. Some old woodsmen 'scorched' or scored the bark, i.e. removed it in patches or strips as an aid to the process.

5. As moisture is given up at a higher rate by the open grain of ends of pieces, these areas can be sealed with wax or varnish to reduce any tendency to split.

6. If wood is to be cleft it is best cleft when green, then stacked to season. Rough shaping or turning can take place at this stage, due allowance being made for shrinkage.

7. For seasoning sawn boards bought not fully dry, refer to notes 1, 2 and 5 above. Boards should be stacked flat with sticks (spacers) between each board at about 12in (300mm) intervals to allow free circulation of air.

8. Thorough seasoning is essential for good work, and material should not be used until really dry. Modern home heating will soon remove excess moisture, often with disastrous results. If in doubt, wait.

Iron

Wrought iron is now in very short supply and expensive, and for almost all blacksmithing work mild steel is the material in general use today. Unlike most of the other craft materials discussed here, steel is a manufactured material bought in as required from specialist stockists.

There are several different types of steel available, all alloys of pure iron with a little carbon; they vary mainly in the amount of carbon which they contain, and it is this which affects their working properties. Common mild steel, which

15

should contain about 0.25 per cent carbon, can be forged and welded within a fairly narrow range of temperature, and while it is less malleable than wrought iron and less resistant to corrosion it has the advantage of possessing greater tensile strength. It cannot be successfully hardened or tempered to retain a cutting edge, however; for this work a high carbon steel is required.

Mild steel can be obtained from stockists in the form of flat, square, round, half-round, hexagonal and angle bars in various stock sizes and different lengths.

Leather

Leather is obtained by treating the skins of certain animals in the processes known as tanning. Tanning one's own animal skins on a small scale is not impossible, but it is much more usual to buy material ready tanned. Leather is usually sold as complete skins measured by the square foot ($300mm^2$). The total measurement includes all the irregular shapes such as leg and neck parts, but an allowance is usually made for damaged areas or cuts.

The most important consideration is to obtain leather of the correct type, pliability and, above all, thickness for the work to be done. For harness straps, belts, hard cases and bags etc., cowhide is best; this can be obtained either smooth or artificially grained, natural-coloured or dyed. It is also available as hide split which is thinner, coming from skins which have been sliced through their thickness to provide leathers of varying weights. These vary in quality and usefulness, the undersplit – the layer nearest the flesh side of the skin – often tearing easily. Calfskin is a thin skin usually of good quality. Sheepskin is soft and supple and is useful for bags, clothing and so on. It is often sold dyed in a variety of colours and is generally artificially grained. Suede is the flesh side of calfskin or sheepskin, specially treated to bring up the familiar velvety surface; this is another soft material. Pigskin is extremely soft and supple, and genuine pigskin is also strong and hard-wearing, but it is often imitated. Very thin leather sold as lining leather or lining split is only really suitable for its intended purpose.

Horn

This general term embraces horns from several different animals, mainly cattle of various types, but including also deer and sheep.

Traditionally, hornworkers obtained much of their raw material from nearby slaughterhouses. Although some may still be obtained from this source, modern abattoir methods and the breeding of naturally polled (hornless) cattle have reduced this to a minimum. Horn obtained in this way will require cleaning by boiling in water and common soda, changing the water at frequent intervals. Afterwards it must be thoroughly dried without heating before use, otherwise it will warp. Bone can be cleaned in the same way and then bleached, either naturally in the sun or in a 20 per cent solution of hydrogen peroxide for up to forty-eight hours.

Most of the horn used today is imported, usually from Africa. This comes mainly from Ankola cattle, whose horns grow to over 3ft (90cm) in length. It is sold as ox horn and may be purchased by weight, either as entire horns in various lengths or as flat sections in random sizes. These sections come from hollow horn which has been opened out and pressed in hydraulic presses. It is also possible to flatten small pieces of horn, after first heating them, in a press such as those used by printers or between the jaws of a vice. Solid ox-horn tips arc sold by the piece. Deer antler is also sold in this way, according to size. Of course, if you live in 'deer country' you may be lucky enough to literally pick up antlers for nothing. Some imported ram's horn is available, but it tends to be rather thin and scaly; the heavy, more solid variety which is best for craftwork is now very scarce.

Willow, Rushes and Straw

Salix purpurea

S. triandra

S. viminalis

Willow

There are well over two hundred different members of the willow family (*Salix*), of which the osiers used in basket making are only one branch. Three species specially cultivated for making baskets are *Salix purpurea*, which produces slender rods up to 4ft (1.2m) in length, *Salix triandra*, which gives good quality rods up to 7ft (2.1m) in length, and *Salix viminalis*, which produces a stouter rod up to 10ft (3m) long and is used in coarse baskets, fish traps, hurdles etc.

Specialist growers and merchants sell willow in bundles which traditionally measured an old English 'cll' – 45in (113cm) – in circumference. Today bundles vary, but average about 37in (93cm), the measurement being taken at the base of the bundle. A bundle of 4ft rods weighs about 26lb (12kg), but some retailers will sell smaller amounts by weight. Bundles are graded by their length from 3ft (90cm) upwards. Some of the old names for different types and sizes are still used in the trade – Black Maul, Red Root, Dicky Meadows and many others. Some kinds of wild willow may also be used, including the stems which grow from certain species of pollarded willow trees. Most of these are tough to work with, but even so it is well worth trying them out if one has access to a supply, and especially if they are free. Many are useful as bottom sticks and sometimes also as side stakes. Other wild materials used in what are called hedgerow baskets include hazel, poplar, mountain ash (rowan) and bramble stems.

17

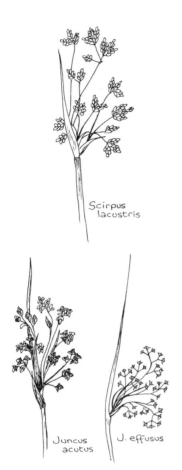

Scirpus
lacustris

Juncus
acutus

J. effusus

Rushes

These are aquatic or semi-aquatic plants, the different kinds being extremely difficult to identify botanically. The English freshwater 'bulrush' normally used for basketwork and seating is now generally considered to be *Scirpus lacustris*, although material does vary, presumably through varietal differences and place of growth. Many rushes are now imported from abroad, and these include Sharp's rush (*Juncus acutus*), which grows in tidal estuaries; known also as the Great Sea rush and the golden rush, it is shorter and thinner than the English bulrush and is used mainly in seating. Another of this genus, *Juncus effusus*, grows near fresh water in Britain, and although generally too short for seating it is useful for weaving small articles such as table mats.

Rushes can be cut in the summer – though not, according to custom, before the longest day (21 June) – or bought from someone who harvests them. The number growing in the British countryside is now very small, owing partly to river pollution and partly to the better drainage of many rivers under the care of the Water Authorities, and harvesting rights are jealously guarded. Most retailers of native rushes also sell imported ones. All are sold in bundles known as bolts, which should measure about 40in (1m) around the base, length varying generally according to the species.

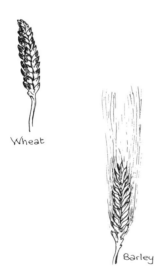

Wheat

Barley

Straw

Wheat straw suitable for thatching and straw decorations should be of the hollow, long-stemmed varieties. For thatching it should be autumn- rather than spring-sown, the longer period of growth making for a more durable straw which will have a longer life on a roof. The old varieties of wheat which had these qualities have generally been superseded by short-stemmed wheats, pithy-centred and more suited to the combine harvester. The straw from these is not suitable for traditional straw work, and in any case it is chopped into short lengths by the combine. Some hollow-stemmed wheats are still grown, some of them especially for thatching, although a fair amount is imported for this purpose. Varieties such as Squarehead Master and Victor are hollow-

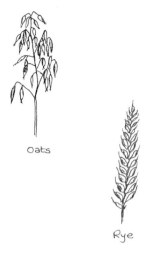

Oats

Rye

stemmed, and more recent ones include Elite Lepeuple and Maris Widgeon. These last are not quite so long in the stem but are suitable for corn-dolly making. Oat and rye straw is also suitable, but barley is not.

Ideally, suitable material should be cut just before the crop is ripe – that is, while the first joint below the ear is still green. Permission should of course be obtained, and even then just a little taken from the edge of the field. Gleaning after the crop is harvested is an alternative, but the straw is usually a little brittle in use when obtained in this way. Straw for corn-dolly making can be obtained commercially – in some places it is grown specially for this purpose – but very few craft suppliers stock it.

Fibres

Wool

There are as many different types of wool as there are breeds of sheep, and there are over forty of those in Britain. Add to this the various mixtures of spun fibres now available and the range is even greater. For spinning, raw fleeces may be obtained, graded according to type and breed. Wool fibre may also be bought in the form of rovings – wool which has been machine-carded and is ready for spinning. A commercial system of numbering from 100 downwards is used as an indication of the length, and thus of the spinning capabilities, of a particular fibre, wool from British breeds ranging between about 60 and 30 – referred to as 60s and 30s. Wool in the 40s to 50s range is easy to spin and makes good-quality yarn.

Machine-spun yarn is readily available and is used by many hand weavers in order to save time. A wide range of yarns can be obtained, some of them virgin wool of one type, others mixtures of virgin wools of different types and yet others which are mixtures of virgin wool and reclaimed wool obtained by shredding discarded woollen garments and factory waste. The quality of these latter mixtures decreases as the quantity of reclaimed material increases. There are also wool mixtures containing varying percentages of synthetic fibres.

Spun yarn is given a number determined by the length required to make up 1lb (.45kg) in weight, this number being known as the 'count'. The count also gives the weaver some indication of thickness and weight; the thinner and lighter the yarn, the higher its count number. The count actually refers to the number of standard-length hanks or skeins needed to make up the pound: for example, a standard skein of worsted wool yarn is 560yd (512m) and if four skeins are needed to make a pound the yarn has a count of 4 (4s). Worsted, with a count of 6 (6s), is therefore a finer yarn and there is more of it in a pound. If a second number is present, either 2/6s or 6s/2, this indicates a two-ply yarn, still a pound in

19

weight but only half the length of a single yarn. A metricated system is now replacing this centuries-old method.

The choice of yarns is dependent on the work to be done and should be suited to the intended purpose of the finished material. Stiff or very coarse yarns are ideal for wall hangings but not for scarves or skirts. Warp yarns must be strong, for they are kept under tension throughout the weaving process; some yarns are marked specifically for warping purposes. On the other hand, weft yarns need not be so strong, and in fact it is possible to weave with a wide range of weft materials.

Rope

All the fibres traditionally used in making rope came from plants. The most important has always been hemp, *Cannabis sativa*, botanically related to the nettle which was itself once woven and made into yarn. Hemp used to be grown in large quantities in Britain, particularly in Dorset, but now all supplies are imported from abroad. Hemp makes a strong rope which can be rather coarse-looking but is reasonably smooth to handle.

Manilla, similar in appearance and strength to hemp, is made from the leaf fibres of a tropical plantain and lays up into a smooth rope which is easy to handle. Cheaper ropes are made of sisal and jute, both of which are rather rough and whiskery. Sisal, which comes from the leaves of a species of agave, is white in colour, while jute is brown. Flax, *Linium usitatissimum*, is used in the manufacture of some cords and lightweight ropes which technically are known as lines — hence clothes line.

When a rope is required to float it is made from the fibres of coconut husks, which are known as coir. Coir rope is hairy and brown in appearance and, having only about a quarter of the strength of hemp, has to be made up much thicker than ropes made from other materials. It is commonly seen woven into mats. Cotton makes a smooth, soft white rope, easy to work but not as strong as hemp. Horsehair was often incorporated into rope where extra softness was required. In the rope trade hemp, jute, flax and cotton are described as soft fibres, manilla and sisal as hard fibres.

A number of man-made or synthetic fibres are now much used in rope making, their main qualities being strength, elasticity and resistance to water. Terylene, nylon, polyethylene and polypropylene are the main synthetic materials being used. Spun yarn of all these natural and synthetic fibres, suitable for stranding and laying up into cords, lines and ropes of various sizes, is available from commercial suppliers. Often, waste material from the spinning factories is suitable, particularly yarn normally used in the manufacture of carpets.

Clay

In most places, if one digs down through the soil, clay will be found. It may be quite close to the surface — just below the topsoil in fact if your garden is 'poor', the soil heavy and frequently wet — or it may be deep down beneath the subsoil. Often the best source is on local building sites or at road works where mechanical diggers have exposed beds or pockets of clay. The clay will vary in substance, of course, according to the geology and the geological history of the area, and in quality according to the amount of impurities which it contains. The distinctive characteristics of the simple ware produced by traditional potteries are the result of these two important features of locally dug clay. Instructions for dealing with clay dug or 'won' in this way will be found in the appropriate chapter.

The winning of one's own clay is satisfying, but it can be arduous, and most people prefer to buy clay from a commercial supplier. Suppliers' catalogues list a wide range of clays specially prepared for specific purposes. Clays are usually referred to as clay bodies, and those ready for use as plastic (in the broad sense of the word).

For general purposes, clays come in three main types. Ivory or white clay is intended mainly for commercial production methods; it is quite frequently used for hand work but it can be rather difficult for the inexperienced. Red clay is a low-temperature clay which is much easier to work with. It retains its colour after firing and is very suitable for making the familiar red, porous earthenware, which can of course be glazed to render it waterproof. Buff clay is actually grey in colour when purchased, its colour coming from organic materials present in the raw clay. These burn off during firing leaving the buff colour which gives it its name. It works nicely and fires equally well at a range of temperatures from about 1100°C up to 1300°C, making it suitable for both earthenware and stoneware; the higher temperature at which the latter is fired makes it hard and non-porous even before glazing. Some clays have grog (ground-up, fired clay particles) or sand added to them; this reduces any tendency to sag during firing, especially at high temperatures.

Stone

Geologically, rock or stone is divided into three groups: sedimentary (limestone, sandstone, etc.), igneous (granite, etc.) and metamorphic (slate, ragstone, marble, etc.). Some are soft and weather easily (sandstone), while others are extremely hard and durable (granite). From a workability point of view, the important feature is the ease with which stone can be shaped into flat, rectangular or near-rectangular pieces, and this is dependent upon its natural cleavage lines. Certain stones cleave or split readily – slate and ragstone, for example – while others, such as granite, do not. Some walls, however, are built with irregularly shaped stones, and it is these which are the real test of the waller's skill.

Wherever possible, the stone used should be local material, not only so that it will blend well with its surroundings but also in order to keep transport costs to a minimum. Stone can be obtained from stockists or, more frequently, direct from quarries in slab or block form, either dressed – that is shaped into ready-to-use rectangular pieces – or as 'random stone', as quarried. Where it is for wall building this should be specified, otherwise stone intended for garden rockeries may be supplied, and this is not always suitable. Stone reclaimed from old buildings is a likely source of supply, especially in urban areas.

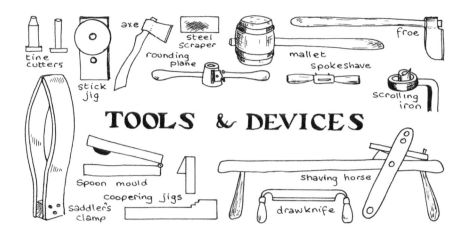

The tools and other pieces of equipment used by many old craftsmen remained unchanged for centuries. Most were of simple construction, in keeping with the technology of their time, and some, in comparison with modern tools, may appear clumsy and difficult to use. In the hands of a skilled craftsman, however, such tools were capable of producing work of a high standard in spite of their apparent simplicity and often crude construction. Some remain in use to this day, and even their more modern counterparts, although perhaps slightly different in construction and appearance, rely on the same basic principles of design and function. Chisels and saws have changed little in a thousand years; many modern boring tools still use the ancient auger principle, and plane blades still have the same cutting angle in their modern steel housings as they did in their beech blocks centuries ago.

Some tools have changed, however, and some are no longer available, while others, little used now, are fast disappearing from manufacturers' catalogues. A lot of tools and devices were never made commercially but were the work of the individual craftsman, or of the local blacksmith if they were made in iron or had a cutting edge. Many such items have now become collectors' pieces and are both difficult and costly to acquire. Not all of the tools and devices traditionally used for the work described in this book will be readily available, therefore, and where items referred to are unobtainable, modern substitutes will have to be used instead. Where feasible, tools may be made specially to suit the work, as they were in former times. This chapter is concerned with tools available from manufacturers, suitable substitutes, and methods of constructing your own simple tools and devices.

The use of certain modern tools, and in particular the use of electrical or other mechanical aids, may be frowned upon by some purists who believe it to be contrary to the whole idea of country crafts. To some extent this is a fair argument; but in practical terms, where items have replaced traditional tools which are no longer obtainable, or where they can save time and unnecessary repetitive effort, there is little harm in making judicious use of them providing that this does not

WALKING STICK BENDING JIG

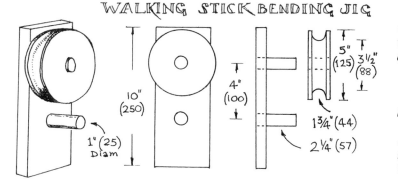

10" (250)

4" (100)

1" (25) Diam

5" (125) 3½" (88)

1¾" (44)

2¼" (57)

Pegs are 1"(25) hardwood dowel. Grooved ring turned on a lathe is made a loose fit. Make several as the ring remains in the stick until it is dry & set

SHAVING HORSE OR MULE

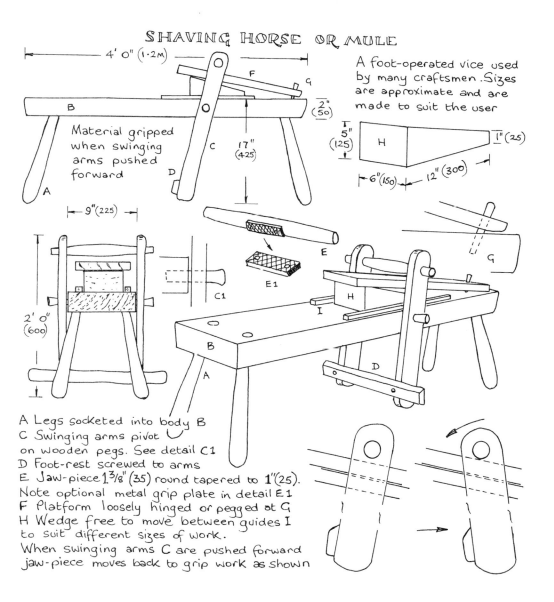

4' 0" (1.2m)

F

G

B

2" (50)

A foot-operated vice used by many craftsmen. Sizes are approximate and are made to suit the user

Material gripped when swinging arms pushed forward

C

17" (425)

D

A

9" (225)

5" (125) H 1" (25)

6" (150) 12" (300)

E

E1

C1

2' 0" (600)

B

A

H

I

D

G

A Legs socketed into body B
C Swinging arms pivot
on wooden pegs. See detail C1
D Foot-rest screwed to arms
E Jaw-piece 1⅜" (35) round tapered to 1"(25).
Note optional metal grip plate in detail E1
F Platform loosely hinged or pegged at G
H Wedge free to move between guides I
to suit different sizes of work.
When swinging arms C are pushed forward
jaw-piece moves back to grip work as shown

lower the standard of craftsmanship. Some of the village craftsmen themselves went over to more up-to-date methods of working and to various forms of powered machinery as they became available. Sadly, it was their inability to compete with even newer and bigger machines which finally put many of them out of business altogether.

One of the most interesting characteristics of the old country craftsmen was their ability to reduce to a minimum, within the limited means available to them, the many problems and difficulties inherent in their work. This is best seen in what might be described as their economy of effort. If a gadget or device could be made to simplify their work or help do the job better, they made it. Often it was a simple device, and in many cases it has never been improved upon. One such aid was the simple jig around which walking-stick handles could be bent and left to set to the desired shape. Another, more widely used device was the shaving horse, mule or mare – its precise name depending upon the area or particular craft in which it was being used. A very effective, quick-release, foot-operated vice, the shaving horse became an almost indispensable aid in a number of crafts. Instructions for making a stick-bending jig and a shaving horse are included in the diagrams.

Of the tools traditionally used in the various wood-based crafts, most are either still available or easily replaced by an alternative. The drawknife, widely used in a number of crafts, is a good example. It is still listed in some toolmakers' catalogues, and although no longer made in as wide a range of sizes and types as formerly, it is well worth searching for. A pleasing tool to use if kept well sharpened, it is suitable for rough shaping and fine chamfering. The spokeshave is perhaps the nearest substitute; the old-fashioned wooden ones, which regrettably are no longer being made, are the nicest to handle. Second-hand wooden spokeshaves can occasionally be obtained at a reasonable price, especially if they are in poor condition. Often the blades (which were hand-forged) are sound, and if the mouth of the stock (the area around the cutting edge of the blade) is badly worn, this can be repaired by cutting it back square and inserting a new piece of wood. Alternatively, a complete new stock can be made from well-seasoned beech. The modern steel spokeshave is adequate, and more easily adjusted for depth of cut, but it is rather heavy in use.

A simple tool still available but little used today is the steel scraper or cabinet scraper. This is a hand-sized rectangle of thin steel used to impart a smooth finish to a wooden surface; the job may be finished by rubbing with glasspaper, but in skilled hands the scraper alone will suffice. The secret of the good steel scraper, apart from the quality of its steel, is the way in which it is sharpened. Its edge should be trued up on an oilstone and then burred over at the correct angle to give a fine cutting edge, just sufficient to take a thin curl of shaving off the wood.

By way of contrast, the tool once expertly used for roughing out – and for some finer work too – was the axe. No self-respecting carpenter would have been without one at one time; its edge was kept razor-sharp, and woe betide the young apprentice who relegated it to the role of chopping firewood! The axe best suited to fine shaping is the lightweight side axe, so called because one side of the blade has a flat face. This type of axe can still be obtained, though the modern hand axe, which usually weighs about 1½lb (675g) and has a wedge-shaped blade or head, may also be used. To be effective both must be kept really sharp. For cleaving short billets of coppice wood the wedge-shaped head is ideal, and for this work sharpness is of less importance. The back of the axe-head is struck with a wooden beetle or mallet — never with a steel-headed hammer, which could cause dangerous splintering of the metal surfaces. Instructions for making a beetle are given in the diagrams. Also used for cleaving was the tool known as the froe, its name derived from the ancient English word 'froward' because its blade cuts away from rather than toward the user. This seems to have been an item made almost exclusively by local blacksmiths to suit local needs, and details of how to make one in the same way are included here.

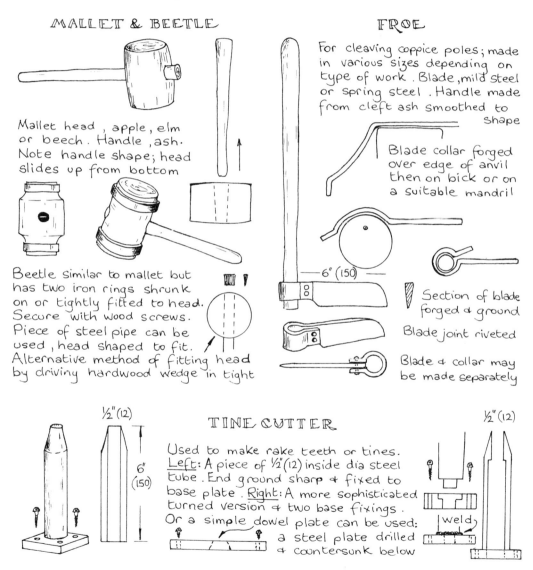

MALLET & BEETLE

Mallet head, apple, elm or beech. Handle, ash. Note handle shape; head slides up from bottom

Beetle similar to mallet but has two iron rings shrunk on or tightly fitted to head. Secure with wood screws. Piece of steel pipe can be used, head shaped to fit. Alternative method of fitting head by driving hardwood wedge in tight

FROE

For cleaving coppice poles; made in various sizes depending on type of work. Blade, mild steel or spring steel. Handle made from cleft ash smoothed to shape

Blade collar forged over edge of anvil then on bick or on a suitable mandril

— 6" (150) —

Section of blade forged & ground

Blade joint riveted

Blade & collar may be made separately

TINE CUTTER

½" (12)   ½" (12)

6" (150)

Used to make rake teeth or tines. Left: A piece of ½"(12) inside dia steel tube. End ground sharp & fixed to base plate. Right: A more sophisticated turned version & two base fixings. Or a simple dowel plate can be used: a steel plate drilled & countersunk below

weld

Still made, though in nothing like the number of different local types which were once obtainable, are the slashers and billhooks used in coppice work and in hedging. Good tool merchants stock them, as do many rural hardware stores. The long-handled adze of the type used by the old carpenters or by chair-bottom makers is rarely seen now, but a heavier type, similar to the shipwright's adze, can still be bought. A small hand adze is also obtainable, marketed ostensibly for roughing out on large-scale sculpture work.

One useful old woodworking tool which has been rescued from obscurity is the device known variously as the stail engine or rounding plane, originally used chiefly for making wooden handles (stails) for rakes and brooms and rungs for ladders. A modern version made entirely of metal – the traditional tool had a wooden stock – has been developed by Mr Fred Lambert of Worcester. Known now as rotary planes, or more simply as rounders, these tools are available in a range of four sizes. Functioning on the same principle as some pencil sharpeners, they will produce long 'turned' cylinders of wood without the use of a lathe. A further tool known as a trapping plane will produce tapered lengths as required.

When using a rotary plane, the wood to be 'turned' is cleft or sawn to between $\frac{1}{8}$in (3mm) and $\frac{1}{4}$in (6mm) over the required finished diameter and the corners are chamfered to fit the large end of the rounder. With the material held vertically in a vice, the tool is placed over the end of the wood and moved round and downward with a turning action. The 'turned' piece may then be tapered if required – to make chair legs, for example – using the trapping plane. For this the material must be rotated while the tool is held still. The tools use standard spoke-shave blades, and full instructions for use are provided by the suppliers, whose address is given on p 248.

The simple stock brace, made chiefly of wood and used, together with a fixed auger bit or, later, a range of different-sized bits, for drilling holes in wood, disappeared from general use a long time ago. It was replaced by various types of steel brace, one variety fitted with a ratchet chuck to take a choice of square-shanked bits or drills – the familiar brace and bit. Other types include the wheel brace and breast drill, both operated by turning a geared wheel by hand. These tools are excellent for drilling small holes in soft wood, but the electric-powered drill is easier on the arm muscles when drilling hardwoods or metal.

Similarly, modern cross-cut and rip saws, if kept properly sharpened and set, are as effective in use as their ancestors. However, for some work, such as sawing down large lengths of timber, the use of the powered circular saw is not to be frowned upon. In this context it should be noted that the laborious saw-pit method of converting timber into usable sizes by hand sawing survived only until suitable powered saws were developed to do the work instead. For sawing curved shapes the traditional bow saw, with its frame made in wood and its blade tensioned by a twisted cord, is still available, although today's models are not quite as large or as robust as the earlier ones. The modern machines which can do this work just as effectively and with far less effort are the electric hand-held jig saw and the powered band saw. For wood turning, lathes driven by electric motor are in general use almost everywhere today, and machines operated by treadle, or by small boys turning large flywheels, are to be found mainly in museums.

COOPERING JIGS

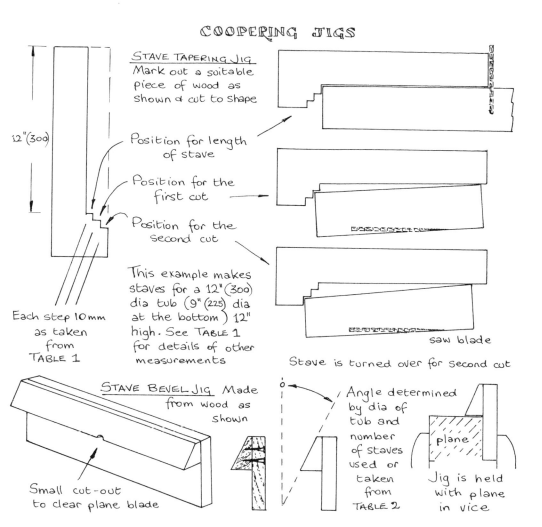

STAVE TAPERING JIG
Mark out a suitable piece of wood as shown & cut to shape

12"(300)

Position for length of stave

Position for the first cut

Position for the second cut

This example makes staves for a 12"(300) dia tub (9"(225) dia at the bottom) 12" high. See TABLE 1 for details of other measurements

Each step 10mm as taken from TABLE 1

saw blade

Stave is turned over for second cut

STAVE BEVEL JIG Made from wood as shown

Small cut-out to clear plane blade

Angle determined by dia of tub and number of staves used or taken from TABLE 2

plane

Jig is held with plane in vice

The specialist tools of the cooper and the wheelwright ceased to be made a long time ago, and most are now collectors' items, figuring prominently in 'what is it?' questions on television and in magazines devoted to mainly rural matters. Both crafts require great skill and no little strength in the manipulation of these special tools, and because of this, and the fact that such tools may well be unobtainable, the practical work described later for these two crafts has been simplified so that it can be carried out with more readily available tools. In addition, two useful coopering aids are described in diagram form.

A number of craftsmen in wood need to bend their material for the work they do: coopers and chair makers are just two examples. Unseasoned wood in small section is easily bent, but for larger-section material the fibres of the wood must first be softened by heating, usually by means of saturated steam at atmospheric pressure. No special tools are required for steam bending, but certain items of equipment are needed: a steam chest in which the wood can be made pliable, a

27

STEAMERS

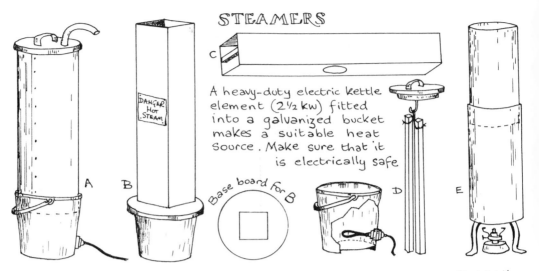

A heavy-duty electric kettle element (2½ kw) fitted into a galvanized bucket makes a suitable heat source. Make sure that it is electrically safe

Base board for B

A   B   C   D   E

In A, above, a piece of sheet metal has been rolled & riveted to fit tightly into a galvanized bucket. It is fitted with a lid & a steam outlet pipe. B is a box section, 6"x 6" (150 x 150), made in marine grade plywood; ½"(6). It fits on top of a bucket on the base board shown & it is fitted with a lid. C is the same type of box which can be used in a horizontal position. D shows the method of suspending pieces for steaming inside the steamers — racks are used in the horizontal box. E is a specially made cylinder with an extension piece, heated by means of a gas or oil stove

BENDING AIDS

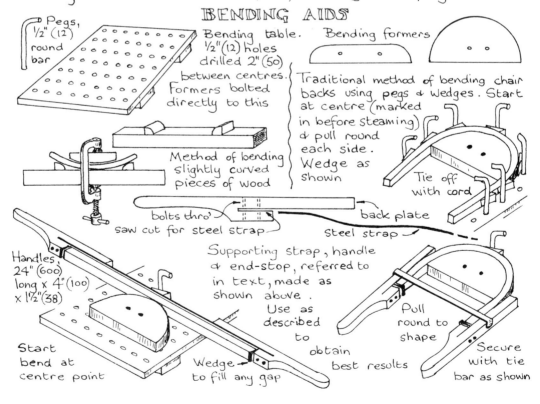

Pegs, ½"(12) round bar

Bending table. ½"(12) holes drilled 2"(50) between centres. Formers bolted directly to this

Bending formers

Traditional method of bending chair backs using pegs & wedges. Start at centre (marked in before steaming) & pull round each side. Wedge as shown

Tie off with cord

Method of bending slightly curved pieces of wood

bolts thro'
saw cut for steel strap

back plate
steel strap

Handles 24" (600) long x 4" (100) x 1½"(38)

Supporting strap, handle & end-stop, referred to in text, made as shown above. Use as described to obtain best results

Pull round to shape

Start bend at centre point

Wedge to fill any gap

Secure with tie bar as shown

bending table or frame and a number of formers or jigs on which various shapes can be bent, together with some means of clamping the work in position until it has set in its new shape. Instructions for making and using these items are given in the diagrams.

Most species of English hardwood can be bent in this way; ash, beech, chestnut, elm and oak are all suitable. The wood should be free from knots, straight-grained, and preferably cleft rather than sawn. Pieces for bending should not be in contact with the sides of the steamer, as this may cause the wood to be badly stained. Approximately one hour per inch of thickness is sufficient to bring the wood to the proper condition for bending. This must be done quickly, before the wood has time to cool, and two pairs of hands are useful at this stage of the work. The wood is bent round the former with a smooth, steady motion, fixed in position by tying or by means of a suitable clamp, and held there until the bend is 'set'. The setting time varies greatly according to the species of wood used, its thickness and moisture content, and so on. At normal room temperature ash of $1\frac{1}{4}$in × $1\frac{1}{4}$in (32mm × 32mm) section is best left for about a week before use. Bends tend to straighten out somewhat even when set, and for this reason it is advisable to bend to a slightly smaller radius than is actually required.

In bending, wood is subjected to two induced stresses which cause the fibres on the convex side of a bend to stretch under tension while those on the concave side are compressed and shortened. It is the first of these stresses which is the cause of most failures when bending wood, and the use of supporting straps and close-fitting end-stops is a means of minimising this problem of stretching (see diagram). The flexible steel strap should have an inner lining of thin aluminium or other plastic material to prevent staining. The back plates help support the end-stops and prevent any tendency for them to swivel under pressure, while the handles provide additional leverage. A simple supporting strap with or without end-stops used with the traditional peg-and-wedge method of bending shown in the diagram gives improved results if the strap is kept in close contact with the convex surface throughout the bend. To hasten drying and thus setting, and to free the bending table for other work, bends may be removed from the former, but the supporting strap should be left in position to avoid fractures on the stretched convex face. Several hours on the former followed by several more with the strap in place gives satisfactory results.

To turn now to the tools and equipment used in other crafts, most of the blacksmith's tools are still listed in makers' catalogues, but the range is small compared to what it used to be. Most blacksmiths made a lot of their own tools anyway, and this is true of many of those still working today. Anvils, swage blocks and some swages, hammers and some tongs were bought in, and these are still obtainable; but a much larger number of tongs of special shape, chisels, punches and so on have always been 'home'-made. Basic forgework requirements can be obtained from the address given on p 248.

Similarly, the hand tools used in the leather trade are still readily available, and instructions are given here for making a useful clamping device. A good deal of leatherwork is still being done by hand, and it seems likely that these tools will continue to be manufactured. General-purpose craft knives, if kept really sharp,

SCROLLING IRON

1

2

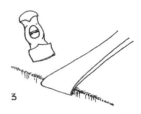
3

4   5

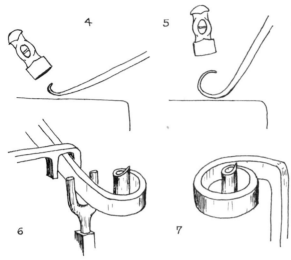

6   7

1. Make a full-size drawing of scroll; scroll tool conforms to inside edge of this drawn shape
2. Forge off   fishtail on end of piece of 3/4" x 3/8" (19 x 9) bar
3. Cut end square & roll tip over edge of anvil as shown
4 & 5. At red heat the scroll is rolled on face of anvil, both metal & hammer blows coming steadily up to near vertical until end is nicely tucked into the centre.
6. Bending continued with horns & wrench. Check against drawing.
7. Completed tool; right-angled bend made to fit hardy hole or for gripping tool in a vice

SADDLER'S STITCHING CLAMPS

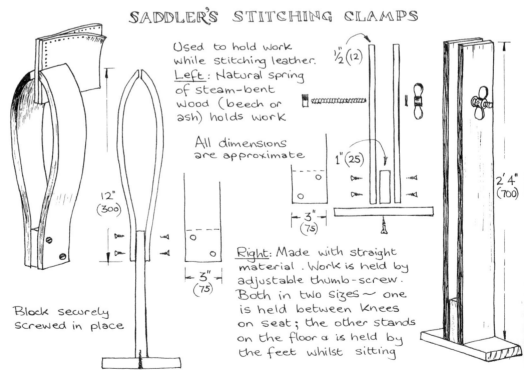

Used to hold work while stitching leather.
Left: Natural spring of steam-bent wood (beech or ash) holds work

All dimensions are approximate

12" (300)

3" (75)

Block securely screwed in place

1/2" (12)

1" (25)

3" (75)

2' 4" (700)

Right: Made with straight material. Work is held by adjustable thumb-screw. Both in two sizes ~ one is held between knees on seat; the other stands on the floor & is held by the feet whilst sitting

HORN SPOON MOULD

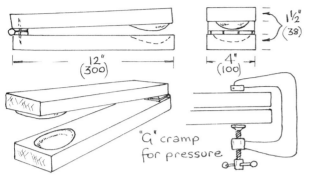

For pressing out hot horn plate; made in a variety of sizes. Hollow cut out with a gouge (as in wooden spoon). Mating piece cut separately & attached by wood screw, countersunk & filled to leave a smooth finish. Make in hardwood

1½" (38)

12" (300)

4" (100)

"G" cramp for pressure

will cut leather adequately, but it is well worth obtaining purpose-made awls, needles and any necessary punches. Conversely, no one now makes tools specifically for hornwork, but ordinary saws (with metal-cutting blades), rasps and files are quite suitable. For finishing and polishing, fine-grade woodworkers' glasspaper and the proprietary polishes sold for plastics are adequate. Instructions for making a simple horn-bending jig are included in the diagrams.

For basket making and for rushwork the tools required are few and simple, and although specially made items can be obtained from craft shops, a great deal of work can be done without. For cutting and trimming willow or cane a pair of electricians' cutters are ideal, and these, together with a sharp knife and a steel bodkin, are all that are required to begin work. The tools required for trugs and spale baskets have already been discussed under tools for woodcrafts.

The thatcher's tools, complicated only by their various names, are likewise simple in construction and few in number. Most were probably made by the thatcher himself or by a local craftsman, and those thatchers still at work today either use tools which have been 'handed on' or make their own. Reference to the relevant chapter heading will give some idea of what they look like. For cutting the straw used in decorative straw work, use a pair of ordinary scissors.

Spinning and weaving require, in addition to a number of easily obtainable hand tools, at least two large pieces of equipment – a spinning wheel and a loom of some kind. Two or three large craft supplies companies stock mass-produced looms and wheels of British and Scandinavian manufacture, and some hand-made wheels are also obtainable. Small pieces of equipment too are available through the specialist suppliers, whose addresses are given on p 248. One of the easiest ways to have the use of the larger items is to join one of the many classes run at colleges and leisure education centres throughout the country.

The rope maker's jack or twister is a piece of equipment which is no longer manufactured, but for twisting short lengths of cord into a rope an ordinary carpenter's brace can be used. A hook, made by bending a short length of round iron bar, is gripped in the chuck of the brace. For extra purchase a loop of cord is taken round the user's waist and tied securely to the brace.

Potters' wheels and kilns are obtainable through a number of firms specialising in a wide range of pottery materials and equipment. Wheels may be of the simple kick variety, but the most popular types are driven by electric motor, some with variable speed control. Kilns suitable for the studio potter are made in a range of sizes, from those about the size of a domestic oven to larger, walk-in models. Electric kilns are the most common, but there are other types which use mains gas, bottled gas or oil. A number of books on pottery techniques describe how to make outdoor kilns using firebrick and fire them with wood, sawdust, coke or bottled gas.

STICKS & CROOKS

Many different kinds of wood have been, and still are, used to make walking sticks: ash, hazel, chestnut, holly, thorn, cherry and the thick, gnarled stems of gorse and ivy – even cabbage stalks. Much sought after are those curious cork-screw sticks which result from stems that have been encircled and constricted by the growth of honeysuckle. There are few rules about what to use and what not to use, or indeed about when to use it. According to an old country saying, the right time to cut a stick is when you see one you like the look of.

Some sticks are in fact just such chance finds, and a careful look along hedge-rows and on the margins of woods will usually reveal something of interest. Neg-lected hedges are good places in which to look, since vigorous growth from an earlier trimming will often have produced nice straight stems which make ideal sticks. Cut these with a portion of the old branch intact if possible, as this can later be shaped into a smooth, bulbous handle. Hawthorn hedges which at one time have been laid (see chapter on hedging and walling) may have suitable stems rising upwards from layered branches. By cutting these in the right place a stick with a natural handle can be readily obtained. Remember to cut off more handle than you need to allow for seasoning and waste, and after seasoning trim to size and shape.

Sticks can be specially grown with natural handles, while others may have handles attached by the maker. These may not always be of wood but sometimes of horn or bone. The most common walking sticks, however, have the familiar hooked handle, and this shape is obtained by bending an otherwise straight stem after subjecting it to heat treatment.

Although many country folk make their own sticks – and it is very satisfying to use one which you have cut and fashioned yourself – some craftsmen specialise in making them in quantity for sale. Young coppice growth of hazel, ash or chestnut has always been the first choice for this large-scale work, especially for hooked sticks. This is usually grown close by the walking-stick 'factory' and cut in rota-tion every three years or so: in good soil, all three species can grow up to 3ft (900mm) in one season. The stems selected for cutting will have butts a little over

33

WALKING STICKS

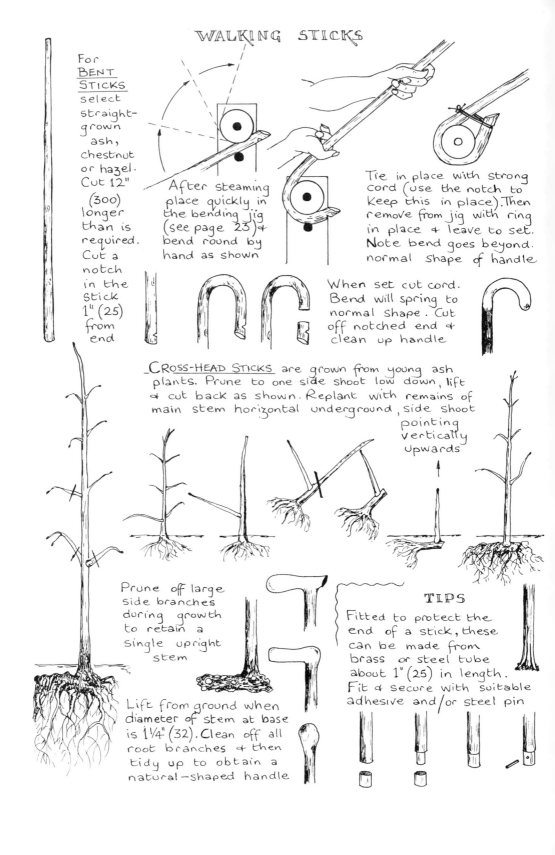

For **BENT STICKS** select straight-grown ash, chestnut or hazel. Cut 12" (300) longer than is required. Cut a notch in the stick 1" (25) from end

After steaming place quickly in the bending jig (see page 23) & bend round by hand as shown

Tie in place with strong cord (use the notch to keep this in place). Then remove from jig with ring in place & leave to set. Note bend goes beyond normal shape of handle

When set cut cord. Bend will spring to normal shape. Cut off notched end & clean up handle

CROSS-HEAD STICKS are grown from young ash plants. Prune to one side shoot low down, lift & cut back as shown. Replant with remains of main stem horizontal underground, side shoot pointing vertically upwards

Prune off large side branches during growth to retain a single upright stem

Lift from ground when diameter of stem at base is 1¼" (32). Clean off all root branches & then tidy up to obtain a natural-shaped handle

TIPS

Fitted to protect the end of a stick, these can be made from brass or steel tube about 1" (25) in length. Fit & secure with suitable adhesive and/or steel pin

1 Sticks placed in hot, damp sand to soften before having their handles bent to shape

1in (25mm) in diameter, and must be straight, strong and free from excessive side branching.

These are carefully seasoned under cover – essential if the bark, which gives these sticks their rustic charm, is to remain intact. On arrival in the workshop the sticks are made pliable, either in damp sand heated over a stove or in a steam chest. The handle can be formed by bending the stick between two wooden pegs set in a post, but most are bent round an iron or hardwood ring which forms part of a bending jig specially made for this purpose. Tied with strong twine to keep it in place, the stick is removed from the jig with the ring in place and left to cool and set to this new shape. The stick maker has a number of these rings to hand so that several sticks can be fashioned at the same time. Instructions for making a stick-bending jig are given on p 23. Walking sticks vary somewhat in length, but one's inside leg measurement may be used as a guide to personal requirements.

Individual stick makers often bend a handle on to a green (unseasoned) stick simply by wedging its thick end high up behind a beam and fastening a heavy weight of some kind to the other end. In this case time and the law of gravity generally produce the right sort of shape. A stick with an undesirable bend in it can sometimes be straightened in the same way, but more often sticks which curve or have kinks are straightened after steaming by gently levering between pegs on a post.

35

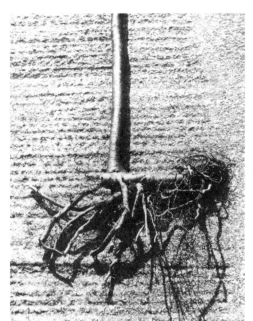

2, 3 (*left*) A naturally grown cross-head ash stick, with its root intact, as dug from the ground and (*right*) the same stick after the handle has been cleaned up

The so-called cross-head stick, usually of ash, is not bent but grown to shape, the root portion of the plant being formed into a strong durable handle at right angles to the main stem by a clever method of artificial cultivation. Plantation-grown ash seedlings are carefully de-budded over a period of about two years, allowing one strong bud to develop low down on the stem. Plants are then lifted, the main stem cut back to just above this single side bud, and transplanted in such a way that the stem lies horizontally with the side bud pointing vertically upwards. In the first season this bud gives rise to a new vertical stem, and a further three years' growth, with careful pruning to discourage side branching, produces a stout, straight stick.

Uprooted a second time, the old underground stem is cleaned up and trimmed to reveal the curious knobbly handle which is such a special feature of these sticks. No two are ever quite alike, and each seems to have a character and a feel of its own. Some can be finished off quite plainly, but others may resemble animal heads and some makers like to emphasise this by a little work with pen-knife and file and even add glass eyes to make the resemblance complete. The cross-head stick's main virtue, however, lies in its strength, for its manner of growth ensures that the grain of the wood follows through the bend of the handle, making it far tougher than it looks.

Sticks with joined handles – that is where stick or shank is separate from the handle to begin with – may not sound quite so strong, but well-made ones can be, and many of these are quite interesting. Gnarled pieces of thorn or vine root, elm

36

burrs, sections of stag antler or pieces of horn or bone make a wide range of curious, even gruesome, handles. Sometimes they are attached to the sticks by means of a simple pegged joint, but more often by dowels of either steel or hard-wood.

Shepherds' crooks have been made in this way for centuries, which proves that jointing, if done properly, must be strong, for a frightened ewe going full pelt down a hillside exerts a tremendous force against the head of the crook which the working shepherd uses to restrain her. In Scotland deer antler is often used for the head, but ram's horn is more common elsewhere. Suitable horns are shaped by heating, as described in the chapter on hornwork; the old shepherds, to whom crook making was a winter evening pastime, made use of the paraffin lamps which lit their isolated homes. Old tup horns are best, with plenty of solid horn at the base to work with; horns from young sheep, which are most readily available, are often too thin and shell-like to be of much use.

First the base is sawn square across the bottom and some of the rough edges are taken off so that it can be gripped in a vice. Rams' horns have a pronounced curl, and this must be straightened by twisting the horn while it is hot. Heating in boil-ing water is simple and uniform, but experienced crook makers prefer to heat over a gentle flame in the traditional manner. Hill farmers used to bend a horn which had curled too much and was growing into a sheep's cheek by boiling a large turnip and impaling it on the horn, which was then twisted away. Whatever the method used to make the horn malleable, it is straightened by gripping the base – or the heel, as it will become – in a vice and levering with a pair of grips or a length of tube. The horn will have to be held in its new shape by tying or clamp-ing for several hours until cool. Two or three straightenings may be necessary.

Mark in pencil the required curve of the head and saw and file to shape. The inside curve is shaped first as this is the most important – the outside line simply follows this curve. Crooks are made with two sizes of head. Neck crooks, which are perhaps the more familiar, are the larger; they measure between $3\frac{1}{2}$in and 4in (88mm and 100mm), or the width of a man's hand, across the mouth, which is just big enough to grip a sheep's neck. The smaller size is made just wide enough to take a sheep's hind leg and is known as a leg crook. An old penny was always used as a general guide for the mouth, which is about $1\frac{1}{4}$in (32mm) across, opening out slightly above so that the leg of the sheep is not damaged.

Before shaping is completed the head is fitted to a suitable shank. Ash or hazel is generally used, the diameter chosen to suit and balance the head, the length varying slightly, tending to increase as one goes further north in Britain. Most shanks are measured hand over hand to give a length of fourteen hands – somewhere between 4ft 3in and 4ft 9in (1.3m and 1.4m).

Careful shanking is essential for the sake of both appearance and strength: head and shank must marry in well together so that the heel is nicely in line with the shank, and the nose should not droop. Usually the head is drilled with a $\frac{1}{2}$in (12mm) hole and a peg cut at the top end of the shank to fit it nicely. The peg may be strengthened by inserting a steel rod – some use a large iron nail but others recommend sound steel. Alternatively, the shank peg or tenon may be dispensed with if both the shank and the head are drilled and joined with a

CROOKS and STICKS

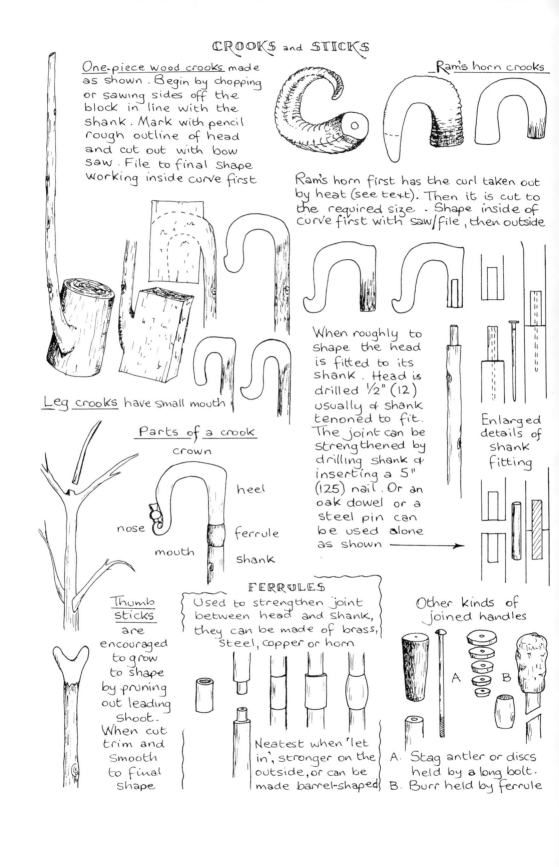

One-piece wood crooks made as shown. Begin by chopping or sawing sides off the block in line with the shank. Mark with pencil rough outline of head and cut out with bow saw. File to final shape working inside curve first

Ram's horn crooks

Ram's horn first has the curl taken out by heat (see text). Then it is cut to the required size. Shape inside of curve first with saw/file, then outside

Leg crooks have small mouth

Parts of a crook

crown

heel

nose

ferrule

mouth

shank

When roughly to shape the head is fitted to its shank. Head is drilled ½" (12) usually & shank tenoned to fit. The joint can be strengthened by drilling shank & inserting a 5" (125) nail. Or an oak dowel or a steel pin can be used alone as shown ⟶

Enlarged details of shank fitting

Thumb sticks are encouraged to grow to shape by pruning out leading shoot. When cut trim and smooth to final shape

FERRULES
Used to strengthen joint between head and shank, they can be made of brass, steel, copper or horn

Neatest when 'let in', stronger on the outside, or can be made barrel-shaped

Other kinds of joined handles

A   B

A. Stag antler or discs held by a long bolt.
B. Burr held by ferrule

steel pin or a hardwood dowel. Finally a collar or ferrule, either of horn or metal, is fitted over the joint: cow horn, stag antler and brass or copper tubing are all suitable for this purpose. The additional use of a good modern adhesive ensures a high rate of success for the present-day craftsman. Given a nice smooth finish and perhaps carved with a simple motif, a well-made crook is an object of beauty as well as being highly functional to the working shepherd.

Another type of shepherd's crook is made entirely of wood. Sometimes called natural neck crooks, these are made from shanks taken with a portion of root or a thicker part of the tree attached. Cut ideally with plenty of wood to spare so that splits do not spoil the piece, they are carefully seasoned before being shaped. The thick handle or head portion is first chopped to size in line with the shank. Then the rough outline of the head is marked in pencil before being cut to shape with a bow saw or similar tool. Remember to cut the inside curve first. The final shape, rounded and smooth to the touch and contrasting well with the bark of the shank, is obtained with a file and glasspaper. Walking sticks can be made in the same way.

Yet another all-wood stick is the thumb stick, usually as long as a crook but having instead of a head or a handle a V-shaped prong at the top. This is obtained by careful selection of natural-grown stems or by encouraging such growth by judicious pruning. The prongs should be of equal length and should leave the shank at similar angles. When the stick is gripped in the hand, the thumb fits conveniently into the notch. Sticks of this type are popular with walkers in fell country.

All sticks may be finished in a similar way after smoothing with glasspaper. Shanks and all-wood sticks are clear-varnished to bring out the beauty of the wood. Polyurethane is suitable, and two or three coats may be necessary if one wants a glossy job. Horn needs careful finishing with fine glasspaper, and some stick makers use a household abrasive cleaning paste or powder and finish off with metal polish. Horn should not be varnished.

Whatever type of stick or crook is made, the bottom end of the shank must be protected by a ferrule or tip, or the wood there will wear and splinter with constant use. Tips can be bought ready-made in brass, but they are quite easily made from steel or brass tubing of suitable diameter, or from horn or stag antler. If a walking stick is to be used by a lame person, a hard rubber tip should be purchased and fitted to prevent slipping.

A well-made stick should outlast several tips, as these will wear out and need replacing, whereas the stick itself, thus protected, is likely to last at least a lifetime.

RAKES & BESOMS

In the days before machinery replaced the scythe, haymaking by hand was a common sight throughout the countryside. The scythes which cut the crop were handmade, the joint product of the blacksmith who made the 36in (900mm) curved blade and the man who made the equally curving wooden snaith or handle. After the cutting came the raking of the crop, pulling the sweet-smelling grass into those long parallel swathes which snaked across the field; then it was turned to open it up more to the drying effects of sun and wind, and finally made into heaps handy for forking up into the carts which carried it off to ricks and barns for use as winter fodder.

The rakes too were hand-made, entirely of wood, and the man who made the scythe snaiths also made the rakes. In fact quite often this same man would make handles for a wide range of other implements and tools, the common factor being the wood most often used for such work, which was, of course, ash.

Rakes made entirely of wood were favoured by farmers and farm workers on account of their lightness and balance in use. Even the wooden garden rake, still obtainable today, has a head over 2ft (600mm) in width, while the old drag rakes used extensively at haymaking were well over twice this size. The factory-made metal head is too narrow to be effective in this work, but would be too heavy if made larger. Weight was an important consideration in earlier times when a day's haymaking often meant working in the fields from dawn until dusk.

As a consequence there was a steady demand for wooden rakes, and country rake makers were to be found almost everywhere, making use of local coppice to produce their wares. There were some regional variations in the methods of working and to a lesser extent in the materials used, all of them related to differences in agricultural practice between the north-west and the south-east of Britain.

Generally the craftsmen cut their own material, sorting the coppice poles into lots according to their use. Straight-grown ash was always first choice for the long rake handle, or stail as it is properly called, on account of its strength and pliability. Willow, hazel and birch would sometimes be substituted locally.

40

4 Shaping rake stails or handles with the stail engine

After being allowed to season for about a year, often with a strip of bark removed along the length of each pole to aid the process, poles suitable for rake stails were cut to length and completely de-barked with the drawknife. If the pole required straightening it would be steamed to make it pliable, then pulled into shape in a device known as a setting pin, a stout wooden post with oak pegs between which the poles were levered straight. Next came the task of rounding and smoothing. In use the stail of a rake has to slide easily through one hand as the other draws it back and forth to gather the hay. Therefore smoothness is essential, and to achieve this the craftsman used a stail engine – a hand-operated tool in spite of its name, the word 'engine' simply meaning an ingenious device. This particular device was a form of rotary plane working on a principle similar to that of the simple pencil sharpener. Basically it consisted of a wooden block with a hole through the centre fitted with an angled blade; a screw adjustment enabled its cutting diameter to be varied so that it could be made to cut a taper as it was worked spirally along the pole. (See p 26 for details of a modern version of this tool.) In some areas cleft or sometimes sawn ash was used for handles, and this was rounded with a rounding plane, rather like an ordinary carpenter's plane but with a deeply concave sole and blade.

5 Rounding rake tines by hammering them through a tine cutter

The rake head was cleft from ash, or sometimes willow, to reduce weight even further. A suitable log some 30in (750mm) in length was cleft with a side axe, which is an axe whose blade is bevelled on one side only. So skilful was the rake maker with this tool that he could trim each head almost to its final size and shape, needing only to finish it off with a drawknife. A number of holes would then be bored, the actual number varying according to the size of the head but with not more than 2in (50mm) between their centres, to take the wooden pegs which form the teeth or tines of the rake.

RAKE MAKING

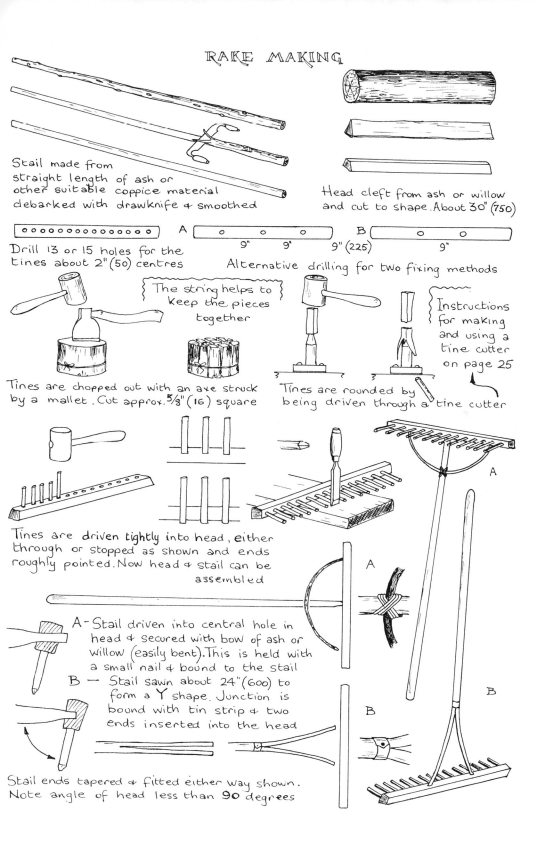

Stail made from straight length of ash or other suitable coppice material debarked with drawknife & smoothed

Head cleft from ash or willow and cut to shape. About 30" (750)

Drill 13 or 15 holes for the tines about 2" (50) centres

A   9"   9"   9" (225)   B   9"

Alternative drilling for two fixing methods

The string helps to keep the pieces together

Instructions for making and using a tine cutter on page 25

Tines are chopped out with an axe struck by a mallet. Cut approx. 5/8" (16) square

Tines are rounded by being driven through a tine cutter

Tines are driven tightly into head, either through or stopped as shown and ends roughly pointed. Now head & stail can be assembled

A — Stail driven into central hole in head & secured with bow of ash or willow (easily bent). This is held with a small nail & bound to the stail

B — Stail sawn about 24" (600) to form a Y shape. Junction is bound with tin strip & two ends inserted into the head

A

B

Stail ends tapered & fitted either way shown. Note angle of head less than 90 degrees

Tines too were cleft and not sawn, for they had to be strong and able to withstand being dragged regularly along the ground. Again ash was frequently used, or sometimes willow, but the best tines of all were said to be those made from the spikes of wood left behind when an oak tree had had a branch torn off in a storm. The word tine is an old English name for thorn, so perhaps this wood too was once used.

The tines, cleft a little oversize from well-seasoned billets cross-cut to the required length, were rounded by being driven through a tine cutter, a piece of steel tube ground sharp at one end. This was set up in a bench with a hole right through it, and cleft pieces of wood were driven through one after the other with blows from a heavy mallet. Just as one tine was almost flush with the cutting edge the next would be placed on top. This way each successive tine was pushed through without blunting the cutting edge or cutting the wooden mallet.

The finished tines – made to be a good fit in the holes already bored in the rake head – were now hammered in good and tight. Here there was some variation in method, for some makers bored right through the head and allowed the tines to protrude slightly on the top edge, arguing that this made them more secure. Others made holes which went only partway through, believing that this kept the head stronger. Often the completed head was soaked in water so that everything swelled up and became even tighter.

All the tines were then trimmed to exactly the same length and given a blunt point – a protruding tooth could spoil the smooth action of the finished rake. For this process the rake maker might use a peg or stock knife, similar to the tool used in tent-peg making and clog-sole cutting. Some used a short-handled axe, while for others a chisel or a drawknife did the job.

There were two methods of fitting heads to handles, one being more common in the north and west of the British Isles, where a tool more suited to the shorter upland grasses of hills or fellside was often needed. Here the tapered end of the stail, driven into a hole drilled centrally in the side of the head, was further strengthened by means of a bow of bent ash, hazel or willow. The ends of the bow were held in holes drilled out towards the ends of the head, and the centre was bound securely with twine where bow and handle crossed. Bows of green wood could be bent to shape quite easily.

Common practice in the south was to saw down the stail for about 2ft (600mm) and to bind the end of the saw-cut with a strip of tin held by a small nail to prevent further splitting. Gypsies employ a similar method when making clothes pegs. The sawn end of the stail was then opened out to form a fork and the ends were trimmed to size and secured in holes drilled in the head several inches each side of centre. Larger sizes of rake had bridge pieces set into the fork. This type of rake, which had a longer handle than those made further north, was designed centuries ago to deal with the long, lush grasses of the southern counties, and there has never been any reason to change it. Those still made today are usually based on this same design.

Seen sideways, heads and stails were always joined up at slightly less than a right angle. A head 'coming in' like this was less likely to jump when drawn over the ground and so gathered hay, or anything else for that matter, much more

44

easily. Balance was important too: a heavy-headed rake could be very fatiguing to use, and if one found its way on to the farm it would as like as not end up getting 'accidentally' broken.

All rakes were put together without glue, and only an occasional nail was used. If anything did work loose the user had only to soak the head in water and all would be well again.

The scythe snaith or snead, as the handle of this particular tool is variously called – its name is said to be derived from the Anglo-Saxon *sneadan*, to cut – must also be well balanced. And it should be curved correctly too, for it is the double curve of the handle which enables the user to keep his hands level and parallel with the ground as he swings the scythe rhythmically to and fro. The curve is obtained by steaming suitable coppice poles or clefts, after they have been de-barked and rounded, and fixing them in a setting frame. This consists of heavy baulks of timber, which lie on the ground, fitted with pegs between which the snaiths are bent. The pegs hold them securely in the required shape and when dry they are set to this new form, which they retain more or less permanently.

The amount of curvature varies: the southern English pattern has deep curves, but the northern or Kendal snaith is less curved. In Scandinavia the *sith* has a handle which is almost straight. In Europe ash is the usual choice for making scythe handles; in America hickory is used.

A scythe is held by means of two little side handles called doles or side pins. Usually of beech with metal rings attached, these can be adjusted and are fixed in place with wedges to suit individual users. There are two or three ways of 'measuring up' for a scythe; one is to place the tip of the blade on the toe of the outstretched foot. In this position the lower or right-hand dole should be fixed at hip level. The upper grip, for the left hand, is then positioned above this by the distance between the elbow and fist of the user.

Gone are the days when a gang of mowers, bodies swinging to the circular sweep of their long, sharp blades, would mow acre after acre with scythes. Now machines turn the grass into neat bundles, or pour out wheat already threshed, its straw neatly baled or more often burnt. But for small fields, especially in the hills, and for awkward places such as orchards and roadside verges, nothing can beat these ancient tools. The same applies to wooden rakes: some are still being made and used, but most arc entirely machine-cut from sawn timber. These may have a more finished appearance but are nowhere near as strong as the well-made cleft variety.

Closely allied to the making of rakes and handles is the craft of besom making. Made entirely from woodland produce, the birch broom or besom is one of the best implements for clearing leaves from a lawn or cleaning up a stable yard. Correctly used, with a sideways movement, it flicks away lightweight debris much better than any other type of broom or brush.

Besoms have been made since Saxon times, and their method of construction has remained unchanged right up to the present time. Before the advent of brushes consisting of bristles of various kinds set with pitch into a wooden block, they were much in demand for domestic and farm purposes as well as providing, so we are told, transport for witches. They consist of a head of twigs bound tightly together with some form of binding material, with a short stick pushed in to form a handle. Although birch twigs are generally used, heads of broom or heather are sometimes made, especially in moorland areas.

Birch brushwood is cut in quantity from the thick crowns of seven to nine-year-old trees during winter and early spring. The cut material is made up into loose bundles, which are stacked head to tail in the besom maker's yard to season. Built up in layers through which the air can circulate, each stack is finished off with a ridge and thatched with more birch bundles, or more recently with sheets of corrugated iron, to keep off the rain and snow until it is ready for use the following year. Thorough seasoning is essential, otherwise the finished article will be brittle and likely to deposit more broken bits than it actually sweeps away.

Material for handles is cut at the same time, although quite often poles remaining after the selection of rake handles can be used. These poles are stored in an open shed or in a covered stack to season.

When the material is ready for use the besom maker likes to prepare sufficient for two or three days' work at a time. This preparation entails first opening up the stack and removing several bundles for sorting. Two separate heaps are made, one containing the long and roughish twigs which are used in the centre or core of the head, while the other consists of shorter, smoother stuff for the outside. Small, unwanted material and brittle ends are trimmed off with a billhook or bille, made up into faggots and sold as firewood. Country bakers often used them for firing their brick ovens in the days when bread was properly baked.

The two lengths of twig are stacked to the left and right of where the besom

MAKING A BESOM

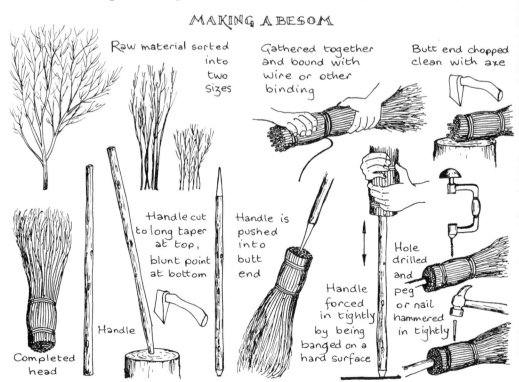

Raw material sorted into two sizes

Gathered together and bound with wire or other binding

Butt end chopped clean with axe

Handle cut to long taper at top, blunt point at bottom

Handle

Handle is pushed into butt end

Handle forced in tightly by being banged on a hard surface

Hole drilled and peg or nail hammered in tightly

Completed head

6 Binding a birch besom with wire which is being held taught in a besom horse

maker does the next part of his work, which is known as gathering. Gathering the prepared material into heads looks easy enough, but it takes long experience to know just how much to gather and how to arrange the longest pieces at the core, the smallest on the outside. Two sizes of head are made, a 10in (250mm) and a 12in (300mm). When his finger- and thumb-tips just meet round a compressed bundle, the maker knows he has the larger size; when they overlap he has the smaller size. Working at speed, he has no time or need for any other form of measuring.

Binding comes next, and there are two ways of doing this; for one method the craftsman sits astride a 'horse', while for the other he stands before a lever-vice. Both devices are foot-operated so as to leave the hands free. The besom horse holds the binding material taut while it is wrapped round the head, gripped tightly by the maker's two hands. The vice, on the other hand, compresses the head while the binding is wrapped round by hand.

Two bindings go on the head, about 4in (100mm) apart, each started by inserting an end into the bundle before wrapping it tightly around four or five times. Finishing a bind varies from worker to worker and depends also on the binding material being used. Galvanized wire is most frequently used today, and this is finished off by twisting with pliers. In earlier times various natural materials, including strips of ash or willow and even strands of bramble shredded of its thorns, were gathered locally and used. These are more supple, have more 'give' than wire, and are less likely to cut into the head. Natural bindings were usually finished off by drawing the end entirely through the head, using a long, home-made needle to do so, looping it through one strand of the binding and back out at the other side, where it was cut off flush. Some finished off with the knot that farmers used to bind corn, the sheaf knot.

Next the base of the head is chopped clean with the short axe, leaving it ready for the handle. This need not be perfectly straight or quite as smooth as a rake stail, for a besom is neither pushed or pulled. Nowadays conifer thinnings are often used. Cut to handle length, which is about 4ft (1.2m), these are first de-barked with a drawknife, then the head end is trimmed with the axe to a gradual taper while the butt end is given a blunt point. The taper helps the handle to enter the bound end of the head more easily as it is pushed in, the blunt point preventing the butt from splitting when it is banged down hard on the ground to force the handle in tightly. Fitting the handle tightens up the head, which is secured to it by means of a wooden peg knocked through a hole drilled between the two bindings. Sometimes a nail is used instead.

Some birch besoms are made without handles; these are known usually as swales. First used by early iron workers to clean the surface of their molten metal, they are still used in some modern steel making to brush flakes from hot steel plates in the rolling mills. Wire brushes can be used for the same job, but the birch swale is still considered best, the charring which takes place apparently giving a cleaner surface. Swales are also used in vinegar brewing to line the bottom of vats, where they help to create acetic acid and act as both aerator and filter.

Heather besoms are made with ling (*Caluna vulgaris*), which of course grows in profusion on moors and heaths. Medium-high and well-branched material is cut in the spring when the sap is rising and the stems are pliant. It is not stacked to season but used immediately, the method of manufacture being the same as for birch besoms.

Besom makers were once as widespread as their materials, and the broom-squires, as they were known in some districts, made a steady livelihood even with besoms retailing at only sixpence ($2\frac{1}{2}$p) apiece. Some worked alone in the woods; others ran two- or three-man village businesses, buying their raw materials from local merchants. Now their numbers have dwindled until only a few remain to carry on this ancient, primitive craft.

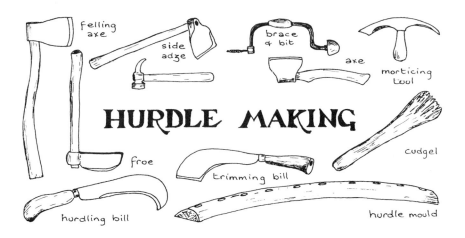

HURDLE MAKING

felling axe · side adze · brace & bit · axe · morticing tool · froe · cudgel · trimming bill · hurdling bill · hurdle mould

Hurdles are a form of lightweight fencing made entirely from coppice-grown material. Large numbers were once made, especially in the southern counties of Britain, where their principal use was in the penning or folding of sheep. Two distinct types were made, the woven, wattle hurdle and the gate or bar hurdle, the main virtue of both being their simplicity and portability. In most, but not all, situations where they were used they formed only temporary fencing and were frequently moved from place to place. Being light in weight and easy to put up and take down, hurdles were an asset in an agricultural system which depended largely on manual labour.

Of the two kinds, the wattle hurdle is almost certainly the older, as well as being the one which is still made today, though in much reduced numbers. It is made of round and cleft hazel rods closely woven together on two stout uprights, also of hazel.

Wattle work, or just plain wattle, as this type of woven work is called, was once put to a great variety of uses besides hurdle making. For building purposes its use goes back to Iron Age round huts, reaching a peak in the wattle and daub of timber-framed houses built in the Middle Ages. It was used for defence purposes in both war and peace — wattle screens protected medieval armies from flying arrows, reinforced river banks and kept shifting sand dunes in check. And when sheep and wool became the mainstay of England's economy the demand for hurdles increased tenfold. So considerable was the use of wattle that at some unrecorded date it became customary in many areas to reserve a certain portion of good land specifically for the growing of hazel coppice. Many of these ancient coppices are now neglected and overgrown, and some have disappeared altogether, cleared and replanted as more permanent woodland of a different type. A few isolated ones survive and are still used in the traditional way.

The hurdle maker works in the hazel coppice, cutting his material and making up the hurdles in the same place, for one of the 'trade secrets' of his craft lies in using the hazel almost immediately it is cut and while it is still pliant. Once it dries out it becomes too brittle to be of much use in good hurdle making. Material

HURDLE MAKING

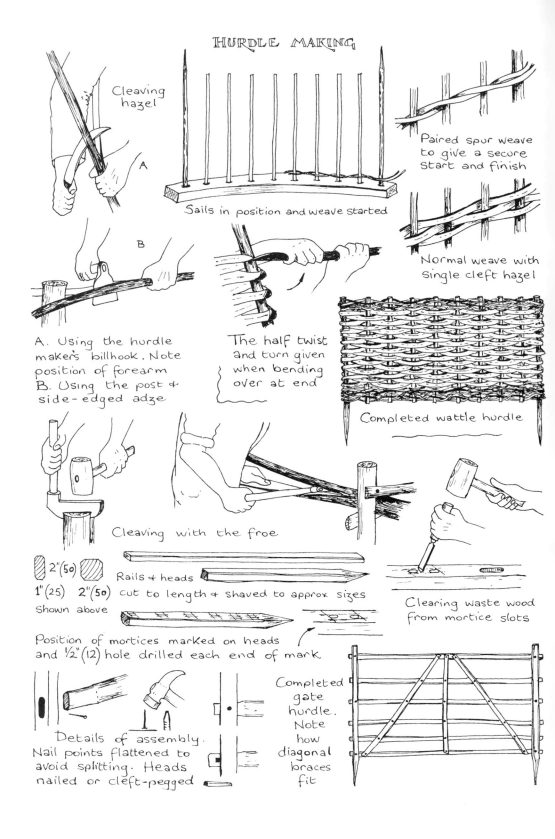

Cleaving hazel

A

Sails in position and weave started

Paired spur weave to give a secure start and finish

Normal weave with single cleft hazel

B

A. Using the hurdle maker's billhook. Note position of forearm
B. Using the post & side-edged adze

The half twist and turn given when bending over at end

Completed wattle hurdle

Cleaving with the froe

2"(50)
1"(25) 2"(50)
Shown above

Rails & heads cut to length & shaved to approx sizes

Clearing waste wood from mortice slots

Position of mortices marked on heads and ½"(12) hole drilled each end of mark

Details of assembly. Nail points flattened to avoid splitting. Heads nailed or cleft-pegged

Completed gate hurdle. Note how diagonal braces fit

is best cut during the winter and early spring months, the wood having at that time just about the right amount of sap in it. Summer-cut hazel is too sappy and causes trouble later, the woven rods opening up and warping as they dry out, while the wood is not as durable as that cut in the winter. Some old-time hurdle makers found alternative work during the summer months, but others made hurdles all the year round.

For hurdle making the hazel coppice is cut every seven years or so in rotation, a patch of about three acres (.03 hectares) providing sufficient material for one man. This is clear-cut – that is, everything is cut down to ground level irrespective of size – and sorted into bundles according to its intended use. Long lengths about 1in (25mm) in diameter and shorter rods up to 2in (50mm) in diameter are reserved for hurdles, the shorter, smaller stuff being put aside for bean poles, thatching spars or crate making, or chopped for firewood. A few selected rods might be kept for walking sticks, and some, cut with a forked branch at one end, for washing-line props. Anything too large goes for fence posts. Cutting is done with a felling axe and billhook when unwanted undergrowth has been cleared away.

All the required hurdle material is stacked close to where the maker has set up his simple, home-made equipment. This comprises first of all a heavy baulk of timber or a half log some 7ft (2.1m) in length, which lies on the ground, and in which have been bored ten equally spaced holes. This is the hurdle mould, and it is always slightly curved along its length. The mould holds the hurdle secure while it is being woven. To one side is a chopping post, sometimes the base of a small tree, and alongside this a post-and-rail arrangement – the gallows – against which the selected hazel rods are laid to be handy when needed. As a ready means of measuring the required length of each rod, several sticks are set in line in the ground nearby at 1ft (300mm) intervals; alternatively, a vertical notched post may be used for the same purpose.

First a number of upright stakes are chopped to length and placed on the gallows. Then the longer, more slender rods which will be woven horizontally through them are placed alongside, some cleft along their length, while others, perhaps a little more slender still, are left intact. The cleaving is usually done with a billhook, but in some areas a small adze-like tool with a side cutting edge is used to start the split, which is then lengthened by forcing the two half sections to either side of an upright post while levering with the adze along the grain. When the billhook is used the upper arm of the user sometimes serves the same function as the post. Some use a froe (see p 25) for cleaving, but whichever tool is used the process demands a skill which is only acquired by practice.

The actual method of wattle hurdle making varies slightly from place to place. In most districts the weaving is horizontal, but in some it is partly diagonal. Occasionally it is reinforced by having diagonal braces nailed on, but this practice is condemned by the best craftsmen. The size of hurdles also varies. Those made for sheep penning are between 3ft (900mm) and 4ft 6in (1.3m) high and up to 6ft (1.8m) in length. Other sizes have always been made for a variety of uses, some being up to 6ft (1.8m) square. Finished dimensions seem to have been decided partly by local demand and partly by the size which the maker found to be 'comfortable' for working.

51

7 Cleaving hazel with the billhook to make wattle hurdles

The upright stakes, customarily known as sails and usually ten in number, are placed in the holes in the hurdle mould and tapped down with a mallet. The eight inner ones are sometimes cleft but the two outer ones are almost always left round. Known by some as shores, not as sails, these two end stakes are longer than the rest by up to 12in (300mm), and have their lower ends sharpened to a point so that they can be pushed into the ground to hold the completed hurdle in position when in use. Ash is sometimes used for this purpose as it has extra strength. Because of the uneven length of the sails, sheep hurdles are made upside down in the mould; those intended for other purposes, and made with sails of equal length, are made the right way up.

With all the sails in position the horizontal weaving can begin. The pattern varies from place to place and so too do the names given to the weaving rods and the weaving processes. It is customary to begin and end with uncleft rods which are interwoven in such a way that they grip the uprights and form a secure start and finish. Known usually as spurs or spur rods, these are woven singly by some, but more often in pairs in the manner of the fitch-pairing weave described in the chapter on basket making. Hurdle makers call this wreathing or ethering, the latter term also being used by hedge layers for a similar braided arrangement of rods.

A start is made near the middle of the sails, at the bottom, the rods passing in

8 Fixing sails into the hurdle mould. To the left is the gallows with prepared stakes ready for use, to the right a chopping post and gauge stick

front of and behind each upright, weaving in and out until the end is reached. Here the rods are given a half-twist and turned round the end sail or shore before being taken back across the hurdle. This half-twist as the rods are bent round is most important – another of the hurdle maker's tricks of the trade – for without it the fibres in the grain of the wood would be strained and broken. Twisting and bending at the same time ensures that the fibres are bunched up and remain unbroken, but the hazel must be green and pliant if the twisting is to be effective.

When several inches have been completed in this way a change is made to lengths of cleft material. These are woven singly in and out of the sails and half twisted at the turn as before. As the work proceeds the woven rods, or runners, as these cleft rods are called, are pressed down hard to close any gaps, either with the foot or by beating with the back of the billhook. Many workers wear a leather knee-pad and kneel on the rods from time to time. New runners are let in as required, old and new ends being overlapped between two stakes as in basketwork.

Most hurdle makers take great pride in producing work which is tidy as well as strong, working the cleft hazel so that the bark shows on one side only, the clean, cleft surface on the other.

For sheep folding a small hole is deliberately left in the middle of the hurdle and neatly woven round with a twisted pair of uncleft rods, like the spurs, but known as twillies. The twilly hole thus formed is used when hurdles are being moved from one place to another; several hurdles can be carried easily on a pole passed through the holes. The twillies which strengthen the weave at this point are sometimes continued for two or three rows around the opening, but then weaving with cleft runners is continued.

When the required height is reached, and after finishing off with three or four rows of spur rods as at the start to secure the weave, the hurdle is trimmed over with a special tool. Some craftsmen do this while the hurdle is still held in the mould, others after it has been removed. The trimming bill or bille is not unlike a billhook, but instead of being pointed it ends in a cutting edge about 3in (75mm) wide. A small axe will serve the same purpose. The hurdle maker uses either of these tools in conjunction with a cudgel, a piece of wood with a handle, which is held under or behind the end to be trimmed, a smart chop cutting cleanly through the projecting rod. Projecting ends of sails are trimmed back to within 1in (25mm) or so of the weave in a similar way.

On being removed from the curved mould, the wattle hurdle has a corresponding curve. Stacked one on top of the other, convex side uppermost, they flatten out under their own weight or with help from another weight placed on top, tightening up the weave as they do so. Had they been woven flat they might quickly loosen up and perhaps even fall apart. No nails, are used in their construction, and apart from a few simple tools they are entirely made by the bare hands of a single craftsman working, often alone, out in the woods.

Gate or bar hurdle makers, on the other hand, were workshop rather than woodland workers. Often they would work in the woods during the winter months, cutting their own material, but it would be transported to a village workshop where the summer months were spent in making hurdles and one or two other things besides. Some bought their material from woodcutters, and so do most of the few still working today.

A gate hurdle, or open hurdle as it is sometimes called, resembles a small, lightly made barred field gate. Coppice wood is used, all cleft rather than sawn, the actual species varying according to availability and local custom. Willow is a favourite choice, being light and easy to work, but ash is stronger and is often preferred, while both oak and chestnut are used in some areas. Sometimes two of these may be used in combination, particularly ash with willow.

Preparation of the material and the method of construction are much the same whichever wood is used. Willow is cut at seven- or eight-year intervals, but ash and oak are usually cut from twenty- to twenty-five-year-old plantations, straight-grown and free from large side branches. When all the necessary material is to hand in the maker's yard, it is sorted according to size and stacked ready for immediate use. Wood which is still fairly green is easier to cleave than seasoned material.

Selected poles are first cross-cut to the various lengths required, and then cleft with an axe or, more usually, a froe. This tool – its name comes from 'froward', the archaic opposite of 'toward', and consequently means 'away from' – has a wedge-shaped blade set at right angles to a wooden handle. Its lower edge is the cutting edge, and after it has been started with a blow on its back edge from a

54

mallet it is pushed away from the user with a levering action, splitting the wood evenly along its grain as it goes. For cleaving, and for shaving, which comes later, each pole is held in a curious device known as a hurdle maker's monkey. This consists of two wooden bars fixed across a pair of upright posts. The bars are at slightly different levels and are not parallel, so that when a pole is pushed between them it is held in place at a downward slant; for stability it rests on another upright post set some distance away.

Gate hurdles are generally made with six or seven horizontal rails held at both ends by stouter uprights and strengthened with one centre and two diagonal braces. Completed they measure between 6ft (1.8m) and 8ft (2.4m) long by about 3ft 6in (1.1m) high. The rails are not equally spaced, those near the bottom being closer together, as in farm gates, to discourage animals from squeezing through. In 'lamb creep' hurdles, however, the space between the two bottom rails is made large enough for a young weaned lamb to pass through to reach food intended for it, but too small for the ewe to follow.

After cleaving, rails and braces are shaved with a drawknife until they are flat and roughly six-sided, all corners having been smoothed away without loss of thickness and strength at the centre. The two main uprights, or heads, are left thicker and more square-cut, and are pointed at their lower ends for pushing into the ground. In the course of this shaving all bark and sapwood is removed, leaving the wood, though not always perfectly straight, clean and strong.

The horizontal rails will be fitted into mortice slots cut through the upright heads, and the position of these must next be marked. In some workshops this is done on a raised wooden framework which acts as a kind of pattern or jig, the required measurements being pencilled in on the heads from marks on the jig frame. Then the head is gripped in the monkey again and holes are drilled through with a brace and $\frac{1}{2}$in (12mm) bit, one at either end of each marked position. These holes form the ends of the mortice slots. The wood remaining in between may be taken out with a chisel and mallet in the conventional way, but traditionally it was done with a tool said to be peculiar to gate making. Known variously as a dader, a twivil, a trybill and a two-bill, this was a narrow, twin-bladed axe of sorts. Some had a cutting blade at one end and a hooked blade at the other, while others had two cutting blades at right angles to each other, forming in effect a small axe and a small adze.

With all the mortices cut to size the final assembly can begin. Here the jig already mentioned is used again, the component parts of the hurdle being arranged according to the pattern so that each completed hurdle will be finished square and true. Some manage quite well without this particular piece of equipment, assembling hurdles flat on the ground and relying mainly on eye judgement and an occasional light kick to line everything up.

First the rails, which have had their ends tapered slightly to fit tightly into the round-ended mortice slots, are fixed into one head. Then the other head is firmly tapped on and, with the whole hurdle squared up, the bracing bars are put into position and nails knocked in at their junction with each of the cross-rails. Cut nails were always considered the best, as they gripped better, but ordinary oval wire nails are now used. They should be longer by up to 1in (25mm) than the

9 Putting the finishing touches to a gate or bar hurdle

thickness of the two pieces, and are driven right through, the protruding ends clenched at the other side so that they do not pull out. The nails pass through the thickest part of the rails and braces, and if their points are flattened slightly before use they are less likely to split the wood.

The rails are made to fit tightly into the mortice slots so that they are firmly held without nailing, but top and bottom rails, and a central one, are secured with shorter, unclenched nails. Alternatively the rail may be drilled through and fitted with cleft wooden pegs on the outside of the head. This prevents the hurdle coming apart by accident, but also ensures easy renewal of a head that is broken or split in use. On completion the hurdles are stacked out in the open to season, weighted down with logs or stones so that they stay flat and do not warp.

Finished hurdles, whether gate or wattle, are made strong enough to restrain a flock of hungry sheep, yet light enough to be moved around fairly frequently by one or sometimes two men. Both types are suitable for the folding of sheep, which is the practice of sectioning off part of a large field so that the animals, temporarily confined, can graze without waste a crop of roots or clover grown specially for them. Once an important part of the arable farmer's rotational cropping system, the method ensured that the land was well trodden and naturally manured between crops of cereals.

The hurdles were erected to a set plan, starting at the gate and moving progressively and systematically down and across the field. If the ground was hard or stony an iron bar would be used to make holes for the hurdle legs or feet and a heavy mallet employed to knock them in. Most farmers overlapped the hurdles, and tied them top and bottom with strong twine. Extra stakes might be driven in at intervals to buttress or shore up a long line of hurdles — a possible explanation, incidentally, of the use of the word shore instead of sail for the end stakes of wattle hurdles. The hurdles were moved on daily as one section of the crop was consumed by the sheep, and it was the high cost of the labour involved in doing this, together with the changes in farming practice resulting from the increased use of artificial fertilisers, which brought about the decline of the fold system.

Some forms of folding are still practised, but wire fences have almost entirely replaced wooden hurdles for this purpose. Wired cleft chestnut paling is most often used in their place, brought out by lorry and rolled out across a field in a continuous length as required. The single-strand electric fence used now in the so-called strip grazing method is really another extension of the fold principle.

In some areas hurdles were always erected at lambing time to separate out the in-lamb ewes and to afford them and their offspring some protection from the weather. Wattle hurdles were obviously better for this purpose; where the gate type was used, straw bales were added to form protective walls around the lambing pens.

Neither type of hurdle found much favour in the northern and western part of Britain. Folding was not generally practised there, and hill sheep can easily clear a 4ft (1.2m) hurdle anyway. With plenty of stone available, the dry-stone wall has always been a better proposition in these areas.

Gate hurdles now find a fairly widespread use as jumps for horses, such hurdles being a little more heavily made to withstand being regularly knocked over. They are made in a variety of heights from 4ft (1.2m) to well over 5ft (1.5m). They are also still used, as they always have been, as temporary gates, and occasionally for pens at livestock markets and shows. Wattle hurdles serve similar purposes and in addition make good garden fences and screens of all kinds. Most of those which are still being made are in fact for garden rather than for agricultural use.

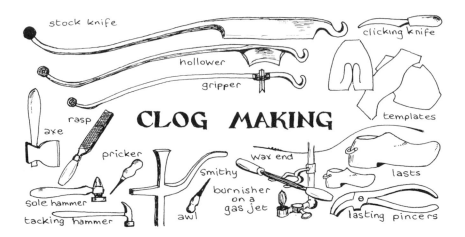

CLOG MAKING

Tools labelled: stock knife, clicking knife, hollower, gripper, templates, rasp, axe, pricker, wax end, lasts, smithy, sole hammer, burnisher on a gas jet, awl, tacking hammer, lasting pincers

The clatter of clogs, and not the cock's crow, was once the sound which began the working day in many a town and village in northern England. One could lie and listen to the familiar iron-shod sound of a solitary early riser going past the house, the noise growing louder as the wearer got closer, then dying away in the distance. Soon there would be a steady thunder as large numbers of people went by to work, and in the hush which followed, perhaps, another solitary sound, quick-step this time, running, late for the mill. Then it was time for school and off we would go, making our own clog sound, kicking sparks off the pavement as we went. In the winter time we could skate along on frozen cobblestones and hard-packed snow. Posh kids had rubbers on their wooden soles and couldn't join in these particular games.

Familiarly associated only with the northern industrial areas, especially Lancashire and Yorkshire, and particularly with the workers in the textile mills, the wearing of clogs was much more widespread than is often realised, and certainly goes back in time to long before the Industrial Revolution. Although the origins of wooden footwear are obscure, the British clog, together with the Dutch *klompen*, the French *sabot* and the *traesko* of Norway, was certainly being worn during the early part of the Middle Ages. Popular with farming communities, clogs became the traditional peasant footwear in many countries, and were common in Wales and other parts of rural Britain long before their adoption by industrial workers.

Unlike the *klompen* and the *sabot*, both of which are made entirely of wood, the interior expertly carved out for the foot, the British clog consists of a shaped wooden sole to which is attached a stout leather top or upper. Some craftsmen made clogs complete from start to finish, but the work was frequently carried out as two separate trades, divided between the sole-block cutting, which took place out in the woods, and the shaping of the soles and fitting of the uppers, which was done in a workshop. The latter practice became the more common as the demand for clogs increased, and in the clog-making factories, which finally put all but a few independent makers out of business, the work was even further subdivided.

58

The wood used for making clog soles varies from area to area, depending partly on the purpose for which the clogs are to be used and partly on the clog maker's preference. The timber must not split when nails are knocked into it, and it must be knot-free so that it does not break in use; yet it must also be relatively easy to work, for although some clog soles are made by machine the best are cut by hand. Alder, sycamore, birch, willow and beech have all been used; most of the old cloggers kept to one, or at the most two, particular species, convinced that no others were really suitable.

Alder was considered best by many, being definitely preferred in Lancashire, and well liked in some parts of Wales, where it grows in abundance. Sycamore seems to have been the choice of many village workmen who made clogs from start to finish, felling the trees locally and cutting sole blocks during the summer months, then making up the clogs in their own workshops during the winter. This wood, they claimed, was more comfortable to the feet and more durable, being closer-grained than alder. And anyway, they said, alder was widely used only because it was of little value to other trades and therefore could be obtained more cheaply. Birch, too, is a close-grained timber, and it withstands moisture better than either alder or sycamore. Soles of birch were fairly common in parts of Yorkshire, both on the farms and in the woollen mills, and they were worn by miners in wet pits throughout the country. Willow was also used where clogs were worn in wet conditions.

Where soles were cut and shaped by machine, beech was – and still is – the timber most commonly used, being quite plentiful and well suited to machine processing. Hand-made soles in other materials have always been considered superior to machine-cut beech, which is cut across the grain and not cleft as hand-worked soles are, and is therefore more liable to split. In addition, machine shaping cannot produce as comfortable an individual fit as can hand cutting.

Where sole-block cutting was a separate trade, it was among the alder groves that one was most likely to find the block cutters at work. Normally these men worked in gangs, living out in the woods in rough, temporary shelters, moving from place to place according to the availability of material. Some gangs were made up of independent men who might or might not be complete clog makers. They sold some of the blocks they cut direct to other cloggers, keeping back sufficient for their own use if required. Some were employed by timber merchants who dealt as 'middle-men', while others worked for firms who had men elsewhere making clogs in their own large workshop. Most of the large-scale cutting took place in Wales and the Midland counties of England, some cutters being local men, while others came from the industrial areas where the clogs were in great demand.

The wood was bought as standing trees, at about six pence ($2\frac{1}{2}$p) a foot (300mm) prior to 1939, and cutting took place during the spring and early summer. After felling the trees were sawn with a two-man cross-cut saw into short logs or billets of four different lengths, corresponding roughly to the four sizes of sole which were required – children's, middles or boys', women's and men's, the latter being cut to about 16in (400mm) at this stage. Each billet was then split with an axe or wedge into suitably sized sections. If coppiced timber

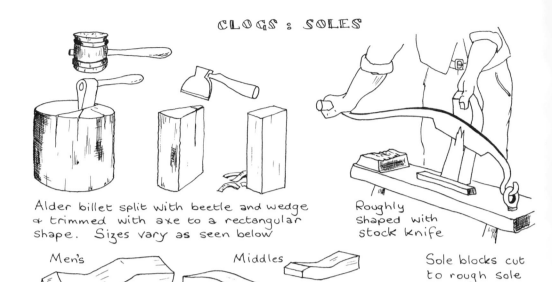

Alder billet split with beetle and wedge & trimmed with axe to a rectangular shape. Sizes vary as seen below

Roughly shaped with stock knife

Men's

Middles

Women's

Children's

Sole blocks cut to rough sole shape in these four sizes

Soles shaped, first with hollowing knife, left. Then groove is cut with the gripper, right

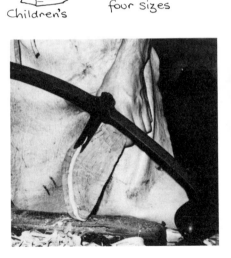

Clog irons, separate ones for sole & heel, are fixed on with tip nails

Irons are nailed on with sole resting on 'Smithy'

Irons in section

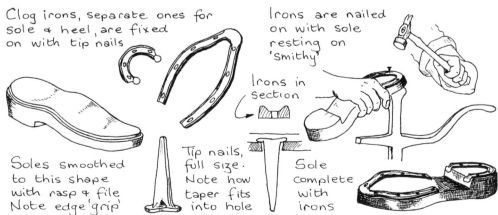

Soles smoothed to this shape with rasp & file Note edge 'grip'

Tip nails, full size. Note how taper fits into hole

Sole complete with irons

was used, material about 6in (150mm) in diameter was chosen, and split once down the middle to make a pair of soles.

Next came the shaping of the clefts, not into completed soles but into over-sized, roughly sole-shaped blocks. This was done with great skill, using the clogger's stock knife. This rather remarkable tool consists of one piece of steel about 30in (750mm) in length, bent slightly towards its middle. The lower half is fashioned into a stout blade and terminates in a hooked projection, while the upper half forms a curved handle with a wooden hand-grip fixed at right angles to its end. By means of the hook the knife is fastened to a steel ring driven into a low wooden bench and, with this ring acting as a pivot point or fulcrum, the knife is used with a levering action, the clogger gripping the handle with the right hand to make downward cutting strokes while his left hand holds the sole block on the bench. The block is shaped by moving it about as the knife moves up and down. At each stroke the clogger has to bend low, and this work, which requires considerable strength as well as skill, can be very tiring if one is not used to it. A skilled man working a ten-hour day could, on average, cut about three hundred pairs of sole blocks in a week.

10 A clog-sole cutters' camp, with newly cut sole blocks stacked to season

Completed blocks were stacked in conical heaps according to size, arranged in such a way that air was able to circulate freely among them. There they were left to season for several weeks before being sent off to the clog makers.

This 'breaking-up' stage, as it was sometimes called, although romanticised as picturesque, was a hard, gypsy way of life. The cutters often lived in crude canvas tents or huts of turf and branches. In sole cutting there was a great deal of waste material – bark, branchwood, wood chips from the knife – and this the workers were expected to sell to local inhabitants as firewood in order to pay for their food while they were away from home. But often they worked in places so remote that this by-product of their work could not be transported economically, and many lived, quite literally, on what they could catch, no doubt becoming expert poachers in the process. The system worked, however, like so many other woodland crafts, because it was easier for the gangs to take their simple tools deep into the woods than it was to transport felled timber to workshops elsewhere. Now the pattern has changed; timber is taken from the woods and delivered in bulk to the few remaining places where clog soles are still made, and there the wood is cut by circular saw and shaped by machine.

In the days when the demand for clogs was high, truck-loads of sole blocks were sent off by train to the clog makers in the industrial towns. The next stage of the work was done either by individual cloggers who ran their own small business and sold clogs direct to the public, often making them to the special order of local customers, or by larger firms who sold clogs both retail and wholesale. The clogger taking special orders would measure the customer's feet and draw up individual paper patterns from which to make the clogs. For ordinary and wholesale work a number of fixed-size patterns would be used.

The final shaping of soles from the rough sole blocks is done with three knives in turn, each similar in appearance to the one used in roughing out the block. The first of these, known as a straight, is almost identical to, although usually a little smaller than, the large stock knife. This is used principally to reduce the sole block to its correct size, and also to shape its outline and lower surface. A second knife, the hollower, shapes the top of the sole, its concave blade giving the finished sole the smooth, hollow curve which fits the foot, supporting the instep and allowing the easy rocking movement from heel to toe when walking. This shaping and hollowing demands great skill, and the good clog maker seems to know instinctively the exact curve required for comfort. The third knife, the morticing knife or gripper, has a narrow V-shaped blade with which the clogger cuts a shallow groove all round the top edge of the sole. The leather upper, when fitted, is gripped into this groove. Finally the soles are trimmed with a short-bladed knife and smoothed with rasp and files.

It is customary to fit the sole 'irons', which are not unlike horseshoes in both shape and function, to the newly completed soles at this stage. They are fixed now rather than later so that if, during the fixing, the sole is split, time and materials will not have been wasted in fitting uppers. Each iron is held in place by several nails, and this nailing-on process soon finds any faults in the wood. Even so, some cloggers prefer to leave it until the clog is finished.

Clog irons were formerly hand-forged, often by local blacksmiths, from flat mild steel bar, each one grooved (or fullered, to use the blacksmith's term) and punched to take the nails. Early this century, however, like horseshoes, they came to be made from ready-fullered bar which needed only to be bent to shape, often cold, and punched to take the nails. Now they are all machine-made, the separate irons for sole and heel being made in a range of sizes.

For nailing on the clogger rests each sole on a smithy, a shaped iron stand which provides a firm foundation. The nails used are called tip nails, but to many old cloggers they were known as sparrow bills on account of their tapered shape. Both these nails and the tacks used in fixing the uppers have blunt points, this shape being less likely to split the wood into which it is hammered. The taper fits

11 A clog maker at work at his bench, nailing irons to a sole

snugly into the punched holes in the irons, the flat heads being narrow enough to fit the fullered groove. After ironing, the soles are blacked around their edges and below the instep with what used to be called Boston Blacking, a concoction consisting mainly of lampblack and turpentine. They are then ready to have the uppers fitted.

The upper may be made from one or two pieces of leather, sometimes even from three. Children's and ladies' clogs often have a one-piece upper fastened with a button, but the traditional clasp-fastening clog needs two pieces, a spade-shaped piece which forms the front and tongue and a longer piece for the back and sides. In order to get a better fit round the ankle the clogger sometimes cuts the back in two, sewing the pieces together again with a slight curve to the back seam. Clogs made in this way are known as split backs or half backs.

Using a paper pattern or a more permanent metal template, the shapes are marked out on a piece of leather with the back of a knife blade, then cut out with a knife which is always kept razor-sharp. This work, known as clicking, is done on a hard, flat surface. Next the inside edges of the leather round the ankle parts and the tongue are thinned down, or skived, to make a softer edge for the wearer's foot. Separate parts are then stitched together, the clogger using a thread known as a wax end which he usually makes himself. Several strands of hemp go to make one of these, each strand separated from the remaining length not by cutting, but by pulling and untwisting the fibres so that they form a finely tapered end. Twisted into a loose cord, the bundle of strands is then rolled on a leather pad placed on the knee, and cobbler's wax is rubbed in. When the strands are tightly twisted together a stiff bristle is attached to each end of the waxed thread. Pigs' bristles were once used for this purpose, the best, so it was said, coming from Russian wild boar. Now a nylon substitute is used to good effect.

The best leather for clog uppers is cowhide which has been treated with wax at the tannery. Known as kip, this is usually dyed black. The leather is hard-wearing yet supple enough to be fairly easy to mould to the shape of the foot. A type of leather known as split kip is sometimes used, but this is of poorer quality.

Stitching is done on a curved wooden sewing block which sticks out from the clogger's bench at knee height. The two pieces to be sewn are held in place by a leather strap kept tensioned by the clogger's foot as he sits at his bench to do the work. A sewing awl with a curved point is pushed down into one piece and up through the other, each hole being about $\frac{1}{4}$in (6mm) from the edge of the joint which, if it is a back seam, is often strengthened inside with a strip of soft leather. The two ends of the wax end are pushed through from opposite directions, as in the harness maker's saddle stitch. Sometimes a sewing machine like the one used by other leather workers is employed for stitching or 'closing' the uppers.

Uppers are shaped over a wooden mould known as a last, which is a sort of wooden foot of the appropriate size. Holding this between his knees, the clogger places the upper on it, fixing it in place with two or three tacks. Then, gripping the leather with a pair of curved lasting pincers, he draws the upper down over the last, shaping it over the instep and toe, where it is secured with a few more tacks. Lasting pincers usually incorporate a small hammer-head so that the tacks may be quickly driven in without the need to change tools. Speed and ease of movement account also for the old clogger's habit of keeping a few tacks held ready in his mouth while he worked.

The upper may be hammered while on the last with a flat-headed hammer or mallet in order to help spread the leather a little, and left on the last for some time until it is set to shape. More often it is rubbed over with a warm burnishing or boshing iron, which is a smooth, half-round piece of steel with a handle at each end. After heating over a gas flame this is used with a stroking movement, mostly over the instep area and down towards the outer edge and over the toe. When removed the upper retains the shape of the last.

Unlike boots and shoes, clog uppers are removed from the last before being

64

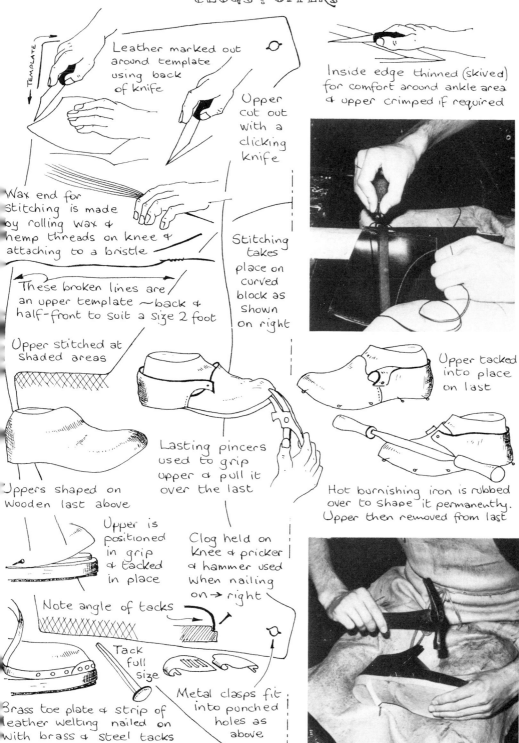

TEMPLATE

Leather marked out around template using back of knife

Upper cut out with a clicking knife

Inside edge thinned (skived) for comfort around ankle area & upper crimped if required

Wax end for stitching is made by rolling wax & hemp threads on knee & attaching to a bristle

Stitching takes place on curved block as shown on right

These broken lines are an upper template ~ back & half-front to suit a size 2 foot

Upper stitched at shaded areas

Upper tacked into place on last

Uppers shaped on wooden last above

Lasting pincers used to grip upper & pull it over the last

Hot burnishing iron is rubbed over to shape it permanently. Upper then removed from last

Upper is positioned in grip & tacked in place

Clog held on knee & pricker & hammer used when nailing on → right

Note angle of tacks

Tack full size

Metal clasps fit into punched holes as above

Brass toe plate & strip of leather welting nailed on with brass & steel tacks joined to the sole. Most of the assembly work is done on the clogger's knee, which is protected by a leather apron. First the upper is placed in the grip of the sole – the groove cut earlier around its top edge – and any unevenness in the edge of the upper is trimmed off with a knife until a neat, close-fitting line is obtained. When he is satisfied, the clogger fixes the upper to the sole with a few well spaced-out tacks – similar in function to the dressmaker's tacking stitch – and then begins to nail it on properly. He uses a short pointed awl or pricker to make holes for the tacks, which are quite different from those used for fixing irons. The pricker is pushed through the leather and down into the sole towards the angle of the grip, care being necessary here to keep the pricker at a downward angle of about thirty degrees so that the tacks will point away from the wearer's foot. Pricking and tacking take place together, the pricker being held in the same hand as the hammer – a further example of the craftsman's economy of effort and movement.

Tacking or nailing on begins at the toe of the clog, and here one of two methods may be used. Ordinary clogs have brass tacks inserted, their heads almost touching, while fancy clogs have a brass toe-plate fitted. A narrow strip of leather, the welting, goes all around the rest of the clog, covering the junction of sole and upper, secured at intervals of about $\frac{1}{2}$in (12mm) with steel or iron tacks. Their blunt ends are pushed into the holes made by the pricker, which here goes through the welting first, and then they are hammered in tightly. The welting strip strengthens and helps to seal the joint along the nail line. Some fancy clogs are nailed with brass tacks all round.

The clasps with which some clogs are fastened were once available in a wide range of designs and styles, in either brass or black japanned steel. Now both their availability and range is limited. Ideally they are fitted while the customer is wearing the clogs, a special punch being used to pierce the leather for the lug which secures the clasp. Not all clogs have clasp fasteners; some, especially children's and ladies', have a button-hole fastener, while many men's clogs are laced through perhaps two pairs of brass-eyeletted lace holes. All these clogs have low uppers and can be slipped on and off fairly easily. There used to be a type of clog with high uppers, similar to a boot; this had several pairs of lace-holes and was generally known as a lace-up. Some were actually made from the tops of old boots.

Clogs were always considered the most practical and the healthiest type of footwear, especially in wet or muddy conditions. Warm in winter and cool in summer, they are not nearly so uncomfortable to wear as they may appear, although it is true to say that they do need a little getting used to. Unfortunately, from the mid-1930s onwards their popularity was overtaken by changes in footwear fashion and social outlook; some people came to regard the wearing of clogs as a sign of poverty, and instead bought cheap and inferior boots which were less practical, and more expensive in the long term, for they did not last as long.

There were others, however, who saw no disgrace in wearing clogs, providing they were clean. They wore their highly polished footwear with pride, and it was not uncommon, particularly among the northern mill workers and miners, to own both a pair of ordinary working clogs and a pair of 'best' clogs for wearing on Sundays and special occasions. These best or fancy clogs would certainly have brass toe-caps and more brass nails than was normal, but in addition many also had designs tooled or crimped into the leather uppers before these were fitted to the sole. Some of the most elaborate of these fancy clogs were worn by clog dancers, both male and female, who performed this northern version of what is basically a type of tap dance either singly or as a dancing troupe.

Clogs and clog dancing are both now enjoying a healthy revival. There is a steady demand from certain industries for machine-made working clogs, and some updated fancy styles have now made their appearance on the fashion scene. Most of the latter are also machine-made, some in coloured leathers and all with beech soles – always assuming they are not of plastic. There are still a few craftsmen making traditional-style clogs by hand, however; some of them use machine-cut soles, which they may alter slightly by hand before fitting hand-made uppers, but others still shape their own soles and make complete clogs, and these remain, as always, the best.

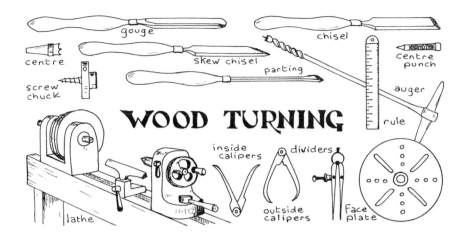

One of life's finer privileges is to stand at a respectful distance and watch an expert wood turner at work at his lathe. There is a fascination in seeing the long shavings curl away from the work, the cutting edge of the tool seeming only to kiss the wood as it revolves before it. As the workpiece takes shape, the contoured outline reveals rich grain patterns previously hidden from view, and a finished surface pleasing to the touch. The floor of the workshop is crisp with clean, new shavings, and the air is filled with the smell of freshly cut wood.

There is an ease about the turner's work which is deceptive, however, for good work comes only with practice and experience. There is considerable skill in the correct manipulation of the cutting tools and in knowing which tool to use at each particular stage of the work.

By comparison with some crafts, the tools used at the lathe are few in number; they comprise a variety of cutting tools, either gouges or chisels, and scrapers. Most of those required can be purchased from specialist tool manufacturers, who at one time marketed a range of over seventy different types. Now about a dozen is considered sufficient. In earlier times it was the local blacksmith who made them to the individual turner's specifications, and each craftsman had his favourite type.

Kept close by the lathe, some of these tools were held in a rack, while others rested on the lathe bed ready for use. Most were of the 'long and strong' variety – heavy-gauge tempered steel fitted with long beech handles, about 20in (500mm) long overall. Similar tools, often simply labelled L & S, are still available, and are recommended for serious turning, since they allow a firm but sensitive leverage against the rotating workpiece and good control of the cutting edge, especially in large-diameter work. Two types of gouge can be distinguished, one shallow, the other deeply hollowed. Both can be obtained in a range of sizes, some ground square across the cutting edge, some curved. All are bevelled to about 45°. Chisels come in sizes from $\frac{1}{4}$in up to 2in (6mm to 50mm) and, unlike ordinary chisels, are bevelled on both sides.

Most curious among the old turner's hand-made tools, and not found in any

68

toolmaker's catalogue, were the hooked knives made specially for bowl turning. These had curved-over blades, like hooks in fact, and some were ground for inside work, some for outside.

Other tools, hanging on pegs along the wall, will include saws, an axe and a drawknife, all used for preparing wood for the lathe. On a nearby bench there will be a small grinding wheel and several oilstones, used in keeping the lathe tools nice and sharp.

The wood turner's lathe, like the potter's wheel and the simple drill, is one of man's oldest machines. It is hard to say when it was first used, but many primitive people knew how to make fire by means of the friction set up when two pieces of wood are rubbed together. The string of a bow wrapped round one piece of wood so that it revolved when the bow was drawn back and forth was a great technological advance in this process. It was not long, presumably, before this turning motion was put to other uses. Both the bow drill and the bow lathe were known in ancient Egypt, where turned and decorated wooden chairs and tables, and also turned ivory ornamentation, reached a high level of sophistication. Primitive craftsmen in a number of countries around the world still use these two simple machines; in parts of Asia the bow is operated by the machinist's foot.

In its simplest form a lathe consists of two uprights, called poppets, supported on a base or bed. The wood to be turned goes between the poppets, and is held on pointed centres so that it is free to revolve. A cord – a bow string – looped round the wood and pulled to and fro causes the wood to turn. The cutting tool, held by the operator against a fixed rest, can only be used on each alternate stroke when the wood is revolving towards it.

The pole lathe is an extension of the bow-lathe idea. The workpiece is again held between centres and revolved by means of a cord or leather strap. But this time one end of the cord is attached to a long springy pole overhead, the other to a treadle below the lathe. The wood revolves when the treadle is pressed, and spins back again, pulled by the pole under tension, when the treadle is released. Still a semi-rotary machine, the pole lathe was widely adopted throughout the world, and in many places continued in use long after the introduction of continuous rotation. In spite of its now obvious disadvantages, it had the advantage of simplicity and portability, and for many woodland craftsman this was important. These men, working out in the woods where their raw material grew, were able to set up a lathe wherever they chose, requiring nothing more than two adjacent stumps as a base and a handy growing sapling to provide the necessary motive power. In any case many of them were accustomed to the pole lathe's peculiarities and would have nothing to do with new-fangled ideas.

In some situations it was the use of water power which first provided continuous rotation for lathe work; in others the treadle, operating through a crank as in old-fashioned sewing machines, did the trick. Many early lathes were linked up to large fly-wheels, and some were driven by small boys in the days of sweated labour. All these methods were in due course replaced by steam and then in turn by the electric motor. Whatever the motive power, the principle of wood turning has remained unchanged; the workpiece is rotated against a sharp cutting or scraping tool held and guided by the skilled hands of the turner.

SPINDLE TURNING

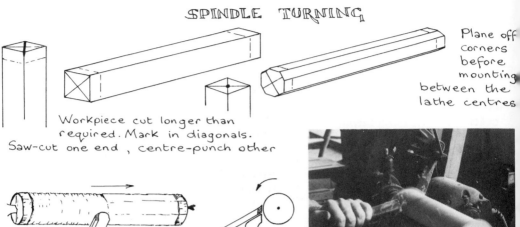

Workpiece cut longer than required. Mark in diagonals. Saw-cut one end, centre-punch other

Plane off corners before mounting between the lathe centres

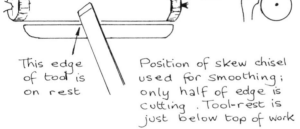

Both viewed from top

Position of gouge for roughing out. Note that bevel of tool rubs the work. Tool-rest is positioned just below centre

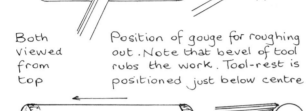

This edge of tool is on rest

Position of skew chisel used for smoothing; only half of edge is cutting. Tool-rest is just below top of work

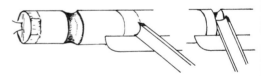

Cutting beads with the skew chisel. Start in the middle and work to the left, then work to the right

Cutting coves or grooves with the gouge. Start on incised line and cut to centre

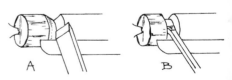

A   B

Tapers are cut with skew chisel working 'downhill' from largest to smallest diameter

Two ways of parting off work on the lathe. A. with chisel B. with a parting-off tool

The lathe should stand before a window so that the work is in full light. The turner centres the wood — a roughly rounded piece to be made into the leg of a table. The tool-rest is positioned as close as possible to the wood without actually touching it, a little above the centre line of the piece. Standing close to the lathe, the turner selects a large half-round gouge and is ready to begin 'roughing in'. He holds the tool against the rest, with his left hand curled round the blade, thumb below, fingers on top, and his right hand holding the handle low down. 'Let the bevel rub all the time; that way it won't dig in,' he warns as, gradually easing the gouge forward, he peels a curl of rope-like shaving from the rotating workpiece. Moving sideways along the rest, the tool continues to remove wood until, quite soon, a completely cylindrical shape is obtained.

Then the gouge is exchanged for a chisel and the shavings come off in a long ribbon, leaving the wood quite smooth. Some workers prefer a skew chisel, which has an angled cutting edge, for smoothing, but our man uses a wide flat tool, holding it at the correct angle himself and allowing only half the blade to cut. 'Gouges and chisels are intended to cut,' the turner tells us; 'the shavings tell you if you are using them properly.'

Chisels can be used with a scraping action, and some instructors teach this method as a safe and easy way for beginners. It is easier to do, but it produces a lot of dust instead of clean shavings, leaves a rough surface on soft wood and quickly blunts the tool edge. For some types of work, though, scraping is a big help, and for others it may be the only way to get a satisfactory finish. Scraping tools are used for fine work in very hard woods and for some faceplate work, and

12 Turning a chair leg

also when finishing the inside of bowls. Old files, suitably ground at the end, make excellent scrapers.

But the table leg is not finished yet. The turner now begins to cut in the beads and grooves and the long central taper characteristic of this type of turned work. The positions of beads and grooves are first incised with the point of a chisel. The beads are cut with a skew chisel, a deft circular movement of the tool cutting each side in turn, the point of the long corner of the chisel doing most of the work. The cut is started midway between the two incised lines, with the cutting edge of the chisel more or less parallel to the axis of the work. The right-hand side of the chisel is raised off the rest, and as the point begins to cut it is rolled further to the left, until at the end of the cut the chisel is on its side, with its cutting edge at right angles to the work. The turner cuts the opposite side of the bead in the reverse manner to form the required shape. Beads cut in this way end up with clean edges. For repetitive work, a specially shaped beading tool in the form of a short-channelled gouge with extended corners is sometimes used.

Grooves, or coves, are cut in two movements with a round-nosed gouge, and the incised lines with which the turner marked his work are of added importance here. The cut is started on one of these lines, the gouge on its side with its bevel square to the work and rubbing as one would expect from the advice given earlier. Without the incised line the tool would skid sideways off the work, but the line supports it until its edge begins to cut. The turner pushes the gouge forward, rolling it over on its back, lowering the handle as he does so in a sort of scooping motion. This first cut leaves the cove half done, the other half being cut in exactly the same way from the opposite side. Coves are not cut in one movement – 'This would mean the gouge going uphill to finish the cut, and that would never do.' Later we are shown what happens when coves are incorrectly cut: the final edge splinters out to leave an unpleasant 'frayed' edge.

Another cut which the turner demonstrates on this occasion is the simple 'V' groove, which is worked with the long corner of the skew chisel. The point of the chisel is pushed lightly into the work at an angle of about 45°, then the same thing is done from the opposite side. Cutting a little at a time from alternate sides, the groove is gradually cut down to its required depth.

The table leg still has to have its tapered portion turned, and again the turner takes up the wide, flat chisel which he used for smoothing the original cylindrical workpiece. First he cuts the top shoulder, then the longer, more gradual taper towards the bottom of the leg. In both cases he cuts from the larger to the smaller diameter, or 'downhill' as he calls it, eye judgement alone telling him when the curve is true and the balance right. Some use the skew chisel for this job too.

A little light glasspapering, done with the work revolving, the tool-rest removed and the glasspaper trailed beneath the work for safety, and the turning is complete. The final job is to part the leg from the waste end-pieces; this is done by cutting a deep groove in the required place with a shaped parting tool, removing the work from the lathe and sawing through the remaining stub.

Such work, which is called spindle turning or turning between centres, is not too difficult providing one does not attempt anything too complicated at the start. The proper way to cut rotating wood, the correct angle at which to hold the

13　A bowl being turned between centres on a pole lathe

tool and the right amount of pressure to apply can only be learned in stages by actual practice at a lathe.

The same applies to bowl turning, which the turner now demonstrates. On a modern lathe it is usual to turn a bowl held on a faceplate which is mounted on the drive spindle of the lathe, the workpiece being fastened to it by means of ordinary wood screws. The old craftsmen originally turned their bowls between centres, as in spindle turning, but later came to rely on a single large screw as a holding device. This screwed into the base of the bowl, gripping it quite firmly.

The turner prepares his wood by sawing it roughly to a little over the required diameter, ensuring that the grain runs across the opening of the bowl. He mounts the block so that the outside can be turned first, again using the roughing-in gouge to obtain the correct shape, and finishes it off with a chisel. Special attention is paid to getting the base of the bowl true, as this is important to the next stage of the work. A slightly concave form is aimed for in shaping the base.

Next he removes the half-completed bowl from the lathe to remount it so that the inside can be turned. 'There are several ways of doing this,' he informs us. 'One way is simply to screw the bowl to the face plate, but that leaves screw holes which then have to be disguised.' He shows us how to avoid this by glueing a false wooden bottom to the bowl, a piece of newspaper between the two. The securing screws go into this without touching the actual bowl. On completion it is easily split off at the paper joint. A false bottom is also used when a bowl is turned in a single operation — that is without removing it from the faceplate halfway through. Here the block is mounted as shown in the diagram; the outside is turned first, then the tool-rest is moved round and the inside turned as follows.

First the turner makes a shallow groove with a scraping tool near the outer edge of the bowl — 'a shoulder for the bevel of the gouge to lean on', we are told. Then a strong, $\frac{3}{4}$in (19mm) gouge is brought into use, and, with the bevel rubbing, the hollowing-out process takes place. A deep groove is opened up around the bowl and progressively made deeper and wider by a circular movement of the gouge which, pivoting on the rest, is rolled gently from side to side. The centre part of the bowl is turned last, and the completed hollow finished off with a scraper. Some turners use scrapers for much of this work, as they can be ground to cut against the grain — gouges tend to lift the fibres of the wood at two points when turning a bowl.

Many of the old craftsmen turned wood while it was still green. For large bowls this speeded up the seasoning process, the bowls being rough-turned oversize and allowed to dry out before finishing. Of course there was a tendency for them to warp and twist somewhat, but they could usually be trued up at the finish.

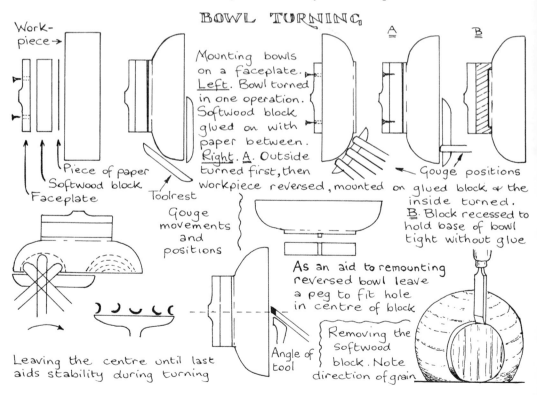

BOWL TURNING

Work-piece →

Mounting bowls on a faceplate.
Left. Bowl turned in one operation. Softwood block glued on with paper between.
Right. A. Outside turned first, then workpiece reversed, mounted on glued block & the inside turned.
B. Block recessed to hold base of bowl tight without glue

Piece of paper
Softwood block
Faceplate
Toolrest
Gouge movements and positions
A
B
Gouge positions

As an aid to remounting reversed bowl leave a peg to fit hole in centre of block

Leaving the centre until last aids stability during turning

Angle of tool

Removing the Softwood block. Note direction of grain

The greatest test of skill was to turn a nest of bowls from a single block of wood. Elm was normally used, and the secret lay in the use of a long curved chisel which cut through to the core of the block, separating each individual bowl.

Most of this early work was utilitarian; large numbers of wooden household utensils were once in daily use in country cottages and farms. Even after the introduction of pewter and earthenware, and then of glass, or silver and porcelain if one were wealthy enough, wooden articles continued to be used in many areas. Country turners were kept busy producing large bowls for storing and mixing, smaller bowls and platters for use at the table, and various other small items of domestic wooden ware now collectively known as 'treen' and including pepper mills, egg cups, mustard pots, tobacco jars and so on.

Sycamore was the most suitable wood for domestic ware likely to come into contact with food: it has neither smell nor taste and will not taint food, and its clean white looks can be maintained by scrubbing. For these reasons boards for cheese and bread and for cutting up meat have always been made from sycamore, as were many of the utensils used in the farm dairy. Beech and sometimes alder were used for similar purposes.

Beech was, and still is, a favourite wood for turning. Rolling pins, brush backs, bobbins and toys all have a nice smooth finish, and are quite durable, when turned in beech. It readily accepts fine turning, and is sometimes seen with a thread cut in it to make wooden screws. A similar species, hornbeam, is actually better for this latter purpose, being harder and denser. Not so easily available now, it was once known as the engineer's wood because of its special properties.

In the early days of the Industrial Revolution, before iron was in general use, wood turners made a variety of wooden machine parts, pulleys, pulley blocks, wheels and shafts, cogwheels and screws in all shapes and sizes. In Lancashire huge quantities of spools and bobbins were required for the growing cotton industry. Locally grown birch was used for this work, and throughout the north of the county water-driven turneries were to be found producing nothing else but goods for the cotton mills.

Birch has fallen from favour as a turning wood, and for craft purposes generally for that matter, being used now mainly in the manufacture of plywood. It also produces a tough veneer, and was used in the construction of Mosquito aircraft in World War II. Birch is still used in Scandinavia and Canada for a number of purposes including turning and furniture making.

For decorative work the turner uses a wide range of woods in order to obtain variety of grain and colour. Because much of his work is on a small scale he is able to use woods not selected by the craftsmen who need large timbers. Fruitwoods such as apple and plum, ornamental trees like laburnum and exotic cherries, and shrub species such as box and hawthorn are highly suitable.

The demand for hand-turned goods is not nearly as great as it once was. Woodware is still quite popular, judging by the articles seen in gift shops, but a great deal of turned work can now be done by semi-skilled labour on automatic lathes. The furniture industry uses this method for repetition reproduction. But there are still a few professional craft turners about, and a great many amateurs, each in his own way preserving this ancient craft.

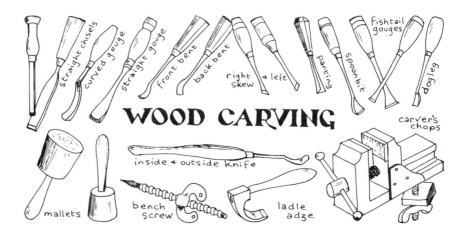

WOOD CARVING

The first thing one notices on entering a wood carver's workshop is the great number of chisels and gouges which he has on his bench. What is more surprising is the fact that these are but a small proportion of the tools available to him. A perusal of toolmakers' catalogues shows that there are in fact well over three hundred different types and sizes of wood-carving tools to choose from: straight, bent and back-bent chisels, spade chisels, left and right skew chisels; front-bent, back-bent and fishtail gouges; fluters, veiners and parting tools; fluteroni, macaroni and backeroni; spoons and doglegs. Each kind comes in a range of sizes, from 1mm up to 25mm and above, and each is numbered in the catalogue for ease of identification when ordering.

No craftsman ever buys all of them. The professional wood carver is more likely to have acquired over a period of time fifty or sixty of the tools best suited to his particular style of work. Most carvers keep those in regular use in a row on a long shelf at the back of the bench, cutting edges to the front for easy recognition. A further aid to selecting the right tool quickly is provided by the handles, which vary both in shape and in the wood from which they are made. They can be of beech, box, ash, yew, holly or rosewood; some are cylindrical, some bulbous and some octagonal, some plain and others with ring markings.

In addition to the strange-sounding names listed above, the carver often has tools which are nameless – chisels and gouges which have been made specially by the local blacksmith, or standard items which have been altered by regrinding – to suit his own individual preference. Often he knows them by the job they do rather than by name.

The amateur carver need not have so many tools in his beginner's kit. Ten or twelve are ample to start with, and many people manage with even fewer; further tools can be added later as the carver and his work improve. It is possible to buy small sets of carving tools, but experience shows that it is better to purchase them individually, as sets always seem to contain some tools which you never use. Other items needed by professional and amateur alike include mallets, saws, holding devices such as a vice or clamps, and equipment for sharpening tools.

76

14 Carving an oak table leg at an exhibition

Carved work in wood dates back over many centuries; it may even be as old as the Neolithic cave paintings. Very little early work has survived, but crude carvings seem always to have played an important part in the superstitions and ceremonial beliefs of primitive peoples, and wood was undoubtedly carved long before stone, being much easier to work with simple tools. Many such carvings had a religious significance; an early biblical reference concerns the building of the temple of Solomon: 'and he carved all the walls of the house round about with carved figures of cherubim and palm trees and open flowers' (I Kings 6: 29). Wooden carvings, and indeed wooden objects generally, have had sacred and sometimes magical properties attributed to them by many different peoples throughout the world. The custom of 'touching wood' as a safeguard against tempting fate originates from these beliefs.

Early carvers used few tools; primitive craftsmen had only axes and knives, first of flint and later of iron. Polynesian face-masks and the totem poles of the North American Indians reflect the use of these crude tools. The carvings of ancient Egypt show a remarkable skill when one considers the limitations of the few tools used, though by this time the chisel was already known. In Europe, Saxon and medieval carving is characterised by a relative simplicity which clearly required fewer tools than later work. The chip-carved patterns, often in stylised, geometric shapes, and the architectural motifs borrowed from the stonemasons, can be readily executed using only a small range of chisels and gouges suited to the particular design.

The carver's craft reached its peak during the Renaissance period (c 1400–1600). The Italian influence on design and the introduction of a freer style of carving, together with a realisation that wood could be carved in more delicate detail than had ever been possible in stone, gave a new direction to the wood carver's work. And it was the interior decoration of the great cathedrals which gave the craftsmen an opportunity to display their skill. The more intricate work required a greater range of tools, and those in use today stem from this period, when chisels and gouges in numerous new shapes were introduced.

The nameless carvers of this period filled the cathedrals and churches of Europe with their masterpieces of delicate tracery and pierced work. Canopied choir stalls, rood screens, pews and pulpits all bear testimony to their artistry and skill. Bible scenes, allegorical beasts and bands of angels, foliage, and fruit and flowers of all kinds decorate their work in a profusion not seen before or since. Large houses and public buildings were likewise decorated, and later individual craftsmen such as Grinling Gibbons made a name for themselves by bringing a new naturalism and an even greater delicacy to wood carving.

The great thing about the carving of this period is the feeling of joy which one can find in it. To the craftsman this work was leisurely, and he seems not only to have enjoyed spending time on perfection, but also to have passed on his enjoyment in what he carved. One has only to look closely at the detail, especially on those parts not too readily seen, such as misericords – the carved ledges on the underside of many old choir stalls – to detect the strong sense of humour in much of the carved work.

The village wood carver had to be skilled in a wide range of work, for he was expected to be able to turn his hand to many different kinds of carving. He had to be able to do ornate work, not only on public buildings but also on house furniture and fittings, and to make a variety of domestic utensils for use in the kitchen and at the table.

In the days before pottery and metal came into general use in the home, and certainly long before the advent of plastics, carved wooden ware of all kinds played a significant part in daily life. We have already seen how important lathe-turned domestic articles were. Some items were part turned, part carved, and in some villages the turner and the carver might be one and the same person. Many other items, not being round, could not be turned, and therefore had to be entirely hand-carved.

The making of certain spoons and ladles was one such job. Often started while the wood was still green, or partly wet, these were roughly hewn to size with an axe, the bowl being partly hollowed with a small, one-handed adze. After further seasoning the bowl would be completed with a rounded gouge or, more often, with a special curved knife. For this work the carver sat astride a low stool, the roughly shaped spoon held against his knee by his left hand. With the long handle of the curved knife held against his right forearm for extra leverage he scooped and smoothed out the hollow of the spoon with a twisting movement of his wrist. Finally the outside was finished off with a spokeshave and a short-bladed hand

78

15 Hollowing a traditional wooden spoon

knife. Alternatively, some spoons were hollowed out with a half-round gouge and finished either in the same way as described above or with a file and scraper. It is this latter method which is described in the accompanying diagram. Small spoons used at the table for eating, and larger spoons and ladles for mixing and serving, were all made by these methods, some of the latter with hooked handles so that they could be hung up when not in use. Sycamore is the most suitable wood for this work because of its cleanliness, but beech may also be used.

In some areas, particularly in Wales, spoons of this kind with handles carved in a most elaborate fashion, were made by young men and given as gifts to the girl of their fancy. 'Love spoons', as these came to be called, date back at least three centuries. Originally, it seems they were intended to be used by the recipient, but as their ornamentation became more and more elaborate they took on a purely symbolic significance. Some were carved with two bowls, or were actually two spoons joined by a linked chain, all cut from one piece of wood. These double spoons symbolised mutual love, while a single carved heart meant 'I love you'. A carved shape like a pair of spectacles meant 'I like what I see', or 'I want to see you again', and so on. Love spoons are still made for the tourist trade, but the genuine old ones are more interesting. Some were crudely carved, but others, their hollow handles containing spheres of wood which moved freely inside, required a great deal of skill to make. These signified, incidentally, that the recipient had captured the maker's heart. Much time and thought must have gone into the carving of these tokens of affection, making them so much more acceptable than even the most expensive shop-bought gift. Most were the work of amateur carvers, farm lads with time on their hands in the long winter evenings or seamen on long voyages.

Many an apprentice wood carver would have made them in his spare time too, no doubt, but mostly he was kept busy at more mundane tasks. In the branch of carving known as coarse carving, beech was used to make a variety of goods for use by other workers. Long-handled shovels were once carved from a single piece of wood, some for handling grain and flour, while others, known as 'peels', were used by the baker to lift loaves of bread from his hot ovens. Saddle makers used 'trees', as they are called, as the foundation for saddles and carthorse collars, and these were hand-carved, usually from beech, to a shape dictated by the anatomy of the horse.

MAKING A SPOON

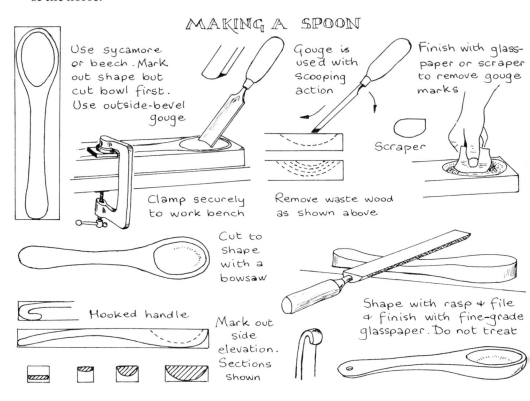

Use sycamore or beech. Mark out shape but cut bowl first. Use outside-bevel gouge

Clamp securely to work bench

Gouge is used with scooping action

Remove waste wood as shown above

Finish with glass-paper or scraper to remove gouge marks

Scraper

Cut to shape with a bowsaw

Hooked handle

Mark out side elevation. Sections shown

Shape with rasp & file & finish with fine-grade glasspaper. Do not treat

One area where the carver had an opportunity to show his artistry was in the making of the butter prints used on dairy farms. These were turned in sycamore or beech, then carved with a distinctive design and used to impress farm-made butter with a sort of maker's label or trade-mark. Some were carved on a simple machine not unlike a modern spindle moulder.

Carved furniture, once much more popular than it is today, gave the carver further artistic licence. In the seventeenth and early eighteenth centuries carved decoration became the dominant feature of the furniture of the wealthy. A piece was considered lacking if it was not encrusted with trailing vines, acanthus leaves, fruit in profusion and a cupid or two. Country carvers remained largely outside this sphere of influence, however, and country-made furniture was more restrained in design and decoration. Often traditional chip-carved patterns were used to good effect.

To achieve some measure of skill in simple chip carving is good practice in the use and control of carving tools. Only two basic tools are used, the straight chisel to produce triangular and rectangular pockets and the straight gouge to make 'thumbnail' notches and curved patterns.

Choose a piece of 'soft' hardwood – lime is ideal – and on its smooth surface mark parallel lines in the direction of the grain. The width of the tool indicates the correct distance between them. Mark in the opposite direction to form squares. Then, using the straight chisel, make near-vertical cuts on the lines and sloping cuts at an angle to meet up with them. In most patterns the cuts will have to be made with the chisel tilted so that it digs deeper at one corner in order to remove a triangular chip. The first cut should not be absolutely vertical, but made at a slight angle towards the second so that the cut surface is more easily seen.

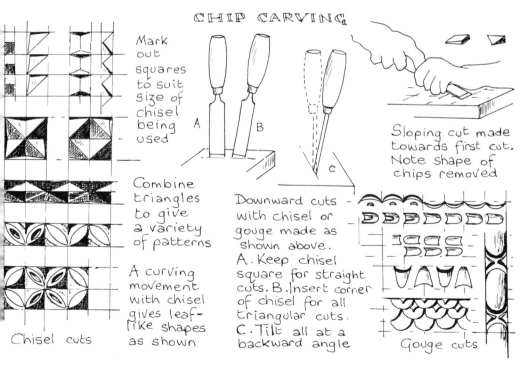

CHIP CARVING

Mark out squares to suit size of chisel being used

A   B   C

Sloping cut made towards first cut. Note shape of chips removed

Combine triangles to give a variety of patterns

A curving movement with chisel gives leaf-like shapes as shown

Downward cuts with chisel or gouge made as shown above.
A. Keep chisel square for straight cuts. B. Insert corner of chisel for all triangular cuts.
C. Tilt all at a backward angle

Chisel cuts

Gouge cuts

Working with the gouge is basically the same; the second cut is usually made towards the convex side of the first.

Chip carving produces a textured surface of simple patterns. Similar work in which the surface is carved with shapes against a background to form a three-dimensional picture is known as relief carving. This can be shallow or deeply cut, the distinction indicated by the terms low or high relief. Here the outline of the design is drawn on to the surface of the work and the spaces between are cut away to varying depths using a variety of chisels and gouges. This is followed by discreet modelling of the remaining surfaces and subtle undercutting of certain areas to achieve the desired effect. Fully three-dimensional work, or carving in the round, produces free-standing sculptural objects, and requires a greater understanding of proportion and form.

Whether carving in relief or in the round, the carver begins by removing the bulk of the waste wood from around the shape to be carved. For this a straight gouge is used – one strong enough to stand up to the blows from the mallet which is usually used at this roughing-in stage. Next comes the more precise work of modelling or cutting in the detail of the piece of work. Here a variety of tools is used: curved and front-bent gouges for hollow sections, veiners for round-bottomed grooves, skew chisels for undercutting. Using two hands now to guide the cutting edge, the carver has more control over where he cuts – and, more important, where he stops cutting. Usually the ball of one hand rests on the work, fingertips resting on or curled round the blade of the tool. This hand acts as a sort of fixed pivot upon which all cutting movement is made, while the other hand, holding the tool handle, provides the forward pressure. Left- and right-hand positions have purposely not been specified, as in carving it pays to be ambidextrous.

It is in lettering that the wood carver shows his greatest skill. Such carved lettering, whether incised into the surface of the wood or raised in relief against a recessed background, calls not only for an ability to produce well-cut shapes but also for a well-developed sense of proportion and spacing. Much of the carver's work in lettering is of a commemorative nature, and knowing what is appropriate to the occasion is also important. Depending on the job in hand, the style of lettering can be light or bold, plain or decorative, large or small; but it must always convey its message clearly, and each individual letter should be easily readable.

After making sketches to determine the best arrangement for the text, the letters should be drawn accurately to full size and transferred to the prepared surface of the wood using carbon paper. The grain of the wood should run horizontally across the lines of lettering wherever possible. For incised work a centre line is needed for each letter; this indicates the deepest point of the cut and acts as a guide for the chisel.

To cut straight line strokes use a sharp, straight chisel, choosing one about $\frac{1}{4}$in (6mm) shorter than the height of the letters to avoid having to join up a number of short cuts. Hold it vertically on the centre line, away from the ends of the letter, and give it a sharp tap with the mallet. Then place the same chisel on one of the adjacent lines at an angle of about 30° and cut down to the full depth of the central vertical cut. Repeat the process from the other side to make a clean V-shaped groove. Curved shapes are more difficult and require a gouge which

82

exactly matches the radius of the curve. Cut the central vertical line with this, overlapping each cut to give a continuous line. For the inside and outside angled cuts of the curve a flatter, more shallow-curved gouge is used, both cuts being made by turning the gouge with a slicing movement to follow the curve of the letter. Care must be taken to prevent the corners of the gouge from digging in too deeply.

Serifs, the curved thickenings on the terminal points of all straight strokes and on the letters C, G and S, are cut with a small spade chisel. Make two downward cuts angling out from the centre line to the corners of the letter, with the chisel tilted so that the cuts are deepest where the three lines meet. Then continue the sloping sides of the 'V' groove on each side up to these intersecting lines, turning the chisel gradually to obtain the correct shape; and finally remove the triangular piece remaining. Chip carving is good practice for this last operation.

When carving with the grain – and this is sometimes necessary – it is wise to make the angled serif cuts early on in the carving sequence, usually when making the central vertical incision. These then act as stop cuts and prevent 'splitting out' of subsequent cuts along the grain and beyond the drawn shape of the letter.

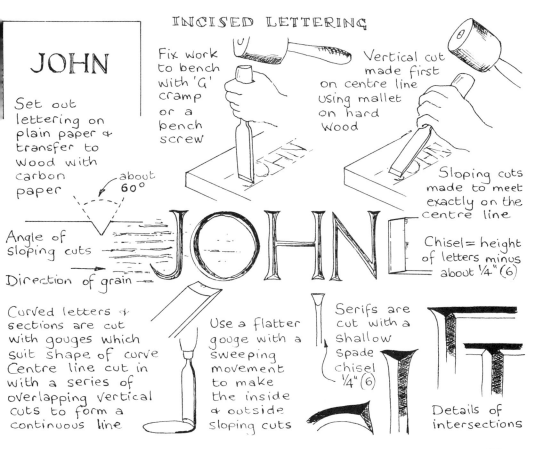

INCISED LETTERING

JOHN

Set out lettering on plain paper & transfer to wood with carbon paper

Fix work to bench with 'G' cramp or a bench screw

Vertical cut made first on centre line using mallet on hard wood

Sloping cuts made to meet exactly on the centre line

about 60°

Angle of sloping cuts

Direction of grain

Chisel = height of letters minus about ¼" (6)

Curved letters & sections are cut with gouges which suit shape of curve. Centre line cut in with a series of overlapping vertical cuts to form a continuous line

Use a flatter gouge with a sweeping movement to make the inside & outside sloping cuts

Serifs are cut with a shallow spade chisel ¼" (6)

Details of intersections

83

When carving in relief the letters are first outlined by making vertical cuts a little way off the drawn shape. Then, working from the 'waste side', an angled cut is made into the outline to produce a channel all round each individual letter. Alternatively this channel may be cut with a V-shaped chisel or parting tool.

Using a shallow gouge, the area between the letters is then cut away evenly to the required depth. If the carving is to be in high relief, the vertical outlining cuts will have to be repeated and more of the background cut away to give the required depth. This background, or ground as it is generally called, can be smoothed or the marks of the gouge may be left to give a tooled effect. Letters are finished to size by means of vertical or slightly sloping paring cuts made with a sharp tool to remove the inevitable nicks made by the gouge during grounding and to give each letter a clean, crisp edge. The initial outlining is done slightly oversize with this final cleaning up in mind.

Some of the carver's traditional woods – oak, sycamore, beech, lime – have been briefly mentioned. These are all excellent, but almost any kind of wood can be carved, although some are, of course, easier or more suitable than others. Colour, particularly the contrasts in colour between heartwood and sapwood, as in yew and laburnum, can be exploited to good effect in carving in the round, as can the grain markings of such woods as elm and pine. For relief work, and especially for lettering, too much contrast in colour and grain should be avoided, as it tends to detract from the carved surface.

Perhaps the most important thing to remember about carving is that chisels and gouges must be kept really sharp. Blunt tools will not cut the wood cleanly but will tear the fibres and spoil the work.

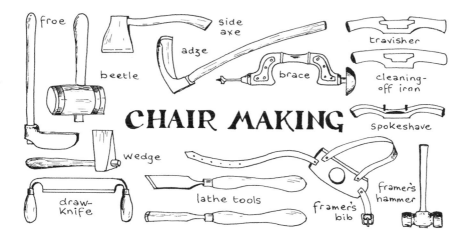

froe

side axe

travisher

adze

beetle

brace

cleaning-off iron

CHAIR MAKING

spokeshave

wedge

draw-knife

lathe tools

framer's bib

framer's hammer

Deep in the stillness of the woods, perhaps on a crisp, cold January morning, the sound of a chair maker's axe cleaving logs heralds the beginning of a chair which, two winters on, will seat someone comfortably by a bright, warm fire. With care and good fortune it will last for a century or more, its wood mellowing with age and polish, its grain still telling of its living, woodland days. It is this sense of continuity, from the growing tree cut there among last year's fallen leaves, through the shaping and assembly of the individual pieces to the finished article, both functional and long-lasting, which brings to chair making a feeling of real involvement and satisfaction shared by few other crafts.

Traditionally there have been few craftsmen making complete chairs from start to finish. Most chairs were made piecemeal by a number of different workers and finally assembled in workshops often quite remote from where the various parts were made. This division of labour suited the very nature of the chair maker's craft, and later lent itself readily to the methods of mass-production which have become necessary as the demand for chairs has increased.

There were, however, and happily still are, some people able to make a chair from beginning to end, combining the skills of bodger, benchman and framer, to name but three of the several specialists working in the chair industry. It is with the complete chair maker that this chapter is mainly concerned.

The most familiar traditional country chair is the one which is now known as a Windsor chair. Its construction seems to have been a natural development from the three-legged stool, which owes its origin to the fact that three legs were more stable than four on the uneven stone floors of early dwelling houses. Frequently associated only with the Chilterns area, Windsor chairs were in fact made in several other parts of Britain, including Lancashire and North Wales. In America a thriving chair industry was established in the Philadelphia area soon after 1750.

The old chair makers chose to work close to the source of their raw material whenever this was possible. Beechwoods or ash coppice were the most favoured places, for it was from these two timbers that the turned parts of their chairs were most frequently made, though yew and fruitwoods such as cherry or apple were

85

also used on occasions. These turned parts comprise the legs, stretchers and back rails. The bow or comb back and the seat complete the chair, the latter usually cut from a solid plank of elm.

Trees were felled on the selection system, those too small for use being left to grow on. Gaps left by felling were soon reseeded naturally from surrounding trees, and the best saplings were allowed to mature. In this way a continuous supply was ensured, literally for centuries. Coppicing was practised in some areas for the same purpose of obtaining a continuous supply over a shorter period.

16 Cleaving billets for chair legs with wedge and beetle

For turned parts, trees of small to medium girth were preferred, quick-grown and straight-grained, without large side branches. After felling, logs were cut into leg-length (18in/450mm) billets with a cross-cut saw. These were then cleft lengthways while still green, first into quarters, using an iron wedge and a heavy mallet known as a beetle. The wedge used has a handle and looks more like a heavy hatchet, while the beetle, a home-made tool widely used in the countryside, has a wooden head ringed at each end with an iron band to prevent splitting.

Further cleaving then took place, this time with a small axe or with the tool known as the froe. The froe has a wedge-shaped blade at right angles to its handle. Its lower edge is the cutting edge, the back of the blade being struck from

86

above by the beetle to start it cutting. After this its progress through the wood is accomplished by levering on the handle, thus splitting the wood along its natural cleavage lines. The quartered billets were cleft in this way on a chopping block into roughly triangular sections, the number obtained depending upon the diameter of the log. The aim was to cut leg pieces with as little wastage as possible, some billets making only four suitable pieces, while a 12in (300mm) diameter log, properly cleft, could yield sixteen or more legs and as many stretchers.

17 Using a drawknife to shape a chair leg held in a shaving horse

Using a side axe, its blade bevelled on one side only, the cleft pieces were trimmed to a six-sided section and tapered slightly at each end. Then, held tightly in the foot-operated vice of a shaving horse, the rough leg was shaped almost to its final size with a drawknife. The pieces were then ready for turning on the lathe.

In the heyday of the country-made chair the felling, cleaving and turning were carried out by itinerant craftsmen known as bodgers who worked and often lived in the woods. Moving from place to place among the trees and setting up temporary workshop shelters, they produced their turned parts to sell to chair 'factories' in nearby villages and towns. The bodger's tools were few and simple; even the

87

18 Turning a chair leg on a pole lathe. Note the treadle and cord

19 Completed legs and stretchers stacked criss-cross fashion to season

lathe which he used was a simple pole lathe, man-powered and easily set up in the woods. It was often easier to erect such a workshop at the source of the necessary raw material than to cut and transport bulk timber to a permanent workshop elsewhere.

The pole lathe was a primitive affair taking its name from the long springy pole which drove it. It had a wooden bed supported on legs, often two conveniently adjacent tree stumps, and this carried the adjustable poppets between which the piece being turned was supported, free to revolve on fixed centres. The butt of the driving pole, a 12ft (3.6m) length of ash or larch, was firmly fixed outside the hut in which the lathe was set up, and the flexible end positioned over the lathe. A cord fixed to this flexible end was wound twice round the piece of wood being turned and then fastened to a foot-operated treadle below the lathe bed. When the treadle was pressed, the cord was pulled downwards, the workpiece revolved and the pole bent like a fishing rod, to spring back up again when the treadle was released. A rhythmic movement of the foot soon had the work revolving at the right speed, first one way, then the other, the bodger's chisel cutting on each forward revolution.

On completion, turned legs, and the turned sticks or stretchers which braced them, were stacked criss-cross fashion outside the hut so that the still green wood might dry and season before being sent off to the chair factory. Working a twelve-hour day, a good man could produce in a week about two and a half gross of legs, together with sufficient stretchers to go with them. That was more than six hundred turned parts, for which, early in this present century, he received the princely sum of 12s 6d (65p). Hand-turned chair parts made from cleft material were always considered superior to the factory-made parts which eventually replaced them, and for this reason a few bodgers were still working in the early 1950s. But when the last of these men died there was no one to replace them, and their craft died with them.

For individual chair makers the turning is best done in the workshop after the shaped pieces have been partly seasoned. A power lathe may be used, and those driven by electric drills are quite suitable for this work. Alternatively, parts may be 'turned' without resorting to mechanical means by using the hand-operated rotary planes described on p 26.

In the larger chair factories, those responsible for making the remainder of the chair and assembling it were divided into bottomers, benchmen, benders, framers and finishers. Each one of these made his own contribution to the finished product, but in some smaller workshops one man might often combine the first three functions and another the last two. Thus the division into benchmen, who shaped chair bottoms and other non-turned parts, and framers, who assembled chairs and finished them off, become established.

The complete chair maker does all this work himself. His first big task is to make the seat, which is the foundation of a good chair. This is generally cut from a single plank of well-seasoned elm, 1½in (38mm) to 2in (50mm) in thickness. A frame or bow saw will serve to cut out the shape marked from a prepared pattern, but a band saw is quicker if available. Elm has always been preferred for seat

MAKING SEATS

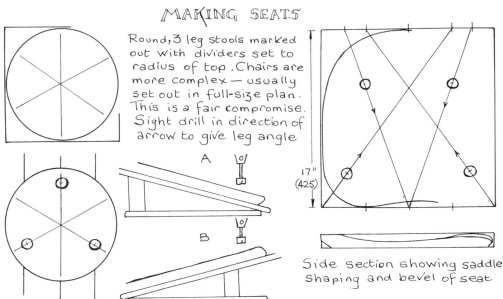

Round, 3 leg stools marked out with dividers set to radius of top. Chairs are more complex — usually set out in full-size plan. This is a fair compromise. Sight drill in direction of arrow to give leg angle

A

B

17" (425)

For wedged joint mark out and drill from TOP (A). For blind joint mark and drill BOTTOM (B). Line up diagonals to centre line of jig

Side section showing saddle shaping and bevel of seat

Seats can be of joined boards as shown. Dowels, if used should be kept low to allow for saddling of the seat

20 Bottoming: using the adze to shape the chair seat

making as it is best able to stand up to the hollowing-out process and the drilling of the holes — six large ones and between six and sixteen smaller ones — which it has to accommodate without splitting. Other timbers, such as beech and ash and some softwoods, may be substituted, and where wide planks are not available, well-joined boards can be used.

The hollowing-out process which creates the comfortable double hollow or saddle seat for which the best Windsor chairs are noted was, for obvious reasons, always referred to as bottoming. Done in the past mainly with an adze, a long-handled, two-handed tool with a curved, razor-sharp blade, this was highly skilled work. The seat blank was placed on the workshop floor and firmly held there by the craftsman's feet as he stood above his work. Cutting across the grain, each calculated swing of the adze scooped out waste wood, reducing the 2in (50mm) thick seat to little more than $\frac{1}{2}$in (12mm) in places.

The adze is now more likely to be seen in a museum than in a workshop, and there are few people who know how to use one properly. Modern routing machines now do what the adze once did, but commercially made chairs are very rarely as deeply bottomed as they ought to be. A large but shallow carver's gouge is an effective bottoming tool where an adze, or the expertise to use it, is not available. Work with the seat blank clamped securely to a bench and strike the gouge with a mallet to rough out, rather as if carving a large spoon or a shallow bowl.

Both adze and gouge leave ridge marks which must be cleaned off. For this a variety of shaves and scrapers are used. A heavy wooden travisher fitted with a curved blade was the favourite tool of the old chair maker, followed by the cleaning-off iron, both not unlike the modern spokeshave but shaped to fit the hollow of the seat. Finally scrapers and then glasspaper are used to smooth off the surface. A neat bevel to its lower edge gives the seat an appearance of lightness.

The several holes required to take legs, back rails and so on are the next consideration, each one needing to be not only in its proper place but at the correct angle. The splay of the legs, with the back ones more pronounced than the front; the rake of the back, where each pair of back rails leaves the seat at a different angle; the positioning of arm rests if fitted — all these have to be taken into account. It was here that the real skill of the master chair maker lay, for he bored these holes by hand, using a wooden stock brace and a simple spoon bit and working by eyesight alone, without the benefit of patterns or jigs of any kind. To improve his accuracy and to increase the pressure when doing this work he wore a breast bib, a recessed wooden block held in place across his chest by a leather harness. The rotating head of the brace fitted into the recessed block and enabled considerable pressure to be applied without injury.

Holes may still be drilled by hand using the modern brace and bit, but elm is a true hardwood, and considerable strength is required to turn and push a 1in (25mm) drill bit through a thick seat at a constant angle. A power drill is easier to use and, for most workers, far more accurate. If the drill is fixed to operate vertically, and a drilling jig is used as shown on p 90, the drilling of holes at a known and constant angle will be much simplified, and symmetry more easily achieved. It is interesting to note in this connection that old hand-made chairs are not always perfectly symmetrical in the way a machine-made, mass-produced

92

MAKING LEGS and ASSEMBLING

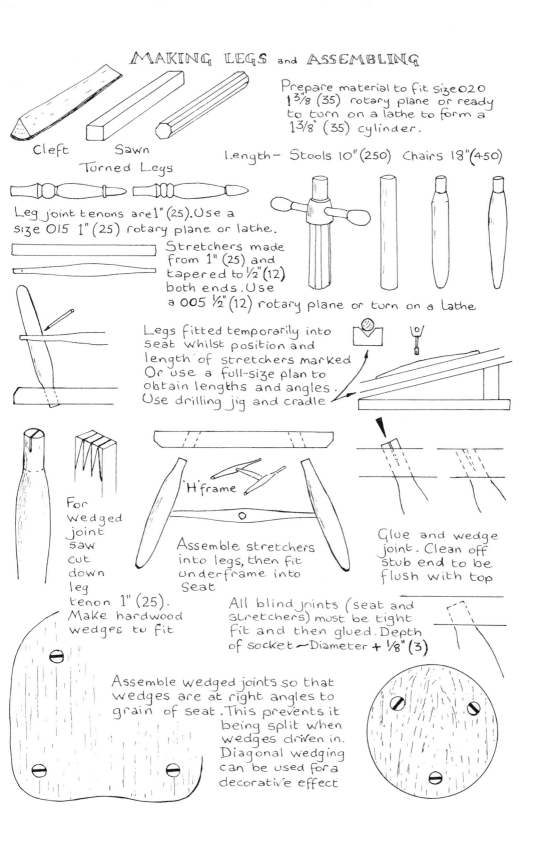

Cleft Sawn

Turned Legs

Prepare material to fit size020 1³⁄₈ (35) rotary plane or ready to turn on a lathe to form a 1³⁄₈" (35) cylinder.

Length— Stools 10"(250) Chairs 18"(450)

Leg joint tenons are1" (25). Use a size 015 1" (25) rotary plane or lathe.

Stretchers made from 1" (25) and tapered to ½"(12) both ends. Use a 005 ½"(12) rotary plane or turn on a lathe

Legs fitted temporarily into seat whilst position and length of stretchers marked Or use a full-size plan to obtain lengths and angles. Use drilling jig and cradle

'H'frame

For Wedged joint saw cut down leg tenon 1" (25). Make hardwood wedges to fit

Assemble stretchers into legs, then fit underframe into Seat

Glue and wedge joint. Clean off stub end to be flush with top

All blind joints (seat and stretchers) must be tight fit and then glued. Depth of socket —Diameter + ⅛"(3)

Assemble wedged joints so that wedges are at right angles to grain of seat. This prevents it being split when wedges driven in. Diagonal wedging can be used for a decorative effect chair is. Any slight errors made by bygone chair makers are now recognised as marks of authenticity and are much valued by collectors of antique furniture.

'Legging up' was how the chair maker described the next stage in the process — the assembly of legs and stretchers and the fitting of them to the seat. First the four legs are temporarily placed in the sockets prepared for them in the seat, and while they are so held the position of the holes for the side stretchers is marked on the front and back legs and the required length of the stretchers themselves is determined. The legs are then removed to have holes drilled in them at the correct angle. After being cut to length, the stretchers are fitted into their respective front and back legs to make two side units.

Stretchers are fitted to brace the legs and so strengthen the construction, the usual Windsor pattern being in the shape of the letter 'H'. This means that the two side units have to be replaced in their sockets so that the central cross-stretcher can be positioned and measured for length. Holes are then drilled in the side stretchers for the cross-stretcher, after which the whole underframe is reassembled and the seat socketed on to it. If the chair maker is satisfied with his work the whole thing is taken apart again for glueing.

With glue applied to all the joints, the legs, stretchers and seat are put together again for the last time. Leg joints are knocked in tightly with a hammer, being further secured by hardwood wedges driven into narrow cuts made in the ends of each of the leg tenons before the final assembly. The wedges are placed at right angles to the grain of the seat so that the pressure of the wedge does not cause the seat to split. When the glue has set, stub ends of tenons and wedges are cut flush with the seat, using first a saw and then a sharp chisel.

Early Windsors had lathe-turned legs, some of the simple reel and bobbin pattern shown in the diagram, while others, made later, had much more elaborate turning. The introduction in the mid-eighteenth century of the cabriole leg provided a further design which was incorporated into the underframing of some of the more pretentious chairs of that and later periods. It is the design of the back, however, which distinguishes one type of Windsor chair from another, and although there is some confusion over some of their names, certain features are universally recognisable.

There are two broad categories into which Windsor chairs can be grouped according to the shape of the back. The first of these is the comb-back, which has basically two uprights or stiles, usually turned, surmounted by a cresting rail or comb. This back frame may then be filled in with turned sticks or spindles, or a combination of sticks and a carved and pierced central splat or baluster. Comb-backs usually have their stiles more or less upright; where these angle outwards to give a wider sweep of comb we have the aptly named fan-back. A late-nineteenth-century variant of the comb-back, the lathe-back, has flattened bars instead of turned sticks, curved to fit the lower part of the sitter's back. Comfortable but heavy, such chairs were more at home in chintzy Victorian parlours than in country cottages.

The second category is the bow-back chair. This has curved parts in its make-up which have to be steam-bent to shape by the maker. In this type the top edge of the back is a hooped or semicircular bow, which may go all the way down into the

94

ASSEMBLING CHAIR BACKS

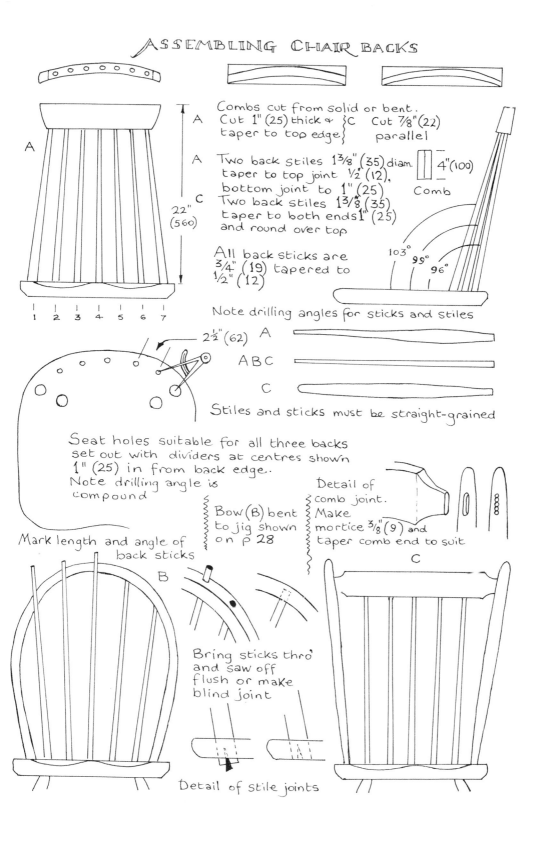

A

Combs cut from solid or bent.
A   Cut 1" (25) thick & }C   Cut 7/8" (22)
    taper to top edge }   parallel

A   Two back stiles 1 3/8" (35) diam.   4"(100)
    taper to top joint 1/2" (12),
    bottom joint to 1" (25)   Comb
C   Two back stiles 1 3/8 (35)
    taper to both ends 1" (25)
    and round over top

All back sticks are
3/4" (19) tapered to
1/2" (12)

22"
(560)

C

Note drilling angles for sticks and stiles

103° 95° 96°

2 1/2" (62) A

A B C

C

Stiles and sticks must be straight-grained

Seat holes suitable for all three backs
set out with dividers at centres shown
1" (25) in from back edge.
Note drilling angle is
compound

Mark length and angle of
back sticks

Detail of
comb joint.
Make
mortice 3/8" (9) and
taper comb end to suit

C

Bow (B) bent
to jig shown
on p 28

B

Bring sticks thro'
and saw off
flush or make
blind joint

Detail of stile joints

seat to give the familiar single-bow chair, which can be made with or without arms. When arms are fitted they are mortised into the back. Alternatively, the back bow may be socketed into another bow running horizontally around the back, its ends pointing forward to form arms. This is known as the double-bow and can only be made as an armchair. The nineteenth-century introduction usually known by the name smoker's bow has only this horizontal bow, generally heavily made and shaped, with nothing above it, and is therefore not really a bow-back at all. The American name of lowback is probably more appropriate. All bow-backs, like comb-back have stick or stick-and-splat infill, so 'stick-back chair' is a misnomer.

Back braces are found on many types of chair. Rising from a small extension, the bob-tail at the rear of the seat, these extra sticks are fitted to strengthen the back.

Back sticks – a mean name for parts which play such an important part in chair construction – should be made from cleft material, for they are often quite slender but must always be strong. At one time these were shaved with a sharp drawknife and cleaned and rounded with scrapers. They can be turned, providing a suitable steady-rest is used, but only with difficulty. Turning such slender lengths, $\frac{1}{2}$in to $\frac{3}{4}$in (12mm to 19mm) in diameter and up to 20in (500mm) long, demands skill if the workpiece is not to 'whip' as it is turned. By far the best method is to use one of the smaller sizes of rotary plane already mentioned. Stiles are made in the same way.

Combs are cut with a bow saw or band saw to a slightly curving shape, thick enough along the bottom edge to accommodate the back sticks, but tapered and perhaps rounded along the top edge.

With each of the back pieces made and cut to length, holes are bored into the top surface of the seat to receive them. Holes for the two stiles go right through so that when they are fitted their joints can be wedged like the leg joints. Then the under-edge of the comb is bored with sufficient holes to accommodate the stiles and sticks. If a centre splat is to be fitted, a narrow mortice is cut to suit it, both in the seat and in the comb. After checking, all the upright parts are glued into their respective seat sockets, and the comb, positioned carefully over their top ends, is tapped into place. Some combs are tenoned into the stiles rather than socketed on to them.

Arms, when fitted to this type of chair, are cut to a variety of shapes. Short sticks to support the arms are required, and additional holes to accommodate them must be bored into the seat. The angle at which these holes are bored is important to the line of the arm when completed. The single arm stick, or the first stick if there is to be more than one, is usually a substantial turned member and is positioned in the seat first. Then the arm is 'offered up' and the position of all other necessary holes marked in, including those in the underside of the arm and the socket into the back stile. All this is done by eye judgement alone. Finally all the arm parts are fitted: first the arm sticks are fitted into the seat, then the arm itself is slotted into the stile, brought down on to its supporting sticks and tapped tightly home.

Chairs with back bows are a little more complex. Bows can only be made from knot-free, straight-grained material that will not break out or split when being bent. Cleft ash is best, although beech, oak and even well-selected elm all bend well. Yew was once very popular, as were some of the fruitwoods, some chair makers using small coppiced material cut in the round and trimmed to size. Cleaving is carried out exactly as for leg making, except that longer billets are required — about 4ft (1.2m), the precise length depending on the size of the chair. Nowadays sawn timber is often used if the grain is straight.

The chosen piece is trimmed roughly to size with a drawknife — for a simple back bow this would be to a section about $1\frac{1}{4}$in (32mm) square. It is then steamed to make it pliable and bent round a shaped block clamped to a bending table. Full details of the steam-bending of wood are given on p 28.

When the bent bow is thoroughly dried out and set to shape, its two ends are shaped to fit the sockets already bored for them in the seat. The bow is cleaned over and has its outer edges slightly radiused with a spokeshave. The bow is then put into place while the chair maker checks it critically for balance in relation to the rest of the chair. In assembling a chair the symmetry of the back is more important than in the underframing; it is the back which forms the most obvious outline of the chair and which takes the eye of the beholder.

After any necessary adjustments have been made, the back sticks are put into their respective seat sockets and arranged fan-wise to lean back against the bow. Working outwards from the centre, these are spaced out evenly by eye and their positions marked on the face of the bow. A compromise is to use both eye judgement and a pair of dividers to mark off relative positions.

It was common practice on many early bow-backs to fit back sticks into through sockets in the bow where they were wedge-jointed rather like the spokes of a wheel. To follow this authentic method the holes are bored with the bow in position in its seat sockets. Bore the centre hole first, using a hand drill or brace, and fit the centre stick. This will help to support the bow while the remainder of the holes are made. Do this with the sticks in position, and leaning against the bow as a guide to the correct drilling angle. When all the holes are made, glue bow and sticks into position, saw off flush all protruding stick ends and wedge across the grain of the bow. The bottom ends of the bow are through-jointed into the seat and wedged also.

Some chairs do not have their back sticks going right through the bow, and for waxed or varnished finishes (many old Windsors were in fact painted) the stopped or blind joint gives a neater appearance. In this case the bow is drilled at the bench from its inner surface.

Baluster splats, where fitted, are cut to a variety of intricate designs with a small coping saw or fret saw. Wood matching the rest of the chair back is used, $\frac{1}{4}$in (6mm) to $\frac{3}{8}$in (9mm) in thickness. Marked out from a paper or wooden pattern, balusters are usually sawn out four or six at a time if required for a set of chairs. Perhaps the best-known design is the popular wheel motif.

Finishing consists of scraping, followed by glasspapering, to get a fine finish, although many old chairs originally received very little of this. The high gloss on many prized antiques is more likely to be the result of countless sitters and the regular application of polish by more recent owners. Often chairs were painted or stained and varnished, probably in some cases to give a uniform appearance to the various woods used in their construction. Some quality pieces were wax-polished when new, especially those made from the more attractive fruitwoods or from yew. Of course, many of those still around today have been 'restored', with varying degrees of success.

Although the separate parts of a Windsor chair, especially the back and arms, often look rather delicate or even fragile, if they are made from sound material, preferably cleft, and properly put together, the finished chair will have considerable strength – enough, in fact, to support well over twenty times its own weight, and to withstand constant stress and strain over a long period of time. The secret lies in the choice of material, in tight joints, and in the tension which is built into the chair during assembly. The old chair makers made their chairs to last indefinitely, and this is the hallmark of all good craftsmanship.

The chair bodgers have disappeared completely from our woodlands now and, although an occasional chair maker may still be found quietly at work, most chairs today are mass-produced in factories. It is interesting to note that a number of successful manufacturers still use traditional materials to assemble chairs in the Windsor styles; but these are produced mechanically and repetitively, and lack the individuality and honesty of the good, hand-made chair.

COOPERING

topping plane · croz · chive · hollowing knife · backing knife · block with hook · adze · downright · broad axe · jointer

Wooden barrels or casks in all shapes and sizes were once as essential in daily life as metal and plastic containers are today. They held everything from beer, spirits and fine wines to apples, gunpowder and nails. Common though they were, the men who made them, the coopers, were a rare breed of craftsmen, for they hardly ever used written measurements or patterns of any kind, relying instead on inherent skill backed by long experience. Yet from tough, seemingly intractable materials they not only made barrels perfectly liquid-tight, but also to specific sizes and capacities accurate enough to be accepted as standard measures.

Finished barrels had to be strong, and so too had the coopers, for theirs was heavy work, all done by hand. They used a number of special tools peculiar to their trade. Most were for fashioning curved surfaces, both convex and concave, and many were suitable for only one particular diameter of work, making it necessary for the cooper to have a wide range of each type. The design of many of these tools is of great antiquity, and the actual tools were often handed on from one generation to the next. Some were made by the craftsmen themselves.

Barrels were made in ancient Egypt, and introduced to Britain by the Romans. By the end of the Middle Ages they were in common use throughout Europe, and they continued to be the standard form of packaging for many centuries. Almost all goods travelling by sea were packed in casks, and coopers were carried as members of ships' crews until the middle of the nineteenth century. Ships sailing out of European ports would be loaded with barrel-making materials, and during the frequently long outward voyage these sea-going coopers would be kept busy making casks in which the return cargo of sugar, spices, whale oil or wine would be carried home. On land coopers were to be found everywhere, some working alone, others organised into small workshops, many later becoming part of larger concerns such as warehouses and breweries.

Three categories of cooper were traditionally recognised: wet coopers, who specialised in making barrels suitable for holding liquids, dry coopers, who made barrel-shaped containers to hold dry goods of various kinds, and white coopers, who were concerned mainly with the manufacture and repair of dairy and domestic utensils of similar construction. By far the most specialised and exacting form of coopering was that of the wet cooper. It was also the most common, and the longest lived, for the use of wooden barrels for storing liquids far outlasted their use for dry goods. For certain liquids they are still considered the best containers, but even here they are becoming rarer all the time. Of the few wet coopers still working, the majority are occupied in repairing old barrels rather than making new ones.

Wet coopering requires much skill and experience. Not only must the parts of a wet or tight barrel fit together exactly and be perfectly liquid-tight, but the completed barrel must be strong enough to bear the weight of its contents and the stresses they exert, and to resist damage to its outer surface when being rolled about and roughly handled, both full and empty, over a period of many years.

The best wet barrels were always made from oak, although chestnut was occasionally substituted. Only oak of a certain type and quality would suit the good cooper; the exact choice varied according to the barrel's ultimate contents. Presumably at one time native oak was used, but when overseas trade developed Baltic oak was found to be best for holding beer, while for spirits American oak was preferred. Latterly oak was imported from a variety of places including the Middle East and Japan.

Oak for barrel making was cut in the forest by woodland craftsmen from the heartwood of trees which might have taken up to two hundred years to grow. It was first cross-cut into logs long enough to make staves, the separate sections used to make up the side of a barrel. These were then split with the woodsman's heavy wedge and beetle into quarters, then cleft again with a froe into radial sections of the correct thickness. Thus the essential requirements of good staves were obtained – a straight grain, with the growth rings running through from front to back and not across the width of the stave. This also left the medullary rays – fibrous membranes impervious to moisture which radiate from the centre of hardwood trees – parallel to the surface of the stave.

A drawknife was then used to cut away the unwanted sapwood and also to trim each piece to a roughly rectangular section slightly more than 1in (25mm) thick. After this initial preparation the rough staves were stacked out in the open until they were thoroughly seasoned. Only then were they sent off to the cooper. More recently, staves would be sawn from seasoned planks.

The first stage in the cooper's craft is the dressing of the staves. Depending on the size of the barrel being made this is done either on a shaving horse of the type used by so many other craftsmen, or with the stave held by a toothed hook fixed close to the top of the cooper's block. This heavy log of beech or elm, some 2ft (600mm) in height, was the cooper's workbench, and 'being at the block' was coopers' jargon for being at work.

First the back or outer face of the stave is shaped with a curved drawknife known as a backing knife. Then the stave is turned over and the inner face is shaped with the hollowing knife, a drawknife with a concave blade. This operation shapes the width of the stave, so that each becomes roughly segmental to the barrel's circumference. The curvature along the stave's length, which produces the familiar barrel shape, is obtained later by bending.

100

21 Shaping a barrel stave with a hollowing knife

22 Shaping and bevelling the stave on the long jointer or jointing plane. In the background is a cooper's block

23 Truss hoops being fitted. Note the trivet fuelled with wood shavings in the foreground

To allow for this shaping by bending each stave is made wider across its middle than at its two ends, the required taper being accurately cut on the cooper's block with a broad-bladed side axe. Next, these tapered edges have to be bevelled so that they are radial to the barrel's centre, the actual angle of the bevel depending upon the size of barrel being made and the number of staves being used. This is done on a jointer, a long plane fixed upside down with its blade uppermost, one

102

end resting on legs, the other on the floor. Made of beech and as much as 6ft (1.8m) in length, the jointer remains stationary while the edge of the stave is moved by hand against the cutting edge to make the necessary bevel. No guide or fence is fitted to the jointer to set the angle of the bevel, the cooper relying entirely on his own judgement.

When sufficient staves to make the barrel have been dressed, the next job is to 'raise the cask'. Raising entails arranging the staves vertically, fitting their top ends into an iron raising hoop or end hoop to form a complete circle. When this has been done the first of several truss hoops is driven down to hold the staves in place.

Truss hoops were originally made by woodland craftsmen from steam-bent cleft ash. Strongly made and cleated with hand-made iron rivets, each hoop had its inside face coned or shaped to fit the taper of the barrel. Like so many woodland craftsmen, hoop makers have now entirely disappeared, and the wooden hoops have been largely replaced by less flexible metal ones. Several of these temporary hoops, which are made in various sizes, are used each time a barrel is set up.

In the next stage the staves are given their familiar barrel shape. One way of doing this is to place the staves in a steam chest until they are sufficiently pliable to be bent. In the traditional method, however, water is poured over the raised cask, which is then placed over a small fire of wood shavings burning in a trivet. Drying from the inside, the wood yields to outside pressure, and by driving progressively smaller truss hoops over and down the barrel with heavy hammers the cooper and his apprentice bend the staves into place. The process is continued until the staves are all tight against each other throughout their entire length. Then a second iron end hoop is fitted at the opposite end to the first one.

More wood is added to the fire, and the half-completed barrel, with truss hoops still in place, is kept over it until it is thoroughly dried out. As the wood dries its fibres shrink and the staves, released from the strain imposed by bending, retain their curved shape.

There are variations on this basic method of trussing, as the process is called. One is to use a block-and-tackle arrangement in which a rope or strap draws the staves together so that truss hoops can be more easily fitted. This particular method was often used in making large wine casks, which have relatively thin staves.

The two ends of the barrel next receive the cooper's attention. First he levels off the ends of the staves using an adze followed by a curious semicircular plane called a topping plane. Then comes something of the mysteries of coopering, told in the craftsman's own words: 'First off I bevels down the chime, then make the howel with the chive. Then the croz all round does for the heading.' The chime is the bevel cut around the inside edge of each end of a barrel, while the howel is the name sometimes given to the wide but shallow channel just below this. The chive and the croz are tools, similar in general appearance and use, each with a blade held in a wooden stock and fitted with a semicircular fence to guide it round the inside of a barrel parallel to its edge. They differ in that the chive has a wide blade, to cut the howel, while the croz has a much narrower but longer blade to

24 Cleaning off the barrel with a downright shave

cut the deep groove into which the barrel ends, or heads as they are correctly called, will be fitted. Both chime and croz are made in a range of sizes to suit the diameter of different-sized barrels.

Inside shaves, which are convex-bladed tools used to smooth off the inside of a barrel, are also made to suit different internal diameters. One of these is used next, special attention being paid to the joints between the staves. Then, as the staves are by now well set, the trussing hoops are removed, leaving only the two iron end hoops to keep the staves together. This leaves an unrestricted surface for the downright shave which the cooper uses to clean off and smooth the outside of the barrel. The downright shave, not unlike a heavy-duty carpenter's spokeshave in appearance, has a concave blade which cuts as it is pushed away from the user.

The bung-hole is made at this stage, before the heads are fitted, for no one wants oak shavings left inside his barrel. The hole is bored with an auger through a stave deliberately made wider than the rest for added strength, then tapered with either a conical reamer or a burning iron. The first stage in heading, or fitting the heads, is to measure the exact circumference of the barrel by stepping a pair of dividers around the inside of the groove cut by the croz. Six equal steps sets the dividers to the required radius for marking out the head.

The heads are made in sections from oak boards joined together with dowels along their edges. Cut to shape with bow saw and side axe and bevelled all round with a heading knife to fit the croz goove, the heads are soon ready for fitting. One is bored first with a hole for the tap. Temporary hoops are fitted again to the bulbous middle section of the barrel so that the end hoops can be removed. Removing these allows the staves to open up sufficiently at each end to enable the heads to be fitted snugly into the croz groove.

Cunningly, barrel heads are not made absolutely circular. They are in fact slightly oval, being widest across their jointed sections. When the barrel is finally hooped, the chime hoops – those at the top and bottom ends – compress the heads at right angles to their joints and so make these even tighter. In addition, the top and bottom heads are fitted so that their jointed sections lie at right angles to each other, thus preserving the barrel's symmetry. All head joints are caulked with rushes during assembly and fitting.

Hooping is the final stage, and for this the cooper must make a number of iron hoops to be fitted permanently to the barrel. First chalk marks are drawn where the hoops will be fixed and the circumference of the barrrel is measured at these points with a piece of string. The iron bands are cut to length from stock material and hammered to shape, for each must be slightly cone-shaped or dished to suit the taper of the barrel's surface. The ends of the hoop are then overlapped, drilled through, and riveted together with mild steel rivets to finish at the required circumference. The cooper carries out this iron working on a tall T-shaped anvil known as a bick iron.

The completed hoops are then fitted to the barrel one by one from opposite ends and driven tightly into place with a heavy hammer and a wedge-shaped drift or driver. This has a sturdy oak handle and a tapered, steel-tipped blade grooved at its narrow end so that it does not slip off the edge of the hoop as it is being driven down. The good cooper takes pride in fitting hoops to lie exactly parallel to one another. There are three each end on a big barrel – chime, quarter and bulge – and four all told on a smaller one. Properly fitted, the hoop joints at each end of a barrel should be on opposite sides. This, and the positioning of the heads, is said to help even up stresses in the barrel and to keep it liquid-tight and in good shape.

Because of the utter reliance on hand and eye and the total lack of any but the simplest measurements, considerable skill is required in this work, and experience counts for a lot. A five-year apprenticeship was always considered necessary, terminating in the centuries-old ceremony which involved dousing the apprentice with soot, flour, wood shavings, water and beer and rolling him round the workshop floor in one of his own barrels.

No machine has ever been invented to do any part of the wet cooper's work, and not until the demands of modern society dictated the introduction of

25 Hooping the completed barrel. Chalk marks are used to indicate the correct positions

machine-made metal or plastic kegs was any replacement found for the individual, craftsman-made wooden barrel.

The dry cooper's work required less accuracy and less skill than that of the wet cooper. At quite an early date machine-made staves and heads were being used in making dry or slack barrels, and most dry coopers did little except assemble parts ready-made for them. Dry barrels have less of a bulge, and the staves fit less tightly together than in wet barrels, and of course they are not required to be liquid-tight. Iron hoops are not normally needed either, the barrels being bound with wooden hoops, usually of hazel. Softwoods were generally used in making the staves, which were quite thin in many cases. Douglas fir was the most popular, but birch, chestnut, poplar and any other locally available wood was also employed.

Slack barrels were used to hold all manner of goods, from dry foodstuffs such as salt and flour to fish and vegetables: tobacco, crockery, nails and gunpowder were all carried or stored in barrels of various sizes at one time. It was to meet the demand for large numbers of these barrels that machine-made parts were introduced, and those dry barrels that are still occasionally used today are made entirely in this way. They are often very flimsy affairs, intended to be used once only, not re-used over and over again as in earlier years.

The hazel hoops used for binding were produced by a woodland craftsman who, like the truss-hoop maker, is no longer to be found. Like the chair bodger, he worked in the coppice where his material grew. Hazel poles were cut and cleft into rods varying in length to make hoops for barrels of different sizes. The bark was left intact, but much of the inner wood was shaved away so that the hoops could be more easily formed. Both for cleaving and for shaving hoop makers used ingenious contraptions of their own making to hold the hazel rods secure.

Bundles of straight hoop-length rods were sent off to those coopers who chose to bend their own hoops. These had to be made pliable by steaming before they could be coiled, but hoops made by the coppice cutters were fashioned while still green and could be coiled without steaming. Methods of coiling varied from district to district; in some areas a device with two hand-operated iron rollers, not unlike the blacksmith's iron tyre bender, was used; in others a mechanical arrangement consisting of a wooden roller and a driven leather belt did a similar job. Some craftsmen soaked their rods in water and coiled them inside a cylindrical tank to dry out, while others used various forms of a frame with pegs arranged on it around which the rods were bent. All rods were finally placed inside a stout ash master-hoop to fix the appropriate size accurately, and the overlapping ends were secured with clenched nails.

The dry cooper assembled his barrel staves in a similar way to the wet cooper, except that his staves were nearly always rendered pliable by steaming. Once the first truss hoop was fitted the thin staves were pulled together with a rope and tackle. A shallow croz was cut to accommodate the barrel heads, which were put together loosely, without dowels. Finally the hazel hoops were fitted, four or six to a barrel, and a head inserted at one end only. Barrels were supplied open at one end, the final head being fitted after filling, and the chime hoop driven down tight to secure it.

There was one other category of cooper, generally known as the white cooper. In many ways his work was as skilful as the wet cooper's, but it was less heavy and far more varied, for he made a wide range of utensils principally for use in the farm dairy and the domestic kitchen. In addition he might also be a wood turner and carver, conveniently combining cooper's work with these other skills.

He worked in a wide range of timbers, using oak, ash, beech and sycamore as well as locally available softwoods. Sycamore was used in large quantities, especially for dairy equipment and utensils, since frequent wetting does it little harm and it does not taint. Its clean-looking, light colour could be maintained by scrubbing, for it was generally left untreated. Perhaps it was from the sycamore wood that the white cooper took his name.

He made coopered vats and bins, washtubs or keelers, kitchen buckets, milking pails and butter tubs. He was responsible for producing butter churns in a variety of sizes and types, some with rotating paddles, others like the simple knocker churn, a tall narrow barrel in which a wooden beater moves up and down. He would also make the small casks or flasks – little barrels in miniature – in which cider or ale was taken out to workers in the fields, and the curious oval casks used chiefly as water kegs in ships' boats, where the oval shape permitted easy stowage under seats and prevented them from rolling about. His work included small bowls and tankards for the table, often combining coopering with lathe work, and he frequently carved the spoons and ladles to go with them. One of his specialities was the making of measures in a variety of sizes and for a variety of purposes, the bushel measure being particularly popular.

Unlike true barrels, many of the items made by the white cooper had straight staves tapering to one end only or not at all. Pails and tubs are good examples of this type of work. The edges of the staves have still to be bevelled to the correct radius, but this simple bevel, and any taper required, both lend themselves to the use of patterns and jigs rather than demanding skilled judgement and accumulated experience.

It was also customary to cut the single croz groove in each stave individually before assembly, thus eliminating the need for special tools with which to do the job later. Providing the end of each stave is cut square to begin with, an ordinary rebating plane fitted with a suitable fence will do the job adequately.

Having prepared the required number of staves, the cooper set up or raised his tub, not in truss hoops but in one of a number of circular metal frames kept for the purpose, each suited to a particular size of tub. Heads (or in this case bottoms, as they were properly called) were made and fitted in exactly the same way as those for wet barrels. Metal hoops too were made just as the wet cooper made them, although some work was fitted with hazel hoops. In the assembly of a tapered tub the largest hoop would be placed in position first, and gradually tightened by being driven down with a wedge until the bottom could just be dropped into its groove from the inside. Then the smaller hoops would be fitted and tightened up. By leaving two staves at opposite sides longer at the top than the others, handles could be provided. In the case of pails and buckets, holes were bored through these two longer staves and a piece of rope was threaded through to form a carrying handle.

Tubs constructed in this way can be made in a range of sizes by anyone able to use simple woodworking tools. Good-quality deal boards are suitable and easy to work, but most hardwoods would be longer-lasting. Tapered stave patterns are easy enough to make and use (see Table 1), or the jig described on p 27 can be employed. Staves for straight-sided articles need no taper. It is not absolutely essential to have each stave exactly the same width, but the correct angle for the bevelled edges is important (see Table 2). These bevels can be accurately cut using the device which is also described on p 27.

108

SIMPLE COOPERING

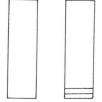
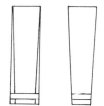

Cut sufficient staves to size. Make groove for base

See Table 1 for number of staves required

Mark out taper as required and saw or plane to shape. If power saw & sawing jig used there is no need to mark out

Bevel both edges~use suitable bevelling jig and hand plane held upside down in a vice. On power saw or plane set fence to appropriate angle

See Table 2 for these angles

Cut base from any suitable material and chamfer edges as shown left not right

Assemble staves on a flat surface, inside down, using adhesive tape. Keep stave ends in line and edges together. Turn over, inside up, insert base into groove and roll together

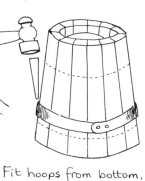

If all is well glue up and reassemble

Tub

Dish hoop by hammering on edge

Make a full-size drawing to find correct curve of hoop BC from centre A

Hoop

Fit hoops from bottom, use hardwood wedge to knock into place

Secure with stout rubber bands until glue has set. Use a waterproof glue

When hoop is dished rivet ends together

Handles can be fitted, as shown on tankard, by dowels

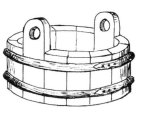

Two staves left long to form handles

Table 1

Outside diameter of work	Number of staves			
	8	10	12	14
	Width of staves (millimetres)			
3in (76mm)	32	—	—	—
4in (102mm)	43	33	—	—
5in (127mm)	53	40	34	—
6in (152mm)	64	49	42	35
7in (178mm)	74	64	47	41
8in (203mm)	80	67	55	47
9in (229mm)	95	75	62	53
10in (254mm)	—	83	69	58
12in (305mm)	—	—	82	70

To make tapered staves, take top and bottom measurements and subtract half the difference from each side of the stave bottom. E.g. tub 12in (305mm) top, 9in (229mm) bottom requires 12 staves, 82mm top, 62mm bottom. Mark bottom of stave 10mm in on either side and cut to this taper.

Table 2

Number of staves	Angle of bevel (degrees)	Angle of jig or fence (degrees)
8	67.5	22.5
10	72	18
12	75	15
14	77	13

When these edges have been cut true, it is hard to make a tub which is not perfectly watertight. The weak spot in such a tub is most likely to be the bottom. This should be cut to a true circle, the actual measurement of which is taken across the inside of the croz groove when the staves have been correctly set up. The edge of the bottom is bevelled off on both sides to fit the groove tightly. If joined boards are used, the wet cooper's trick of making heads or bottoms slightly oval across their joints can be tried, the joints themselves being either caulked or glued with a waterproof adhesive. Of course, in tubs intended for growing plants all this is unnecessary – they have to be drilled at the bottom for drainage purposes anyway. But it would be interesting to try making one which was watertight.

110

Assembly is simplified by the use of adhesive tape and strong rubber bands. Metal hoops are easily made and riveted – strips of copper or brass look well on small items – or wooden hoops cut with the bark intact can be used. Modern adhesives mean that hoops can be dispensed with altogether, although temporary ones (strong rubber bands or tight string) must be fitted while the glue sets. Use a good-quality waterproof glue.

If metal hoops are used on a tapered tub, either to hold it together or purely for decorative purposes, these should be coned or dished. This is done by hammering with even blows along one edge of the length of metal, either on an anvil or on some suitable piece of iron. The metal will be spread slightly where it is struck and will curve away from the hammered edge. The amount of curve required is ascertained as shown in the diagram. Turn the strip over and hammer it on the other side to prevent the metal curling. Check for size and shape against the tub, then rivet securely before fitting.

Plant tubs need not be smoothed off inside, and if glued and not hooped can be left segmented on the outside too. Some roundness inside can be achieved by the use of a suitable curved-sole plane or spokeshave before assembling the staves. For rounding and smoothing the outside a spokeshave is used, or small tubs can be turned on a lathe if one is available. First a tapered wooden plug is made to hold the work between centres. Do not remove too much wood, especially where the groove is holding the bottom in place.

Paint iron hoops black and finish the whole tub with a clear varnish for a pleasing and durable finish. Treat plant tubs with a wood preservative not toxic to plants. If sycamore or beech is used for kitchen or table ware, leave it untreated.

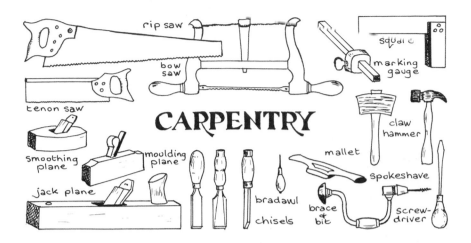

rip saw · square · marking gauge · bow saw · tenon saw · claw hammer · mallet · smoothing plane · moulding plane · spokeshave · jack plane · bradawl · brace & bit · screw-driver · chisels

CARPENTRY

The old village carpenter did all manner of work in wood. He was capable of building a barn or putting up the framing for a complete cottage. Then, after making and fitting doors, door frames and windows, he might go on to make much of the furniture and interior fittings for the occupants. The ladders which he used in his construction work would have been made in his own workshop, as often would most parts of the cart or wagon on which he carried his materials from place to place. There would be hardly a farm in the neighbourhood that did not have a gate which he had made or a shed which he had built or rebuilt.

Throughout his life he not only made new things but carried out repairs to the many old ones which he and generations of carpenters before him had made. He was, without doubt, an essential part of the rural scene, and it was he who made not only your cradle, your cupboard and your carriage, but also your coffin, for he was often the local undertaker as well.

Carpentry began when man first found ways of fashioning wood with tools and making simple joints. Carpenters were originally known as treewrights, for they worked trees as the blacksmith works iron. Later came the distinction between carpenters and joiners – a distinction not always easy to establish even today – and later still the separation of specialist craftsmen into cabinet makers, wood turners, chair makers and so on. In the north of England the name joiner is the general term for any woodworker; elsewhere a man making doors, window frames, staircases etc. in a workshop is a joiner, while the man fixing them on site is usually a carpenter. These subtle shades of difference were not part of the old carpenter's less complicated way of life; he did all these things and much more besides.

In his stockyard he kept a wide variety of timbers, each destined for a particular type of job. Most were English hardwoods – oak, elm, beech, ash and sycamore. These were usually purchased as standing timber, which means that the carpenter went out into the woods and selected and bought a whole growing tree. After felling, this would have to be converted into usable timbers, either by cleaving or by laborious work at the sawpit. Often the carpenter took account of the

112

26 Sawing timber at the saw-pit

natural growth of the trees he bought, making use of naturally curved or forked pieces to give strength and support in certain constructions in just the same way that boatbuilders did, and indeed still do. All the timber would be stacked in the carpenter's yard to season, some not being brought into use until several years after it had been felled; some choice pieces, like old acquaintances, remained there throughout most of the carpenter's life, saved for some extra special job.

Pit sawing was usually carried out by travelling sawyers who moved about an area working at different yards in turn, or sometimes even in the woods themselves. They worked in pairs, a top sawyer and his pit man. The top man was the senior partner, and it was his job to arrange the work and set out, in consultation with the carpenter, the cuts to be made. He was also responsible for sharpening the saw. Seven feet in length and double-handled, the saw tapered in width from about 10in (250mm) at the top to 3in (75mm) at the bottom. This kept the weight at the top where it was most needed and could more easily be controlled. A well-sharpened, well-set saw was the crux of this work.

First the trunk was hewn flat top and bottom with an adze and cutting lines were marked on both surfaces in either chalk or lampblack, depending on the colour of the wood. Then it was laid over the pit, supported on cross-beams and held in place by iron spikes or dogs. The top man stood on top of the trunk holding the saw by a long handle called the tiller; it was he who steered the saw along its cutting line, while down below the assistant grasped his end of the saw by a second handle which was removable so that the saw could be withdrawn as necessary.

The saw, cutting on the downward stroke, showered the pit man with sawdust, and his could not have been a pleasant job, down there in the gloom. But the two usually worked well together, making a series of parallel cuts through the trunk until they reached the first cross-bearer, then levering it forward and resuming the process. Steadily they worked, unhurried and accurate, in spite of a reputation for ale-drinking. 'Thirsty work, and dusty too' was the sawyers' claim – and, by modern standards, poorly paid. According to an account of 1813 they could expect, for 'sawing of oak, ash, elm, beech and poplar, under eighteen inches [450mm] in width of board, from 3/6 to 4/- [17$\frac{1}{2}$p to 20p] per hundred feet [30.5m]'.

Pit sawing continued long after the introduction of power saws, mainly because it was cheap and convenient. Many small firms could not afford expensive machinery, and anyway the 7ft (2.1m) saws could tackle trees which, until quite recently, would have been impossible for most machines. Pit sawing is still customary in some underdeveloped countries for these same reasons.

The carpenter learned much at this sawing-up stage about the tree he had chosen. As it was 'opened up' its true character was revealed and he discovered how good – or bad – his judgement had been. He selected and allocated each piece as it was cut, setting some aside for those special jobs already mentioned.

For building work, the carpenter chose oak for the main frame and roof beams, and in this case cleft timber was preferred to sawn wood because of its greater strength. Roof trusses and beams were usually hewn to size with an adze, and beams bearing the characteristic scoop marks of this tool are much sought after today, the marks being regarded as proof of genuine age. One even sees poor attempts at faking such marks for this purpose.

The framing was prefabricated, the carpenter laying out the necessary pieces flat on the ground and there marking out and cutting them to shape and size so that each would fit its neighbours correctly. Mortice-and-tenon joints were marked and cut, the mortices bored out with an auger bit, then squared with an axe-like tool or with chisel and mallet. Tenons were sawn to size. Holes were then bored through both to receive securing pegs of cleft oak.

Such pegs, an inch or more thick and cut on the taper, are much more effective than nails or screws. The tannic acid in oak reacts with iron and causes it to corrode, while brass screws, which should always be used in oak cabinetwork, are not strong enough to be used in large structures. In the days when ships were built of wood, shipwrights used oak pegs, some as thick as a man's arm, to fasten knees to ribs and stern posts to keels. The stone slabs on many a country-house roof are held with similar oak pegs, or tree nails as they were sometimes called.

The carpenter's greatest skill was demonstrated in the laying out of roof timbers. First the pitch of the roof and the positioning of joists and trusses would have to be calculated, and the carefully angled slots and joints cut out to size. Then, with the aid of helpers with levers and block and tackle, the heavy timbers were raised one by one and put into their proper place. Identification marks cut into each piece determined its exact position in the building.

Many timber-framed houses were finished in traditional daub and wattle or hand-made brick. Some, however, were clad in weatherboarding or clapboarding, the first formerly of sawn elm, the second of cleft oak, though both names are now used indiscriminately. Tapered in cross-section and left with the bark intact along one edge, the 'waney edge' (a practice started by the pit sawyers to save time), weatherboarding was popular in several counties of southern England and became a traditional style of the early American colonists. It is still used for its decorative effect on the gable ends of some modern buildings, though too often this is not true weatherboarding but painted or creosoted softwood.

Turning from such heavy work, the carpenter might next be called upon to make an item of furniture for a customer, perhaps an ornate cupboard for the squire's house or a simple table for a cottage kitchen. For the cupboard he would again use oak or perhaps beech, selecting well-seasoned material which was nicely figured or grained. The framing would be securely jointed and slotted, and panels put in loose to allow for any movement. Sometimes the panels would be carved and the cupboard made to stand upon nicely turned legs.

The kitchen table was usually made with a top of sycamore or wide boards of pine. Early tables were simple affairs, little more than trestles supporting a number of loose boards, and indeed tables were originally known as boards. As social conditions improved, the trestles and boards developed into the more permanent refectory table of the type still seen today, with solid ends braced by a stretcher rail across the bottom. This rail, tenoned through the end-pieces, is held by means of a wedge passing through a hole in the end of the tenon. This type of joint is of great antiquity and is known as a tusk tenon.

Tables made for the medieval nobility and highly placed clergy were heavily constructed in oak, frequently reflecting church architectural styles. Village craftsmen simplified the design to suit their own tastes and the needs of their locality. Sycamore was used for the top because it could be scrubbed clean after use – polished oak would have been out of place in country cottages. Later, pine was used, and this too was kept clean by scrubbing, as many an old kitchen table still bears witness. Pine furniture was to be found in almost every kitchen at one time; tables, benches, cupboards and dressers all had a charm and robust simplicity which has remained unaltered through the years. Pine is popular again today, though now it is generally seen with an easy-clean surface of polyurethane.

The traditional designs are not difficult to construct in solid pine, which is readily available. Use substantial material − nothing less than 1in (25mm) boards for the items described here − and do be sure that the wood is dry and not warped before the work begins. For large surfaces such as tabletops, edge-joint narrow boards together as shown; wide boards will have a greater tendency to twist.

Because of its clearness, sycamore was used by the carpenter for a whole range of domestic and farm dairy goods, including spoons, ladles, plates and platters, bread boards and rolling pins. For such work small pieces of branchwood could often be used.

By way of contrast ladders or, to be more precise, ladder sides are made from a complete tree. A straight-grown spruce or a Scots pine, sawn up the middle to make the two parts, is planed smooth on its flat surfaces, but the bark is left intact for the present. Both parts then have holes bored out at 9in (225mm) intervals to take the ladder rungs. These holes, which go right through the ladder sides, are then opened out with a tapered auger. Rungs, cleft from oak or sometimes beech, are shaped with a drawknife and then rounded and tapered with a rung engine, a hand tool similar to the rake maker's stail engine. The wood used must be bone dry to ensure that further shrinkage does not take place, and sometimes in the past sound old wheel spokes of cleft oak would be used. Loose rungs spell danger to anyone on a ladder. Often roughly shaped rungs were laid out in the sun to 'bake' before being passed through the rung engine.

Rungs are driven home into one side first; then the second side is put into place, the rungs being eased in one by one, and the whole thing hammered together tightly. Protruding rung-ends are drawknifed flush and only then can the bark, left on to protect the sides, be shaved off and the sides planed smooth. Metal rods screwed in at intervals brace the completed ladder and add to its safety, which must always be uppermost in the maker's mind. A coat of paint on the sides, but not on the rungs where it would soon get worn off, finishes the job off properly.

Like that of so many rural craftsmen, the carpenter's work was closely linked with farming. From barn building to making dairy utensils, he was kept busy. Ploughs were once made largely of wood, oak and ash being used for the main part, the heavy plough beam. For this a naturally curved bough would be selected, trimmed to shape with adze and axe and smoothed with the drawknife. The final assembly of the plough, like that of carts and wagons, was a joint task for the carpenter and the blacksmith who had made the metal parts.

Gate posts, gates and fencing materials of all kinds were also the work of the carpenter. Gate posts were massive timbers of oak or elm with up to half their total length below ground. This was left rough, while that above ground was hewn square in section. Gate designs varied from place to place, but all were built to last, firmly braced and jointed. The traditional 'five-bar' design − though some gates have more and some fewer bars than this − consists basically of two uprights, a diagonal brace, a top rail, and a number of secondary rails, usually four.

116

COTTAGE FURNITURE

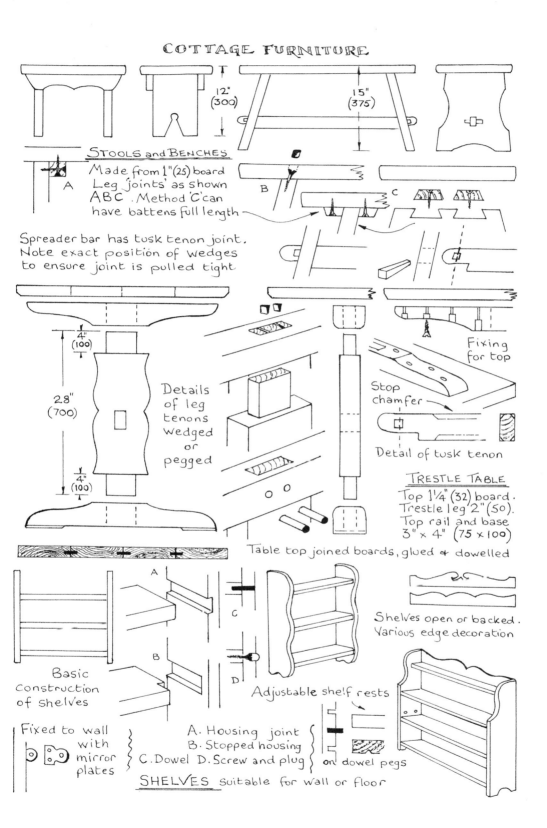

STOOLS and BENCHES
Made from 1"(25) board
Leg 'joints' as shown
ABC. Method 'C' can
have battens full length

12" (300)

15" (375)

A

B

C

Spreader bar has tusk tenon joint.
Note exact position of wedges
to ensure joint is pulled tight

4" (100)

28" (700)

4" (100)

Details
of leg
tenons
wedged
or
pegged

Fixing
for top

Stop
chamfer

Detail of tusk tenon

TRESTLE TABLE
Top 1¼" (32) board.
Trestle leg 2" (50).
Top rail and base
3" × 4" (75 × 100)

Table top joined boards, glued & dowelled

A

C

B

D

Shelves open or backed.
Various edge decoration

Basic
construction
of shelves

Adjustable shelf rests

Fixed to wall
with
mirror
plates

A. Housing joint
B. Stopped housing
C. Dowel D. Screw and plug

on dowel pegs

SHELVES suitable for wall or floor

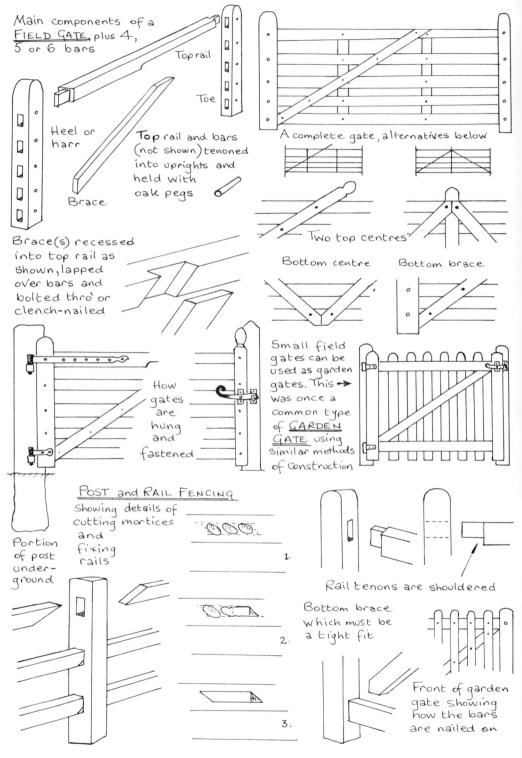

Main components of a
FIELD GATE, plus 4,
5 or 6 bars

Top rail

Toe

Heel or
harr

Top rail and bars
(not shown) tenoned
into uprights and
held with
oak pegs

Brace

A complete gate, alternatives below

Two top centres

Bottom centre

Bottom brace

Brace(s) recessed
into top rail as
shown, lapped
over bars and
bolted thro' or
clench-nailed

How
gates
are
hung
and
fastened

Small field
gates can be
used as garden
gates. This →
was once a
common type
of **GARDEN
GATE** using
similar methods
of construction

Portion
of post
under-
ground

POST and RAIL FENCING

Showing details of
cutting mortices
and
fixing
rails

1.

2.

3.

Rail tenons are shouldered

Bottom brace
which must be
a tight fit

Front of garden
gate showing
how the bars
are nailed on

27 Trimming an oak gate rail from a cleft log, using a large drawknife

These are unevenly spaced, being closer at the bottom to keep in (or out) those young, small animals which are generally inclined to wander to the other side of the fence where the grass is, of course, always greener.

The upright at the hinge end, variously known as the heel, harr or arr, should be the strongest piece of timber in the gate, for it carries the whole weight. For a field gate about 9ft (2.7m) wide, a piece 5½in by 3½in (138mm by 88mm) would be about right. Its opposite number at the latch end is known as the toe or the head; this must be a lighter piece, measuring approximately 3in (75mm) square, in order to reduce weight at the unsupported end of the gate. Both uprights are carefully mortised to take the cross-rails or bars, which are pegged into position. The top rail in particular must be rigidly jointed if the gate is to maintain its shape. In the best gates this rail is tapered, or more frequently stepped, from 5in (125mm) at the heel end to 3in (75mm) at the toe, to match the difference in

119

thickness of the two uprights to which it is joined. This further reduces weight at the free end of the gate. The top rail is braced firmly with a diagonal strut running from about its centre to the bottom of the heel. Other diagonal struts may be added, and it is here that one gets such a variety of designs. All are held in place with either clenched nails or bolts where they cross the horizontal bars. Struts and bars are usually 3in by 1in (75mm by 25mm). Smaller garden gates can be made in exactly the same way.

Hinges need to be substantial for a large gate, and in earlier times were individually made by the local blacksmith. The top hinge, being under tension, should be of a good length, extending some 20in (500mm) along the top rail. The bottom hinge is under compression, and so can be quite short, confined to the width of the heel.

If you have ever wondered why some gates close by themselves, it is because of the clever way in which they are hung on their hinges. The hinge pin at the foot of the heel projects more than its counterpart at the top; therefore the gate is slightly top-heavy and will swing shut by virtue of its own weight from every position except one – when it is fully opened.

The body and underframe of farm carts and other horse-drawn vehicles were often built in the carpenter's shop. Although there were specialist builders, known as wainwrights, and although some wheelwrights built complete carts, normally a team of men would be involved: a blacksmith to produce all the ironwork, a wheelwright to make the wheels, a carpenter for the undercarriage and body, and finally a painter. Each one contributed his own special skill and expertise.

28 A group of carpenters at work on a farm cart

The carpenter used practically the whole range of his timbers in cart and waggon building. The rigid cross-pieces of the heavy undercarriage were of oak and iron-hard beech. The latter was used to make the axle bed to which the wheels were attached; at one time they were fixed directly to the wooden bed itself, later to iron arms bolted to it. The fore-carriage of a four-wheeled waggon had, above its bed, a heavy beam of beech or oak known as the bolster. Separating these two, a pair of parallel pieces called hounds ran at right angles to the two main members. These were made of oak or ash and were in turn braced at the front by oak rails and at the back by the slightly curved slider bar. The hind carriage was built in similar fashion.

Between bed and bolster of both carriages came the centre or coupling pole. This pole, which joined the two carriages together, was always made of ash, specially chosen for strength and flexibility because of the torque or twisting to which it was subjected in use. Shafts too were made of ash, for the same reason; they were curved to suit the shape of the horse, and tapered from back to front, being thick and strong where they joined the vehicle but thinner and quite flexible at their front ends.

The shape of waggon bodies varied from place to place – so much so in fact that it was possible to recognise regional types. There were basic similarities, however, and it was mainly in design details that pronounced differences existed. A typical waggon construction is shown in the diagram on p 131.

Quite often the body of a waggon merely rested by its own weight on its under-carriage, the only point of attachment being a long bolt $1\frac{1}{4}$in (32mm) in diameter. This passed through the fore-carriage and the front end of the coupling pole, and on up through a stout cross-member known as the pillow. The pillow, made of oak, was part of the body frame, which in its simplest form consisted of parallel pieces joined together by a number of cross-bars, all of oak or ash.

Built on this basic foundation were the body sides, which might be of spindles or panels, or a combination of the two, or of plain planks. A variety of timbers was used in body sides, but the flooring was always made of elm, long-boarded, front to back, so as not to impede unloading. Later, when sawn softwood boards became available, these were used for both sides and floors.

Skilful and sometimes elaborate chamfering – the shaving or bevelling off of all outer edges of wooden members – could save up to one-eighth of the total weight of wood used in a cart without loss of strength. It was in the interests of weight-saving that this practice was followed, and not, as one might assume, purely for decoration. It did, however, allow for a little artistry in the carpenter's otherwise very functional work, and some craftsmen must have enjoyed the opportunity to show off a little.

The separate parts of a vehicle were put together in such a way that each could be fairly easily removed for repair or replacement – a wise precaution when one remembers that they were used on rough, unsurfaced roads, often deeply rutted, and frequently driven across open fields.

Before machinery, all this work was of course carried out with hand tools. The ones mentioned already are only a few of the many which the carpenter used to fashion his materials. Many would have been locally made, years before, at the blacksmith's, to be passed on from father to son, each acquiring its own 'feel' for its owner. Chisels in numerous sizes and shapes, each with its well worn handle probably fitted to the blade by the user himself, were kept in racks behind the bench, those in regular use laid flat along the back of the bench itself. Planes of different patterns, including a wide range of special planes for making mouldings, would be kept ready for use below the bench, while braces with their wooden stocks and fixed bits were hung on pegs along the wall. Several types of saw were used, some similar to those used today, but including a number of wooden-framed bow saws now only seen in one small size, as well as a whole range of different drawknives and spokeshaves. All were kept extremely sharp, for the good craftsman knew that a keen cutting edge not only improved his work but also made it easier and safer.

It may truly be said that the old-time carpenter was a jack-of-all-trades where wood was concerned. To achieve this versatility a long apprenticeship and wide experience were necessary. Even this was not enough, however, if he lacked a true affinity with wood – the most familiar of all materials, yet a natural one subject to the infinite variability of all nature's products.

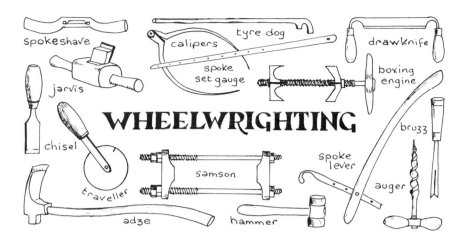

WHEELWRIGHTING

Of all man's discoveries, the wheel may well have been the most significant, giving a whole new shape to civilisation. A rolling log no doubt inspired its design, and the earliest wheels were in fact solid discs, made of a section of log or of joined boards cut to a solid circular shape.

The origin of the spoked wheel is shrouded in mystery. Its evolution as a series of modifications to the solid disc wheel is doubtful, and it seems more likely to have been an independent development related to the problems of weight and manoeuvrability in certain early vehicles. Persian chariots of war had spoked wheels as early as 2000 BC, and although solid disc wheels, being easier to construct and very durable, continued in use on heavy goods and farm vehicles and may still be seen in this role in remote areas even today, it was the spoked wheel which proved the better design for all uses. There is evidence to suggest that wheelwrights making spoked wheels were established craftsmen in Iron Age Europe by about 500 BC; wheels and fragments of wheels found in Britain show that, long before the Romans came, wheels were being made here in ways which have remained basically unchanged for over two thousand years.

The spoked wheel is truly a masterpiece of design and good craftsmanship. Few other wooden constructions are subjected to the stresses and strains, or are able to withstand the heavy loads and sudden shocks, to which the wheel is exposed. Only through a combination, born of long experience, of top-class workmanship and the skilled selection of best-quality materials can the necessary strength and 'truth' be built into a wheel.

There is much more to making a wheel than is apparent to the casual eye. The finished product is not just a flat circular shape, nor is its attachment to the vehicle as straightforward as it may appear. When a cartwheel is looked at end-on the hub or nave seems to be recessed, each spoke slanting outwards from hub to rim, the whole wheel slightly concave like a saucer. The descriptive term for this shape is 'dished'. Furthermore the wheels on a cart lean outwards at the top, some quite considerably, as though about to fall off. This arrangement has the effect of

123

making the wheel stronger and thus increasing its load bearing capacity, and also improves its resistance to wear and damage.

As a horse moves forward in the shafts its gait causes the waggon or cart to sway slightly from side to side and to follow a somewhat sinuous course. This tends to throw the whole weight of the loaded vehicle sideways against the wheels, sliding it along the axle arms with considerable force, first to one side, then to the other. On rough surfaces this movement is increased. Flat wheels have been known to collapse under this constant ramming. Dishing counters this sideways movement because the wheel's cross-section forms a triangle with its apex opposed to the direction of lateral thrust — in engineering terms a very strong structural feature. The thrust is also partly offset by mounting wheels so that they run slightly inwards, not unlike the toe-in alignment on the front wheels of some modern cars.

The outward angle is necessary to enable the dished wheel to present its lower spokes vertically to the ground. Thus the weight of the load is always carried by spokes which are at right angles to the road surface.

Arguments about the scientific principles underlying the dished wheel have gone on for centuries and have never been properly resolved, although the physics department of a British university has shown by calculation that a dished wheel is in the order of twenty times stronger than a flat one of equal size. Two aspects of practical value to the wheelwright are that the dished wheel gives more space above the axle for the body and allows for a better turning circle.

The wooden parts of a wheel comprise the hub (also known as the nave or stock), an even number of spokes which radiate from it, and an outer rim which is generally made up of a number of separate sections called felloes.

WHEEL CONSTRUCTION

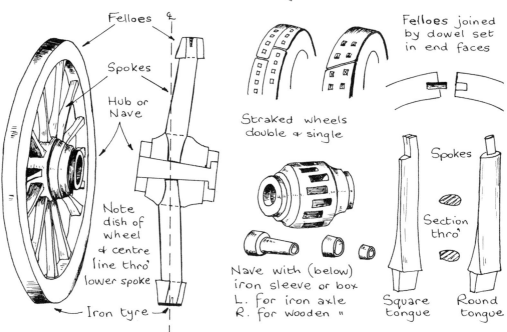

Felloes &

Spokes

Hub or Nave

Note dish of wheel & centre line thro' lower spoke

— Iron tyre —

Straked wheels double & single

Nave with (below) iron sleeve or box
L. for iron axle
R. for wooden "

Felloes joined by dowel set in end faces

Spokes

Section thro'

Square tongue

Round tongue

Elm was the choice for naves or stocks on account of its resistance to splitting. A large hole had to be bored through the centre to take the axle arms, and between eight and sixteen close-spaced slots cut around it to accommodate the ends of the spokes. This meant the removal of a considerable amount of wood, and only elm can be weakened in this way and still stand up to long periods of stress and strain. Elm was bought 'in the round', cross-cut to length and stacked to season for between five and ten years before use. A hole was usually bored through its centre to aid this process. While seasoning, elm exudes a sap which encourages mildew, and this can result in fungal damage. Periodically, therefore, the wheelwright would brush off the white mildew, and so over the years he came to know his elm stocks well.

When ready for use the wood was first hewn to shape with an axe or adze, removing the sapwood in the process to leave only the solid heart. Then it was turned on a huge lathe, often hand-powered. Older types of nave were turned to a barrel shape – these were always considered stronger – but later cylindrical naves were found to be adequate, and, being easier to handle, came more into general use. In turning both types, provision was made for the nave bonds – iron hoops – which enclosed the outer ends. On cylindrical naves the bonds were fitted at this stage, but with barrel naves it was customary to leave this job until the wheel was finished.

After turning, the nave was laid across the mortising cradle – a heavy wooden contraption which held it firmly in place – and had the slots for the spokes cut into it. These were carefully marked out and numbered – a wise precaution taken by the careful worker to avoid finishing up with more or fewer slots than spokes. First three holes were bored with an auger to remove the bulk of the waste wood, and then, using a three-cornered chisel called a buzz or bruzz, each slot was cut at the correct angle for the dish of the wheel and tapered to take the end of the spoke. For this the wheelwright used a gauge stick which could be set to suit each individual wheel. With the gauge in place, each mortice was finished correctly by careful chiselling.

In an average-sized cartwheel nearly 5ft (1.5m) in diameter the finished nave would have a diameter of between 12in and 14in (300–350mm) and would measure about the same from front to back. Mortice slots would be about 3in by 1in (75mm × 25mm) and would go through to the centre.

The number of spokes was decided to some extent by the size of the wheel, and varied from eight to sixteen. These were always of oak, cleft in the forest from the heart of the tree where the wood is strongest and the grain straightest. After careful seasoning each piece was drawknifed down to a diameter of about $3\frac{1}{2}$in (88mm). Next the 'feet' were cut and tapered to fit the hub mortices, then the spoke was trimmed along its length until it was roughly egg-shaped in section, the thicker part to be fitted to the inner side of the wheel where most strength would be needed. An axe was used for the bulk of this trimming, together with a spokeshave and a hollow-bladed plane known in some areas as a jarvis.

With the nave held in position over a wheel pit – a narrow, rectangular trench in the floor of the workshop – each spoke was then driven hard home into its respective mortice with blows from a large hammer, each one making the tapered

125

29 Fitting the spokes to the nave over a wheel pit

tenon tighter. After every two or three blows the spoke would be checked with the gauge stick to ensure that its angle was correct.

Then, with all the spokes radiating from the nave, the next job was to set out the position of the spoke 'tongues' – the top joints fitting into the rim of the wheel. The shoulder of each tongue was marked off with a scribe. This was simply a length of wood with a sharp steel point set into it at the required distance from the nave. The shoulders were cut with a tenon saw and the waste wood split away with chisel and mallet, the battered wood resulting from the heavy hammering each spoke had received as it was driven tightly into the nave being removed in the process. Early wheels always had spoke tongues cut square for extra strength, but changes in wheel tyring later made round tongues, which are easier to shape, acceptable. Tongues were not cut in line with the spoke but at a slight angle so that they were radial to the axis of the wheel.

The rim of a wheel, in most cases, was made up from a number of segments, each curved piece known as a felloe – which was always pronounced to rhyme with belly. Some very early wheels were apparently made with one-piece rims, steam-bent to shape, and occasionally one may still come across lightweight wheels made by joining two semicircular felloes with metal clamps. Since the sixteenth century, however, wheels with one felloe to every two spokes have been the most common.

Felloe blocks made from ash were often roughly hewn to shape with an adze whilst still green, and after seasoning they would be trimmed to their final size and shape. More recently, seasoned wood was sawn to shape either with thin-bladed frame saws or with power-driven band saws. The usual practice was to work to shapes pencilled in from one of the dozens of felloe patterns kept in the wheelwright's shop.

When all the spokes had been tongued and the felloes cut to size, the half-completed wheel was placed face down on a low wheel-stool or on top of half a barrel. The felloes would then be put on, each resting on the backs of two spokes close up to the shoulders of the tongues to which they were soon to be fixed. The

30 Fitting felloes, using a spoke dog to draw the spokes together

position of the tongues was then pencilled in from below on to the face of each felloe. Holes were drilled through in line with these marks with a $1\frac{1}{4}$in (32mm) auger to form sockets for the tongues. Holes for the dowels which bound each felloe to its neighbour were also bored at this time, one at each end. Each of these had to be square to the face of the felloe end and aligned to meet up accurately with its neighbour. Dowels 1in (25mm) in diameter were cut from cleft heart of oak, usually from old, sound spokes.

Because of their radial form, the ends of spoke tongues are at a greater distance apart than are the shoulders. Therefore the spokes, at their widest spread, have to enter the holes prepared for them in the felloes where these are closest together. The wheelwright overcame this problem by using an ingenious implement called a spoke dog with which he was able to force two spokes close enough together for a felloe to be slipped over their ends. Spoke dogs varied in construction, but consisted basically of a stout ash pole to which was attached either a long, adjustable iron hook or a length of chain with a hook at its end. Placing the end of the ash pole behind one spoke and adjusting the hook so that it fitted over the next, the wheelwright could, by getting his shoulder against the long handle of the tool, lever the spokes just sufficiently close together to tap a felloe into place. As he proceeded he had to make sure that the end dowels were engaging correctly, and then, with all the felloes in place and everything lined up, all the parts were knocked into position with a heavy hammer.

Projecting spoke tongues were cleaned off with a chisel and oak wedges driven into their ends to secure them. These were always at right angles to the grain of the felloes so as not to cause splitting.

The whole wooden wheel was now cleaned up with jack plane and spokeshave. Important in this process was the way in which the skilful wheelwright could reduce the weight of his wheel without any corresponding reduction in strength. This was achieved by chamfering – the careful shaving of exposed edges between joints. Felloes were left full where the spokes entered, but were chamfered both sides in between. Spokes too were often chamfered along their length. In addition, the rim of the wheel was often given a pronounced taper so that its outside face was up to 1in (25mm) narrower than the inside.

The wooden rim of a wheel was always shod with iron to protect its wearing surface. For centuries separate curved sections called strakes were nailed on, each one arranged to overlap a felloe joint, but in more recent times a continuous iron hoop was introduced. This hoop tyre was much better for general use, but in some areas strakes continued to be used, and some wide wheels were even fitted with strakes and a hoop.

Both types were made by a blacksmith, either working alone or employed in the wheelwright's shop. Stock widths of $\frac{3}{4}$in (19mm) flat iron bar were used in each case, strakes being cut to length with sledge-hammer and chisel. Heated in the forge, these were beaten to shape over the bick of the anvil. After a second heating, they had four or more square holes punched at each end to take the nails which held them in place. The blacksmith made the nails, each one tapered to fit the tapered holes he had made, so that, like horseshoe nails, they continued to hold the strake tight even when they became worn. A heavy, screwed clamping

128

device known as a samson was used to draw the ends of adjacent felloes together while the separate strakes were being nailed on.

Hoop tyres were measured for length with a revolving measuring wheel known to the trade as a traveller. Having first ascertained the size of the wheel by means of the traveller, the blacksmith cut his metal according to a formula which he kept in his head – the circumference of the wheel, plus an allowance for the joint, less a bit for expansion and shrinkage. The iron had to be joined into a continuous hoop made a shade smaller than the wheel as measured. Expanded by heating before it could be fitted over the rim, it had to shrink to a perfect fit on completion.

The ends of the tyre were first scarfed down, or flattened, so that the overlapping joint did not result in any extra thickness at that point. Then the strip of iron was passed through the rollers of a bending machine to form the hoop, bringing the two ends together. These were then placed in the forge fire, and when almost white hot were welded together by quickly striking the overlapping ends on the anvil with a heavy hammer. This was fire welding, a method perfected by blacksmiths long before oxy-acetylene made welding comparatively simple.

For the next stage the wheel was securely fixed, face down, to an iron tyring platform by means of a long bolt which passed through the hole in the nave. Meanwhile the tyre had been heating either in a special narrow, upright furnace or in an open fire on the ground nearby. When the right temperature was reached, the tyre was raked out of the hot embers and carried quickly to the platform by two, or more usually three, men using long-handled tongs. There it was dropped over the wheel and eased on by means of levers and resounding blows

31 With the tyre in place, water is poured on to cool the hot metal and shrink the tyre on to the rim of the wheel

129

from a sledge-hammer if necessary. There was no time to waste during this operation; the hot metal immediately began to burn the wooden rim, and water, kept handy, had to be quickly poured over it. Amidst clouds of steam and hammer blows and shouted instructions the tyre was positioned, and more water was poured over it to cool everything down. As it cooled the iron tyre shrank, bracing the whole wheel together in a vice-like grip, binding felloe to felloe and spoke to nave. For the wheelwright and the blacksmith this was the moment of truth. Both would then discover if their calculations had been correct and their workmanship sound; a mistake by either and the wheel could burst apart, or at least be pulled badly out of shape.

One further, very important task remained before the wheel was finished. This was the fitting of a cast-iron bearing — or box, as it was called — into the nave of the wheel. First a hole was made in the nave, larger in size than the box to be fitted, using either a gouge or a tool known as a boxing engine, a hand-operated boring bar fitted with prongs to hold it in position and an adjustable revolving cutter which bored the hole to the required size.

The wheel, with the box loosely in position, was then mounted on an axle arm fixed in such a way that the wheel could be swung just clear of the ground. A marker (a small block of wood) was placed there to show when the wheel ran true as it was turned, and the box was then centred, and finally held in place, by means of oak wedges driven into the end grain of the nave so as to tighten the elm against the cast iron.

Last of all the wheel was given a final clean-up before painting, and provision was made for the fitting of the lynch pin, a metal peg which prevents the wheel from running off the axle.

Whatever size of wooden wheel was made, and for whatever size or type of vehicle, this was the basic method of construction. There were certain variations, of course, some between individual wheelwrights, others of a regional nature. These regional differences were more pronounced in cart and waggon design than in wheel construction, however, and were often, though by no means always, the result of geographical features such as highland or lowland country, soil type and land use.

Two-wheeled carts were the earliest form of wheeled vehicle, and although the four-wheeled waggon was not unknown, even in prehistoric times, it did not come into general use until well into the sixteenth century. Even then carts continued to be favoured in many areas, waggons being found mainly in the lowlands where arable crops predominated.

The design of many of the early farm waggons was basically that of the heavy carrier's waggon, which was capable of hauling between four and eight tons and was pulled by a team of up to twelve horses. For farm work a lighter vehicle was needed. In adapting to local needs some craftsmen stuck closely to the original design, while in other areas distinct changes were made, often producing quite elegant-looking waggons with clean, graceful lines. It was these differences in design which gave rise to the various recognisable regional types. Closely linked to these regional differences in design was the variety of different names given to the same parts of carts and waggons, which were sometimes most confusing.

130

WAGGON CONSTRUCTION

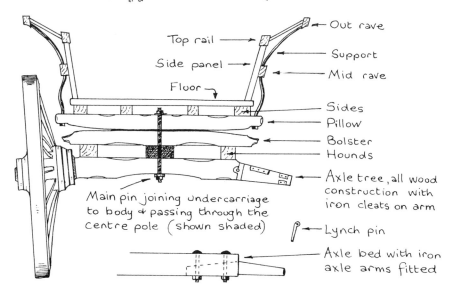

Out rave
Top rail
Side panel
Floor
Support
Mid rave
Sides
Pillow
Bolster
Hounds
Axle tree, all wood construction with iron cleats on arm
Main pin joining undercarriage to body & passing through the centre pole (shown shaded)
Lynch pin
Axle bed with iron axle arms fitted

Section through fore-end of a typical waggon

Despite these variations in design and designation, the general principles of construction, like those of wheel construction, were similar throughout the country. Sometimes the body of the vehicle was made by a carpenter, and the wheels by the wheelwright, as his name suggests. Alternatively, the wheelwright might make the complete vehicle. Certainly most wheelwrights could, and often did, turn their hand to other aspects of work with wood. During the nineteenth century, however, many carts and waggons were made by a team of men, each carrying out his own part of the work in an employer's workshop.

In addition to making new wheels and building carts and waggons, wheelwrights were kept busy with repair work. Fitting new spokes after a breakage, replacing a felloe which was worn out of shape, or re-tyring a wheel which had shrunk during a hot spell and had cast a strake or developed a loose hoop, were common jobs. Replacing boards in a cart floor, or even a complete floor; stove-in side panels; a broken shaft – all these kept the wheelwright busy. Indeed, it was often this work which kept him in business, for 'jobbing', as repair work was called, was often the only sort that paid. New work showed little profit – a new waggon sold at £30 or thereabouts in the latter part of the nineteenth century. This new work was generally carried out during the winter months, just to keep busy when there was not much repair work to be done, farmers being notorious for not bothering about a broken waggon until it was urgently needed for harvesting.

Often the wheelwright carried out general carpentry work or did jobs allied to his own. One of these jobs might be to make a wheelbarrow for a local gardener or

131

WOODEN WHEELBARROW

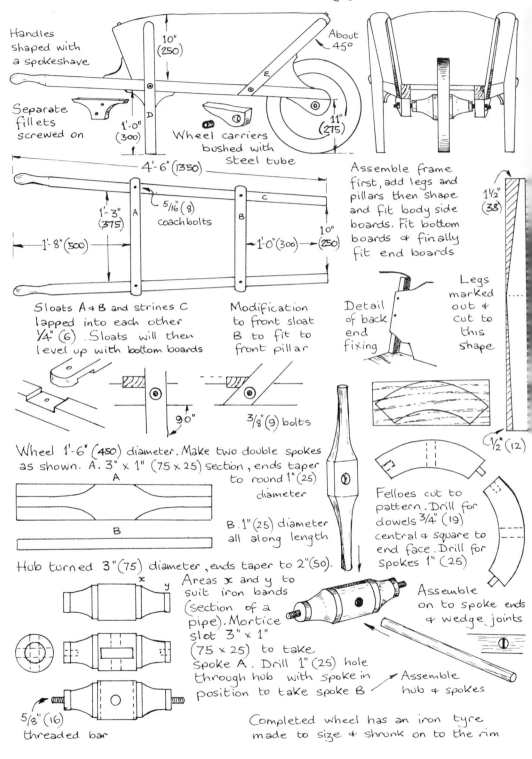

Handles shaped with a spokeshave.

Separate fillets screwed on

10" (250)

About 45°

1'-0" (300)

Wheel carriers bushed with steel tube

11" (275)

E

D

Assemble frame first, add legs and pillars then shape and fit body side boards. Fit bottom boards & finally fit end boards

1½" (38)

4'-6" (1350)

5/16" (8) coach bolts

1'-3" (375)

A

B

C

1'-8" (500)

1'-0" (300)

10" (250)

Legs marked out & cut to this shape

Detail of back end fixing

½" (12)

Sloats A & B and strines C lapped into each other ¼" (6). Sloats will then level up with bottom boards

Modification to front sloat B to fit to front pillar

90°

3/8" (9) bolts

Wheel 1'-6" (450) diameter. Make two double spokes as shown. A. 3" x 1" (75 x 25) section, ends taper to round 1" (25) diameter

A

B

B. 1" (25) diameter all along length

Felloes cut to pattern. Drill for dowels ¾" (19) central & square to end face. Drill for spokes 1" (25)

Assemble on to spoke ends & wedge joints

Hub turned 3" (75) diameter, ends taper to 2" (50).

x y

Areas x and y to suit iron bands (section of a pipe). Mortice slot 3" x 1" (75 x 25) to take Spoke A. Drill 1" (25) hole through hub with spoke in position to take spoke B

Assemble hub & spokes

5/8" (16) threaded bar

Completed wheel has an iron tyre made to size & shrunk on to the rim a nearby estate. These old-style barrows were made entirely of wood, elm often being the choice for the barrow body and ash for the shafts or handles, while wheels were made of the same materials as cartwheels. Wheelbarrow wheels were said to be the most difficult of all to make; according to an old saying current among those who worked in wood, if you could make a wheelbarrow wheel you could make anything. With that challenging thought in mind, some details of construction are given here.

WOODEN WHEELBARROW CUTTING LIST

A	sloat	cut 1	1ft 9in × 2in × 1¼in	(525mm × 50mm × 32mm)
B	sloat	cut 1	1ft 6½in × 2in × 1¼in	(463mm × 50mm × 32mm)
C	strines	cut 2	4ft 6in × 2in × 2in	(1350mm × 50mm × 50mm)
D	legs	cut 2	2ft 0in × 2in × 2in	(600mm × 50mm × 50mm)
E	pillars	cut 2	1ft 7in × 2in × 1¼in	(475mm × 50mm × 32mm)

All above items in ash. 'Sloat' and 'strine' are traditional names for these parts of a wheelbarrow. Body sides, and boards and bottom boards are of elm or good-quality deal, ¾in (19mm) thick and shaped to fit. Support fillets can be ¾in (19mm) or thicker. Wheel carrier is cut from 2in (50mm) thick hardwood. Four $\frac{3}{8}$in × 4½in (9mm × 114mm) and four $\frac{5}{16}$in × 3½in (8mm × 89mm) coach bolts required. Wheel hub turned from elm, 3in (75mm) diameter, 10in (250mm) long. Spokes and felloes of ash, felloes 2¼in (56mm) to 2½in (63mm) in thickness.

The hub is solid – that is, it has no axle passing through it – and it is much longer, compared to its diameter, than the average cartwheel nave. Sometimes the centre boss is left square, and turning confined to the area either side of where the spokes lie. Another peculiarity is that it has four felloes and what appear to be four spokes – in other words, one spoke to each felloe, unlike cartwheels which normally have two to each felloe. The spokes themselves, however, are most peculiar. There are in fact only two of them, both double-length but quite different in shape. Both are normally round where they enter the felloes, but one is flattened and rectangular at its halfway point. This fits into a corresponding slot cut in the hub. The second spoke is round along its entire length and passes through a hole bored right through both the hub and the other spoke.

The felloes are dowelled together and the whole wheel secured with an iron hoop tyre held in place with four nails. The turned ends of the hub are sometimes bonded with iron straps, and the wheel is hung in carriers mounted on the main frame of the barrow.

This main frame carries the floor and the end and side panels, extending forward to take the wheel and backwards to form the handles or shafts, the ends of which are shaped into hand grips. Two legs are fitted which serve also to strengthen the sides, and often provision is made to extend the sides to increase the barrow's capacity when carrying bulky loads such as leaves or straw.

Hand-made wheelbarrows of this kind were common until the introduction of factory-made barrows, first of wood with metal fittings and later entirely of metal. Factory-made carts and waggons first appeared as early as 1850, using wheels made from machined parts. It was this which brought about the decline of the wheelwright's craft. The change-over from horses to the internal combustion engine, and especially the use of tractors for farm work — tractors pulling trailers with rubber-tyred metal wheels — caused his final demise.

Many wheelwrights turned to other forms of hardwood carpentry, in some cases to the building of trailer and lorry bodies. Some are still in business, and here and there it is possible to find a man who still knows how to build wooden wheels as they have been built for over two thousand years.

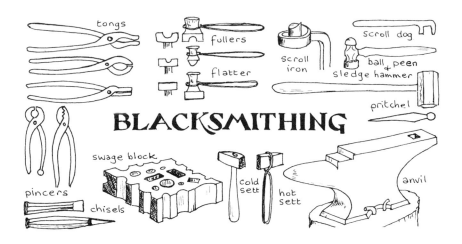

BLACKSMITHING

The blacksmith is a worker in iron, and every village and town once had its smithy where he worked. Immortalised in poetry and in music too, he was for centuries a central and essential member of every community; the village smith in particular was a vital part of the rural economy. Like that of the saddler and the wheelwright, his work was closely linked to agriculture and to the horse as the main source of power and transport.

Although, strictly speaking, a man who shoes horses is a farrier, the village blacksmith always included shoeing among his other skilled work in iron. Many took the examination of the Worshipful Company of Farriers to become Registered Shoeing Smiths, a test requiring not only manual skill but also a precise knowledge of the anatomy of the horse's foot, together with its diseases and treatment. The smith had to be something of a mechanic too, and familiar with farm machinery, for he was often called upon to repair machines or to make complete new parts. He made the fittings for waggons and carts, and tyred their wheels, and later turned his hand to making and repairing springs for vehicles of all kinds. Medieval smiths forged weapons and made armour. In addition, all kinds of agricultural and domestic ironware were made or repaired in his workshop: gates, hinges, fasteners and latches, oven bottoms, complete grates, fire-irons, and brackets, hooks and hangers of all shapes and sizes.

Before veterinary surgery became a profession, the smith was the local horse doctor as well, and some extended this aspect of their business to treating the minor ailments, pulling the teeth and even cutting the hair of the local population too. Some people believed that smiths had magical powers, and certainly the horseshoes which they made have long been regarded as lucky charms. Many thousands must have ended up nailed to doors to ward off evil spirits. The blacksmith was truly a man of some stature in a village community, and his smithy a natural meeting place for all and sundry.

Perhaps it was the smithy itself which gave the smith and his trade their aura of mysticism. Its dark interior, lit only by the glowing hearth of the forge, sometimes a gentle light, at others a shimmering white heat; the glow of hot iron; the

135

ringing sounds of hammer blows; sparks, smoke, the acrid smell of burning hooves and the steam and hiss of hot metal being quenched in water – all this made it a somewhat awesome place. And it was fascinating, too, to see a material as hard as iron made malleable and shaped, as if magically, by heat and hand alone.

Pure, wrought iron was the traditional material of the blacksmith, but in recent times mild steel, which is an alloy of pure iron and carbon, has been extensively used owing to the limited availability and high cost of wrought iron. Wrought iron was produced by stirring molten iron in a special hearth – a process known as puddling – then hammering and squeezing the mass of material to form a strong, fibrous structure. It is mainly in this structure that it differs from the mild steel which is now used. Mild steel is granular in structure and thus less ductile and malleable than wrought iron, but it possesses greater tensile strength and, being more even in texture and quality, is considered easier to work by some. It is obtainable in lengths of various size and section – round, square, hexagonal, flat bar, half-round and angle.

The most important piece of equipment in the blacksmith's shop is the raised hearth or forge in which is built the all-important fire. Most old ones were of brick, but others are of iron, and all have a canopy or hood and a chimney above to take away the smoke and fumes. Good-quality coal or coke is the fuel used. Air to keep the fire burning brightly is blown through a water-cooled pipe or tuyère which projects into the hearth from the back, the air supplied either by a hand-operated bellows or a blower motor. A range of heats can be produced for different types of work by careful regulation of the air flow. The good blacksmith likes to keep a clean fire, without which good work is impossible, and his greatest problem is the build-up of clinker, a sticky black mass produced by the combination of oxygen with impurities in the fuel. This has to be allowed to harden – it sets to a hard, glass-like substance when cool – and is raked out from time to time using a hooked poker made specially for the job. New fuel is banked up at the back of the hearth and pulled on to the fire as required using another special forge tool, the slice. At the front or to one side of the hearth there is a water trough, or bosh as it is called, used for cooling tools, quenching metal or damping down the fire when needed.

Close by stands the solid iron anvil, usually mounted on a block of wood to improve its resilience, since the rebound from each hammer blow struck on a springy anvil contributes towards the next. Anvils are made in two or three patterns, the London pattern being the most familiar. It is obtainable in different sizes, the largest weighing about 3cwt (150kg). Its flat upper surface, made of hardened steel, is known as the face; the cone-shaped projection is the bick, and between these two is a small flat area, the table, which has not been hardened like the rest of the anvil's surface. This part is used when metal is being cut with a chisel, the softer surface preventing damage to the edge of the chisel if it cuts through. At the blunt end of the anvil there is a square hole and a smaller round one. The first, the hardy hole, is used to hold the shanks of a variety of tools used in cutting and shaping the metal, which is placed on them and struck with a hammer from above, either directly or through another tool. The round hole is the pritchel hole over which holes are punched into hot metal; this was always used when making nail holes in horseshoes. The anvil is usually positioned with the bick pointing to the left as the blacksmith faces it, at a height to suit the individual, and sloping slightly away from the user so that scale from the metal and other hot debris falls away safely.

Although most shaping is done on the anvil, many smiths have in addition a curious cast-iron 'swage block', rectangular in shape and with different sizes of half-round and angled notches in its edges and variously shaped hollows and holes in and through its surfaces; this complements the anvil in the forming of hot metal. Similar in function are the smaller swages made in pairs: one of the pair, the bottom tool, fits into the hardy hole in the anvil, while the other, the top tool, which has a handle, is struck from above to shape the hot metal in between. A large floor mandrel — a cast-iron cone used in rounding off hoops and large rings — is sometimes to be found, especially in older smithies. A bench with a heavy-duty leg vice and a rack containing a range of hammers, chisels, punches, setts and tongs of many different shapes and sizes completes the blacksmith's principal equipment.

The tool most frequently used by the blacksmith is the ball peen hammer, which may vary in weight from $1\frac{3}{4}$lb (0.79kg) to 3lb (1.35kg); for heavier work the long-handled sledge-hammer of either 7, 12 or 20lb (3.2, 5.4, or 9kg) is used, wielded by the blacksmith's chief assistant, the striker.

Methods of working iron have hardly changed since prehistoric times when the metal was first discovered, and although techniques have improved as knowledge of metallurgy has increased, nevertheless the Iron Age smith would be familiar enough with much of the work of his modern counterpart. Basically, black-smithing consists of the forging or working of iron and steel, heated to the correct temperature, by means of hammers and other tools; the main processes are few in number, comprising drawing down, upsetting or jumping up, bending, cutting, punching and welding.

The correct temperature for each stage of the work is judged by eye, the change in colour of the hot metal giving the smith the information he needs. The colours are best seen in subdued normal daylight, away from direct sunlight and against a dark background. Heats range from dull or blood red through bright red to bright yellow (near welding heat) and finally to nearly white (full welding heat). If iron gets too hot, either because it is left in the fire too long or because the air blast is too high, it burns, and scaly lumps are formed which spoil the work.

Drawing down increases the length of a piece of metal and reduces its cross-section. It is done at a near welding heat by hammering the bar to shape on the face of the anvil. Round and rectangular bar may be drawn down to a point or to a chisel end in this way. Heavier work is done between top and bottom tools called fullers, the latter in the hardy hole, the former struck from above by the sledge hammer. Upsetting or jumping up is also done at near welding heat; this process causes metal to swell in one particular place, reducing the overall length of the bar at the same time. The skill lies in getting the swelling in exactly the right place, which is done by cooling part or parts of the workpiece with water,

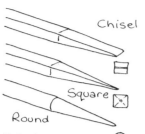

Chisel

Square

Round

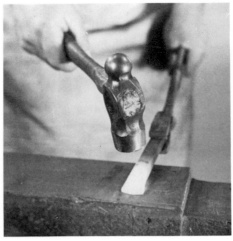

DRAWING DOWN ⊙
Chisel end. At near welding heat bar is held on anvil at a slight angle. Strike square on without 'pushing' the metal. Begin at tip & work backwards

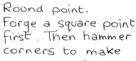

Correct tendency to fishtail by turning bar on edge. Then continue working on both sides alternately until chisel completed

Start with an abrupt point & work backwards, turning the bar a quarter-turn between hammer blows ↗

Round point. Forge a square point first. Then hammer corners to make 8 sided & round up point

Square point.   Note wrist movement to achieve an accurate quarter-turn quickly

UPSETTING   Done at near welding heat by striking bar down on anvil face. Correct buckling as work progresses & keep end square. Centre of bars upset in a similar way

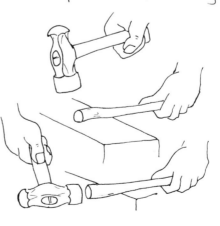

Short lengths can be held in tongs & end hammered as shown above

FORGEWORK - 2

Radius bends made over the bick of the anvil. All bends made at bright red or at near welding heat

BENDING Marked position is placed on anvil edge. Strike hammer blows just off the anvil working out towards the end. Keep square & even as shown above

TURNING AN EYE Mark off 5" (125). Shape at mark over edge of anvil as shown below

Move work as shown by the arrows

PUNCHING At near welding heat drive punch almost through on anvil face. Turn over to reveal small black spot and punch there to go through. Enlarge by punching over hardy hole

Heat eye again, cool at first bend in water, then shape over bick of anvil to an inside diameter of 1¼"(32)

FIRE WELDING Carried out at high temperatures from light welding heat up to white heat

STRAIGHT SCARF WELD

End forged to a short 45° bevel

With bevel down end is forged over round edge of anvil

First end of bar is upset to provide extra metal for weld

Completed, ready to weld

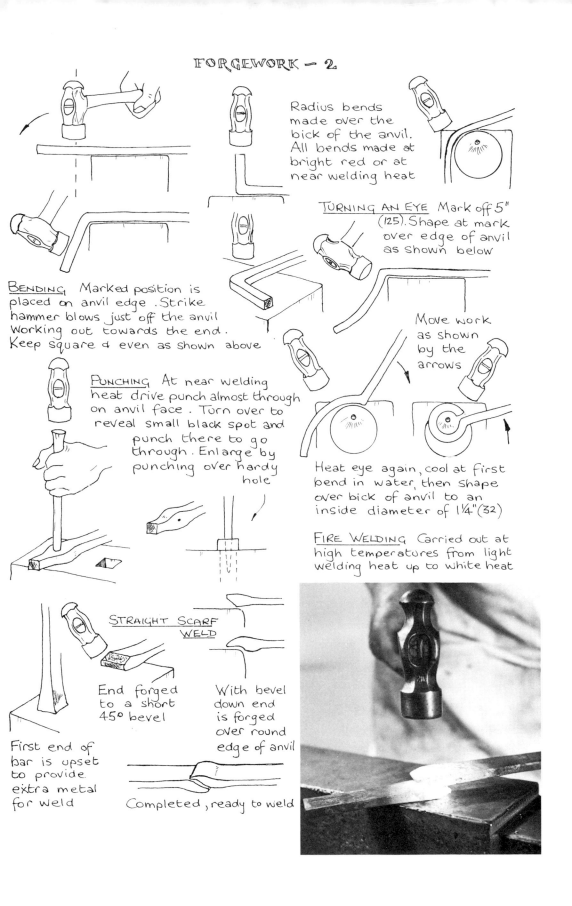

thus confining the heat to the required area. The end of the bar is then brought sharply down on to the anvil face. Shaped ends can be formed by placing the bar in a suitable swage and hammering the opposite end.

Mild steel, especially in light section, can be bent without heating, but it is usual to do it at a bright red heat to even out stresses caused by the bending. All kinds of bends are made by hammering over the anvil – angle bends over the edge of the face, curves on the bick – or a swage block or mandril can be used. For repetitive work and complex bends, as in ornamental ironwork, special bending tools are often made by the smith.

Cutting can also be carried out cold with a chisel or over a hardy, a chisel-edged tool placed upright in the hardy hole; the metal to be cut is laid over the hardy and struck with a hammer. Cutting right through is unnecessary; nicking all round is sufficient to allow the bar to be snapped clean by striking over the edge of the anvil. Metal is usually cut cold when being prepared to length prior to forging. Hot cutting is a forging operation carried out at a bright red heat using hot chisels or setts. Hot chisels have a sharper cutting edge than cold chisels, and are longer, to keep the hand well away from the hot metal being cut. Hot setts are similarly ground but are hafted like hammers, and their use is a two-man operation. The blacksmith holds the workpiece on the table of the anvil, the hot sett placed on it in the correct position for cutting, while his assistant strikes the back of the sett with the sledge-hammer. Hot cutting is carried out when portions of metal have to be removed completely during forging, or to start a split when opening up or dividing a bar lengthways.

Holes, round or square, are made during forging using pritchels or punches of various sizes. Like hot chisels, pritchels should be long enough to keep the hand clear of the hot metal, since the process is best carried out at near welding heat. Punching is started on the anvil face and completed over the pritchel hole to enable the punch to pierce right through the workpiece. If the hole being punched is deep, the punch must be withdrawn after every three or four hammer blows and quenched in water to cool it, otherwise it will be held fast by the contracting metal. Some smiths sprinkle a little coal or coke dust into the hole; gas is formed when the punch is driven in, which in effect blows the tool clear again. Holes are enlarged and their edges smoothed by means of a drift, a suitably tapered piece of steel which is driven into and sometimes through the previously punched hole. Punching is preferred to drilling in most forged work in order to retain the maximum strength of the metal.

Chisels, setts, punches and drifts are almost always made by the blacksmith who uses them. Chisels, which he makes not only for his own use but for a variety of other tradesmen such as welders, builders and quarry workers, are made from steel with a fairly high carbon content. Suitable steel is available in distinctive octagonal bars which are not easily confused with bars of ordinary mild steel.

As a skilled ironworker, the blacksmith traditionally made a wide range of tools for himself and for other workers. Indeed, the claim was made that without the blacksmith to make tools, no other craftsman could begin his work – the motto of the Worshipful Company of Blacksmiths, formed in 1571, being 'By hammer and hand all arts do stand'. Many smiths acquired a reputation locally, if not over a wider area, for making certain tools, especially cutting-edge tools such as billhooks, scythe blades, axes, carpenters' chisels and plane irons. Such tools depended for their quality on the hand-forging methods used in their manufacture, the hammer blows tightening up the metal, compressing and aligning the fibre of the iron so that, after tempering and grinding, the final sharpening 'kept its edge' in a way no longer possible with modern tools, most of which are rolled and pressed out by machinery.

All edge tools need hardening and then tempering after forging, and this is done by carefully controlled heating and cooling. First the steel is heated to a dull red, then plunged quickly into oil or water. This leaves the metal hard but brittle and easily broken. The brittleness is reduced by re-heating the metal to a lower temperature than that required for hardening, the exact temper being judged by subtle changes of colour in the metal as the heating takes place. First the workpiece is rubbed with a piece of stone or a file to clean the surface so that the colours can be seen. Then it is heated, not in the fire but by placing it on a hot bar of iron so that heat is transferred into the tool. As it absorbs heat it will change colour from what is described as straw (a sort of dull yellow) through brown and purple (pheasant's breast) to blue. These colours serve as a rough guide to temperature: the lower the temperature, the lighter the colour and the harder the tool. As the temperature rises, the colour darkens and the tool becomes softer. Experience, or reference to a colour chart, tells the blacksmith when the required temperature is reached, and he plunges the hot metal quickly into water, thus fixing the temper at that stage.

One important tool which the smith makes for his own use is the tongs used for gripping hot metal during many forging operations. Quite a number of different types are required, some with plain jaws, others with hollow round or hollow rectangular jaws, some straight, others angled. To hold work tightly some tongs are fitted with hoops which slide into place to form a self-grip device and keep the jaws closed. The two separate halves of a pair of tongs are forged to shape, then joined together with a large hand-made rivet.

Some blacksmiths may do quite a lot of riveted work, but a more common method of joining parts is by welding. Nowadays this generally means either oxyacetylene or electric arc welding, but the traditional way was by fire or forge welding, which produces the strongest form of joint when properly done. Briefly, fire welding involves heating two pieces of metal to the point of fusion and then hammering them quickly together into one solid piece. It requires considerable skill and much practice to perfect the co-ordination of the several factors essential for good work. These are the proper preparation of the metal according to the type of weld to be made, a clean-burning, clinker-free fire and clean joint surfaces, and accurate colour judgement of the correct welding heat, which varies from bright red and yellow changing to white for most mild steels, to bright sparkling white heat for wrought iron. When the metal is at the right temperature, speed is an added requirement, both in withdrawing the two pieces from the fire, checking their joining surfaces and cleaning off unwanted scale if necessary, and in positioning them on the anvil and delivering a series of rapid and accurate hammer blows to the hot metal before it has time to cool. Silver sand is

141

sometimes used to help clean the metal surfaces, or a proprietary flux may be used.

Some smiths are able to tell from the sound of the first few hammer blows whether the weld is going to be a success or not; a hard, ringing sound indicates that it has not 'taken' and will have to be done over again. Plain joints are usually scarf-welded, the two ends tapered and overlapped so that they pair up when placed together, while other joints may be cleft or pocket welds, where one piece is made wedge- or chisel-shaped and held in a cleft or pocket formed in the other. Before most welding operations it is necessary to upset the ends to be joined to provide the extra metal required in fusing the two parts together.

Most of what the blacksmith produces is of a purely functional nature, but often he is able to add some form of simple decoration to his work. One of the simplest forms of decoration is the twist, frequently seen on an otherwise straight piece of bar, perhaps a supporting rail on a cart body or the handles of a set of fire-irons. Square bar up to $\frac{1}{2}$in (12mm) can be twisted cold, but it is best done at a dull red heat. The portion to be twisted is marked with a punch and the bar placed in the fire. When the correct temperature is reached the parts of the bar not to be twisted are cooled in water and the cool part of the bar gripped in the vice up to one of the marks. A wrench is used to grip and twist the bar at the other mark. More elaborate composite twists are made using bundles of rods welded together at their ends prior to twisting. If a twist forms unevenly, more water is poured on the part which is overtwisting, and if it becomes necessary to twist back again to even up, the part twisted correctly is cooled so that it is not affected.

Many smiths could, and often did, turn their hand to ornamental ironwork of the type now known as wrought ironwork. There are a number of craftsman-blacksmiths working today who specialise in this type of work, but a good deal of the so-called wrought ironwork now available is crudely formed in lightweight material, spot-welded and gloss-painted or, worse, plastic-coated. Genuine, ornamental wrought ironwork is a vastly different thing, and one has only to look closely at the many examples to be found in the gates and grilles of historic houses and the chancel screens and altar rails of ancient churches to see the difference. Only work done in true wrought iron, whether decorative or otherwise, can correctly be called wrought ironwork.

Scrolls often figure prominently in decorative ironwork, and the ability to make them well is of prime importance for good work. An acute sense of proportion is necessary, for the beauty of scrollwork lies in the way in which each piece fits and flows gracefully within the overall design. Shape is determined largely by eye, and even when the craftsman is following a full-size drawing he works freehand; 'mechanical' shapes are to be avoided. In addition to their graceful beauty well-made scrolls give added strength to open tracery ironwork. Without them, gates and similar items would have to be of far heavier and less attractive construction.

There are several patterns of scroll, all formed by forging and bending, each defined by its central termination. The simplest type is the ribbon-end scroll, its terminal point being the same width as the rest of the scroll but finely tapered, with rounded corners. This is done by drawing down the end of the bar before

142

MAKING SCROLLS

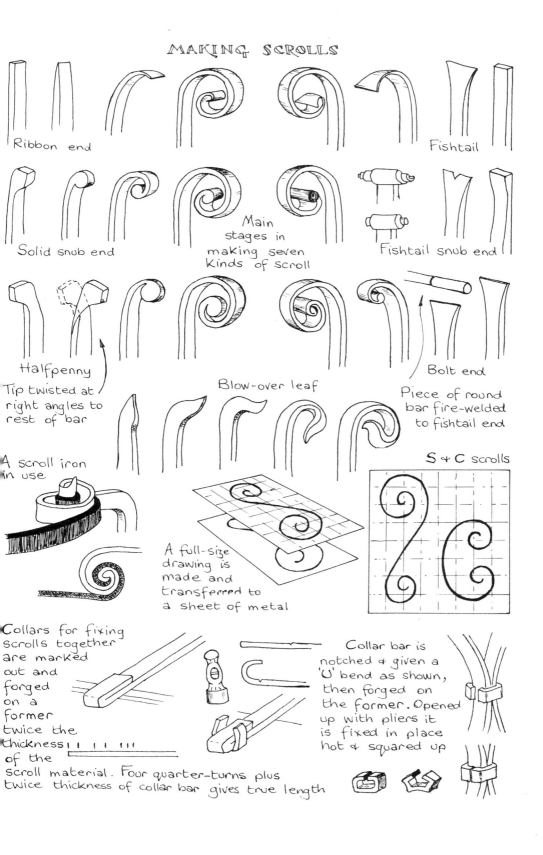

Ribbon end

Fishtail

Solid snub end

Main stages in making seven kinds of scroll

Fishtail snub end

Halfpenny

Tip twisted at right angles to rest of bar

Blow-over leaf

Bolt end

Piece of round bar fire-welded to fishtail end

A scroll iron in use

A full-size drawing is made and transferred to a sheet of metal

S & C scrolls

Collars for fixing scrolls together are marked out and forged on a former twice the thickness of the scroll material. Four quarter-turns plus twice thickness of collar bar gives true length

Collar bar is notched & given a 'U' bend as shown, then forged on the former. Opened up with pliers it is fixed in place hot & squared up bending. The fishtail-end scroll is formed in the same way, except that its end is allowed to fan out during the drawing-down process. The snub-end scroll has a cylindrical end formed over the edge of the anvil, the bar then being drawn down to a little over half its original thickness but kept parallel for some distance behind the termination. There is a fishtail version of this scroll too. The bolt-end scroll also has a cylindrical termination, but of a larger size. This is obtained by drawing down the bar to a thick fishtail and fire-welding a piece of round bar across its end.

Two attractive terminations are the halfpenny snub and the blow-over leaf scroll. The first ends in a disc shape formed partly on the anvil and partly on a special shaping tool. First an offset neck is forged – that is, to one side of the bar rather than centrally – leaving the end roughly square, as shown in the drawing. This end is then given a half twist so that it lies at right angles to the width of the bar. Before twisting, the corners of the neck are rounded off so that the metal does not appear twisted at that point later. Next the end is forged to the required disc on the anvil and the neck squared up again. To finish, the radius between the neck and the disc is closed using the specially shaped tool fixed in the hardy hole of the anvil.

The more difficult blow-over leaf is started by rounding over one side of the end of a bar and forming a neck on the opposite side, leaving the edge between tip and neck a little longer than the bar is wide. Thin the neck and then bend, on edge, over the bick of the anvil. After bending the tip slightly outwards in the opposite direction, thin both edges, using a ball-faced hammer and working out from the centre 'rib' of the leaf. Next the leaf is curled over, hammered surface uppermost, working the metal with light hammer blows over the point of the bick. Knowing what leaves really look like is a big help in getting the right kind of reflex curve here and so avoiding ending up with something which looks more like a dead spear-head than a living leaf.

Most scrolls can be bent into the familiar shape on a scroll tool or scrolling iron, as it is sometimes called, but all should be started on the anvil. Plain ribbon ends and fishtails have their tips rolled over the edge of the anvil into a hook-like curve with light hammer blows. Turned over, the roll is continued on the anvil face, both the bar and the direction of the hammer blows steadily coming up to near vertical as the roll is formed. It may be necessary to repeat this movement two or three times to obtain a good shape.

Scrolls can be made entirely in this way with the aid of a scroll wrench or scroll dog, but more often they are completed on a scrolling iron made for the purpose by the blacksmith. This is a substantial piece of steel shaped into a well-made scroll of the required size, with a raised centre formed by forging an offset fishtail termination; it is held firmly in a vice or in the hardy hole. The raised centre provides an easily accessible anchor point for the start of the scroll. The rolled tip, placed on the centre of the scroll iron, is held there by means of round-nosed pliers while the end is pulled to shape. Once the centre has gripped, the scroll is lowered and pulled round the main part of the scrolling iron. If the bar section is not too heavy this can be done by gripping it with the hand; usually a wrench is used to keep the scroll tight. Small scrolls of light section can be bent cold.

144

32 Making a wrought-iron gate. The smith is fixing the collars which hold the decorative parts together

Solid and fishtail snub-end scrolls and bolt-end scrolls can all be shaped on the same scroll iron, but halfpenny snub-end scrolls require a special tool with an open centre. Blow-over leaf scrolls are formed entirely with scroll wrench, pliers and light hammer blows.

Scrolls may be either S-shaped or C-shaped, both shapes, for the sake of symmetry, being most frequently used in pairs or to form repetitive designs of pairs. In making a large piece of work, a gate for example, it is best to join scrolls in pairs and then to fix pairs together as the work progresses. Of the various methods of fixing scrolls together, collars are the most satisfactory. These are cut exactly to length from light-section flat bar and forged to shape on a former twice the thickness of the scroll bar. The true length is obtained by rolling the former along the collar bar four quarter-turns and adding twice the thickness of the collar bar. After forging square the collars are removed from the former, opened up with pliers, placed hot over the scrolls to be joined and squared up again with pliers and hammer. Alternative fixing methods include riveting, bolting and, nowadays, welding.

Decorative ironwork intended for use out of doors must be well protected against rust, although genuine wrought ironwork is much more durable than mild steel in this respect. After thorough cleaning and de-greasing, a good-quality lead undercoat followed by matt black paint or lacquer applied fairly thinly is recommended for both. For indoor work a finish known as 'armour

145

33 Shoeing a horse in the village smithy

bright' is sometimes used. For this the forging must be done with great care and the metal kept clean. On completion, the work is pickled in a solution of five parts of water to one of sulphuric acid, then washed in sulphate of ammonia to 'kill' the acid. After drying it is polished and may then be given a coat of clear lacquer to preserve the finish.

Despite the great variety of his work, it is as a shoer of horses that the rural blacksmith is most renowned. Horse shoeing as we know it today has been practised for over a thousand years, and for most of that time blacksmiths have not only fitted shoes but have made them as well. At first horseshoes were just flat iron plates, but soon the familiar shape evolved, forged from heavy bar over the bick of the anvil, the square tapered nail holes punched through with a pritchel. Blacksmiths made their own nails too, the distinctive wedge shape made to fit nicely into the shoe's tapered hole, thus ensuring a firm hold on the shoe even

146

when it has worn quite thin. Some shoes, especially those intended for heavy draught horses, were fullered – that is, grooved right round the line of nail holes – both to lighten the shoe and to give some protection to the nail-heads. Later it became possible to buy straight bar already grooved which the smith then simply cut to size and bent to shape. Earlier this century factory-made shoes in various weights and sizes became available, and it is these which are now most frequently used by those who still shoe horses.

When a horse is being shoed the smith or farrier begins by examining all its hooves, beginning with the fore feet. Next the old shoes are removed and the hooves trimmed and smoothed with a rasp and paring knife, for hooves, like fingernails, grow and need regular attention. Then the new shoes, ready-made or hand-forged, are tried for fit and any necessary adjustments made. In the old days all shoes were fitted while still hot in order to seat them snugly on the hoof. In spite of the acrid smell and the clouds of smoke, this does no harm to the horse. Nor does the nailing on of the shoe, unless it is done badly – and the horse would quickly let the smith know if this was the case – for the horny substance of the hoof is quite insensitive. The nails are accurately driven in so that they do not touch the sensitive inner area, and in order that the points shall protrude on the outer surface of the hoof where they can be clenched and thus remain secure. A final rasping to smooth hoof and iron, and the job is completed.

The village blacksmith, busy from dawn till dusk, with two or three big cart-horses always waiting to be shod and a group of curious children looking on, has now become almost a legendary figure. The increased interest in horse-riding, now generally for recreation or in competition rather than from necessity, has kept some busy shoeing; but these men, for the most part, travel out to stable-yards in vans and shoe the horses with ready-made shoes fitted cold. Some smiths have adapted to modern needs, and with new techniques and up-to-date machinery produce forged work for engineering and industrial use, while yet others have specialised in making decorative ironwork of infinite variety. Happily, there are still a few good, all-round smiths in business who really understand their material and are well skilled in its manipulation. Longfellow's mighty smith, beneath his spreading chestnut tree – which was traditionally grown for the shade it cast on hot, sunny days – may have gone forever, but the blacksmith's craft remains.

HARNESS MAKING

When all agricultural machines were horse-drawn, and both road transport and the canals depended entirely upon the horse, the saddler or harness maker, whose basic raw material is leather, was one of the busiest of craftsmen. Throughout the country thousands of them were kept busy making and repairing the heavy harness and equipment required for working horses. Large quantities of collars, ridge pads and saddles, bridles and all the necessary strapwork were needed by all those people who used horses for carrying or pulling.

While this work kept many in full employment – and although some specialisation also took place, especially in the towns – the village saddler undertook all kinds of work in leather. Some might specialise in equipage for horses, and a few, if close to racing stables or in hunting country, might even concentrate on light-weight riding saddles, but most could, and in fact still do, turn their hand to any branch of their craft. The saddler's workplace would often be combined with a small retail shop where all kinds of leather goods made by him would be on sale: leggings, heavy gloves and leather aprons for hedgers, lighter ones for the garden, travellers' trunks and cases, shopping bags and purses, cases for guns, binoculars, and whisky flasks, dog leads, collars and whips, belts and general-purpose straps of all descriptions. Indeed, the term 'saddler' is really too narrow to do justice to this craftsman; he certainly made saddles, but he made much more besides.

When one considers the skilled workmanship required for so great a variety of jobs, it is hardly surprising that the old craftsman had to serve a long and often difficult apprenticeship. One old-timer recalls how, sixty years ago, when he began his working life, he received three shillings (15p) a week and a rise of one shilling each birthday. An older man tells of starting at the age of twelve at only sixpence ($2\frac{1}{2}$p) per week. He began work at 6 a.m., cleaning out the workshop and the master's stable, milking the cow and feeding the horse. Breakfast at 8 a.m. was followed by more skivvying until about 10 a.m., after which he spent the rest of the day twisting and waxing threads and doing simple sewing jobs, with half an hour off for lunch. At 6 p.m. he put up the shop shutters, milked the

148

cow, bedded down the horse and went home for his own supper. This continued with little variation until another apprentice was taken on, setting him free for more bench work, mainly repairs. In this way he handled a wide range of work, and so learned his craft thoroughly, but only in his last two years was he allowed to make the more difficult cart saddles and occasional collars.

Tanning, the process in which animal skins are preserved and converted into leather, has long been a separate craft. In the distant past, however, the same man killed the animal, tanned the skin and then went on to make things from it, and in some areas the saddler was called a knacker, a term now reserved for someone who buys and slaughters horses. Traditional tanning was a lengthy process involving the soaking of skins in a solution of tannic acid, which was extracted mainly from the bark of oak trees. First the raw skins were soaked in lime, then scraped clean over a wooden beam, the hair so removed being used for making felt, and the flesh and fat to make gelatine and glue. Then the skins were neutralised in a solution reputed to consist of water and animal droppings. Next they were washed clean in revolving drums of running water before being suspended in pits containing the oak-bark solution. Over a period of about four months the skins would be passed through a succession of these pits, starting with a weak solution and ending with a strong one to ensure thorough tanning rather than just the colouring of the outside. The whole process could take up to nine months, depending on the type and thickness of the skin. After tanning, the skins were dried ready for curing.

This final process varied according to the use to which the leather was to be put, and this still applies. First the skin was scrubbed with clean water and scoured with stiff brushes and blunt scrapers. It was then set out on a beam and shaved to an even thickness. Next, if it was intended for harness leather or general purposes, it might be rolled to compress the fibres and remove wrinkles, stained black or brown on the hair side and bleached on the flesh side, or the whole skin might be treated with cod oil, tallow or mutton fat. For boot and shoe making additional processes are needed to prevent shrinkage or undue stretching.

Oak-bark tanning is rarely practised today, modern tannery methods having speeded up the process by the use of other active solutions. One of those most widely used contains chrome, and has reduced the working time from several months to only a few days, but it has the disadvantage that the chrome residue creates pollution problems. Oak-tanned leather remains the best for high-grade work, though some of the chemically tanned leathers are of good quality and are much used in present-day goods, including footwear. Good leather should be supple and for certain work needs to be waterproof, yet it must remain porous so that it is able to 'breathe'. Although numerous substitutes have been tried, none has been found to beat 'real leather' as it is now so often labelled.

The saddler would normally buy in whole cured skins and hides direct from the tanner to provide a wide range of leathers for his various types of work – heavy cowhides for harness straps and heavy leather goods, softer calfskin for saddles, bags, purses, and so on. Sheepskin was often used for items of clothing, while the more supple pigskin was used not only for saddles but also for a variety of fine leather goods.

149

34 Cutting out straps with a plough gauge to make harness for a heavy carthorse

Each skin provided a range of material, the back furnishing the strongest and best leather, the sides a strong but softer material and the belly the thinner stuff used where strength was less important, for example in linings.

Few tools are needed to work leather, and although each craftsman may have a large number for each particular job, there are basically only three categories of job, cutting, punching and stitching. For making long straight cuts, or for parallel cuts such as are needed when cutting out harness straps or making belts, a plough gauge is used. Fitted with an adjustable double cutter, this tool can be set to the required width and then pushed along with one hand while the other pulls aside the strip being cut off. For cutting out irregular shapes many people prefer to use a curious knife with a broad, half-moon blade, while others may choose a knife with a more conventional blade. Whatever kind of cutting tool is used, it must be kept razor-sharp if it is to do its job efficiently and safely.

The indentation seen along the border of many straps is made with a tool called a creaser, its blunt iron point being heated in a flame and drawn along to make a permanent mark in the edge of the strap. Decorative patterns are sometimes made using special modelling tools or shaped punches to produce tooled or embossed work. Sharp punches, either round or oval and available in various sizes, are used to make holes for buckles, lacing or riveting. The hammers used with these different punches serve also to secure the metal rivets and to attach small pieces of ornamentation.

The leather worker's main skill lies in stitching by hand the various parts which together go to make saddles, harness fittings etc. For this he uses a variety of needles, some straight, some curved, and all generally diamond-shaped in section. They range in size from the $2\frac{1}{2}$in (63mm) straight needle for stitching straps to the 8in (200mm) curved waling needle used when making horse collars.

150

STITCHING LEATHER

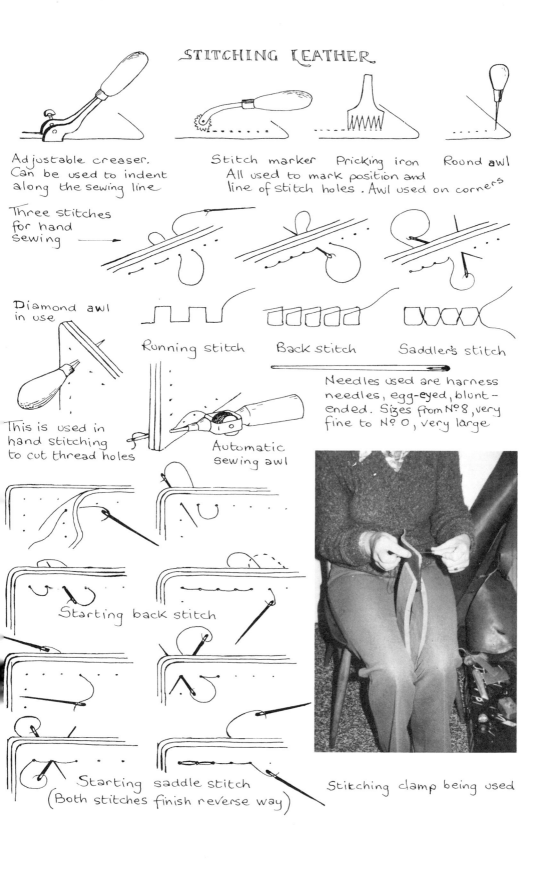

Adjustable creaser. Can be used to indent along the sewing line

Stitch marker   Pricking iron   Round awl
All used to mark position and line of stitch holes. Awl used on corners

Three stitches for hand sewing

Diamond awl in use

This is used in hand stitching to cut thread holes

Running stitch   Back stitch   Saddler's stitch

Automatic sewing awl

Needles used are harness needles, egg-eyed, blunt-ended. Sizes from Nº 8, very fine to Nº 0, very large

Starting back stitch

Starting saddle stitch
(Both stitches finish reverse way)

Stitching clamp being used

The parts to be sewn together first have a row of stitch holes marked with either a sharp-toothed pricking iron, if the edge is straight, or a rotary pricking wheel if it is curved. The pricking iron is a type of punch with a number of sharp points, which, when struck with a hammer, punches a row of correctly spaced holes in the leather. The leather is placed on a board or a piece of linoleum for this work, and regular spacing is ensured by placing the first point of the punch in the last hole of the previous row. On thick leathers the punch is used only to mark a guide, the actual holes being made with an awl. The wheel is almost always used in this way. Stitch punches and stitch wheels, as they are sometimes called, can be obtained in several sizes to give between six and fourteen stitch holes per inch (25mm).

The pieces of leather being sewn are held between the knees or, if the pieces are small, in a wooden clamp, so as to leave both hands free for working. Some clamps rely on the natural spring of two pieces of curved wood; alternatively, they can be tightened by means of a threaded bolt. (See p 30 for instructions on how to make a clamp.)

A variety of stitches may be used, but saddle stitch is the strongest. Sometimes called cobbler's stitch or double-hand sewing, this stitch is made using two needles, either one at each end of a single thread or with two separate threads. The needles are passed through the same hole in opposite directions, one from the front, one from the back, and pulled tight. For additional security each stitch can be locked by passing the needle through the loop of the opposite thread each time. The seam is finished by working back over the last few holes and bringing both threads out between the sewn pieces before cutting them off tidily.

Success in stitching depends largely upon the tension of the thread. It should not be too tight or it will cut the leather or crinkle the edge; too loose and it will be both impractical and untidy. Neat, regular work is important; stitching, while primarily functional, can add much to the appearance of a finished article.

The thread used has to be strong and, above all, hard-wearing. The old saddlers made most of their own thread by twisting together a number of strong linen strands coated in beeswax; in this way they could make up a variety of threads of different strengths and thicknesses to cover all needs. As we have seen, this was often the apprentice's job, or it might have been done by members of the saddler's family after work. Today it is possible to buy a wide range of threads made from both natural and man-made fibres. Good-quality linen thread is still preferred to the artificial threads; the latter may have greater tensile strength, but they lack the resistance to abrasion of the former.

Leather may also be joined together by lacing with leather thonging. Narrow strips of leather, cut usually from calfskin, are threaded through holes or preferably slits, made along the edges of the pieces to be joined. Slits made with a thonging chisel, a three-or four-pointed punch not unlike the stitch punch to look at, give a better appearance than the round holes too often seen on much modern thonged work. These round holes are usually made with a tool called the six-way punch plier. Holes or slits should always be made through both pieces at the same time.

Thonging through slits requires the use of a thonging needle, which is a double

152

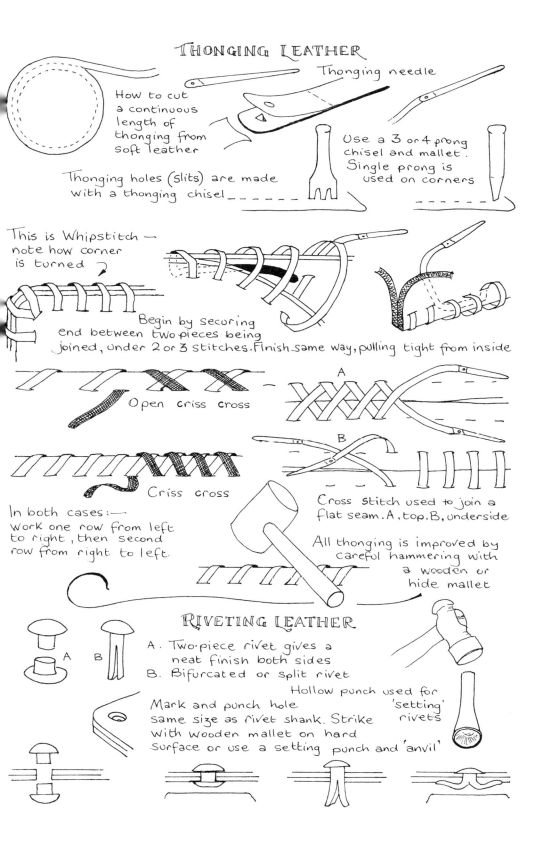

THONGING LEATHER

Thonging needle

How to cut a continuous length of thonging from soft leather

Thonging holes (slits) are made with a thonging chisel _ _ _ _ _ _

Use a 3 or 4 prong chisel and mallet. Single prong is used on corners

This is Whipstitch — note how corner is turned

Begin by securing end between two pieces being joined, under 2 or 3 stitches. Finish same way, pulling tight from inside

Open criss cross

Criss cross

A

B

Cross stitch used to join a flat seam. A, top. B, underside

In both cases:— work one row from left to right, then second row from right to left.

All thonging is improved by careful hammering with a wooden or hide mallet

RIVETING LEATHER

A. Two-piece rivet gives a neat finish both sides
B. Bifurcated or split rivet

Hollow punch used for 'setting' rivets

Mark and punch hole same size as rivet shank. Strike with wooden mallet on hard surface or use a setting punch and 'anvil' piece of flat steel open at one end to accept the end of the thong. An ordinary eyed needle is not suitable. Regular spacing of the holes is as important for thonging as it is for stitching; particular care has to be taken with corners.

Joining leather by thonging gives a decorative but rather bulky finish, and although much used for 'fancy goods' and clothing it forms little part of the saddler's work with equipage for horses. Here a strong but smooth, uncluttered finish is essential, for strength combined with comfort are the main requirements of this work.

It has been said that the good saddler, like the good blacksmith, is the horse's friend. Poor workmanship by either craftsman can cause a great deal of discomfort to an animal, leading perhaps to permanent injury or ill-health. To distribute the weight of a load or the strain of pulling, saddles and horse collars are built on a firm but hard foundation of wood and metal. The saddler's job is to see that these unyielding materials are adequately padded and securely fastened within a well-shaped leather cover which is both hard-wearing and comfortable for the horse.

Riding saddles vary in size and weight according to their use, but most are built up of five main parts. First the wooden foundation, usually of beech, and known as the saddle tree, is covered with a protective layer of felt. Fitted to the tree on each side is a steel bracket to which the stirrup straps will be attached. On top of the tree goes the leather flap, and then the seat and the skirt which covers up the stirrup bracket. These parts are all hand-stitched together, and then the seat, usually made from soft pigskin, is carefully stuffed with flock for the comfort of the rider. Below the tree goes the pad, also carefully stuffed with flock, this time for the comfort of the horse. This rests directly on the horse's back, unless a saddle cloth is used, and in the best saddles it is made of calfskin. Cheaper saddles have pads of serge, expertly quilted to prevent chafing.

Carthorse saddles, or ridge pads, as they are more usually called, have a much stronger trough-shaped tree, deeply grooved to take the chain which supports the weight of the shafts. This tree too is well padded, usually with straw, and then covered with leather on top, with a pad of serge below to protect the horse's spine.

Straw is also used to stuff the collar, and it is here especially that good craftsmanship counts. For this is where the strain of the load is taken, be it cart, plough or canal barge, and whether it is pulled by shaft or trace harness. A badly made collar, or one in bad repair, can cause chafing and a great deal of pain to the horse, making it unco-operative and reluctant to pull.

A horse collar is basically two leather tubes, the wale and the body, firmly filled with flock and straw, fastened together and shaped to suit the horse's neck. To this is fitted the hames, a special frame made either of wood and metal or wholly of metal. To each side of the hames are attached the tug or trace chains with which the load is pulled. In pulling its load the horse pushes its shoulders and the whole weight of its body into the collar, so a nice snug fit here is essential. The filling of a collar is highly skilled work, the flock and straw being properly arranged inside the leather tubes by means of a long metal stuffing rod. A lining of quilted serge inside the collar adds to the horse's comfort and is renewable when worn.

154

35 Repairing a horse collar

The shaping of the collar is carried out on a wooden beam shaped like a horse's neck. The leather is worked in a damp condition, using a heavy wooden mallet to beat it into shape. As horses vary in size the collar must be made to measure, and the beam is tapered to give a range of sizes.

All leather needs careful attention if it is to give good service. Periodic treatment with one of the proprietary brands of leather preservative is recommended, especially where horses are concerned. Their sweat is acidic and mildly corrosive, which is why the old carters rubbed their working harness with grease to keep the leather supple and the metalwork bright. For this reason too working harness was usually made from leather which had been dyed black so that the regular greasing did not spoil its appearance and colour.

Decoration by the saddler was usually limited to the use of brass studs and decorative buckles. Attaching horse brasses to harness straps was the work of the horse owner or driver. The practice seems to be very ancient; originally brasses were believed to ward off evil, but in time their use became purely decorative.

155

Many were of a commemorative nature, while others were show awards, and the men who placed them on headbands – and more especially on the martingale, the strap suspended from the collar down between the front legs of the horse – were very proud of them.

Sadly, the heavy working horse has all but disappeared today. Oddly enough the railways were the last to use them in any number, for deliveries to and from their goods yards; but now they are rarely used, except by a brewery or two. Some of the old-type Shire horses still appear at shows throughout the country, harnessed to restored carts and waggons or engaged in ploughing matches, and a number of people have maintained small breeding stocks. Army and police horses may still be seen, of course, resplendent in their ceremonial gear, and saddler and farrier are still recognised army 'trades'. But by and large the modern saddler has maintained his foothold in the contemporary scene by virtue of the increase in the number of horses and ponies now kept for pleasure riding and competitive sports.

His products are again in great demand, both at home and abroad, and this in spite of apparently high costs. A good-quality hand-stitched saddle can cost £150 or more, and a full set of working harness anything up to £400. Secondhand equipment, some of it made over fifty years ago, also fetches high prices at sales and auctions, proving that the initial cost in relation to useful life is not really all that bad. Perhaps this is why some saddlers complain mischievously that what they make, they make too well.

HORNWORK

For thousands of years, horn has been one of the basic raw materials used by man. It has formed the handle for his knife, tipped his bow, and held the powder for his firearm. It has been his drinking vessel and his spoon, held ink for his pen and covered his books. Armies and hunters were once summoned by it, and herds and flocks collected, while the ancient *Shofar*, or booming ram's horn, is still used today in Hebrew ceremony. Combs, buttons and shoelifts, boxes for snuff, tobacco and trinkets, and ornaments and jewellery of all kinds have been made from horn. Before glass, it was used for the windows of buildings, ships and lanterns.

The craftsmen who came to specialise in this ancient craft made full use of the particular qualities which horn possesses, and like all good craftsmen they developed their techniques to suit the nature of the material. Horn can be cut and sawn and, by the application of gentle heat, made sufficiently malleable to be shaped and moulded. When heated it can be pressed out into flattened plates or split lengthways into leaves of various thicknesses, this sheet material later being put to a wide variety of uses. It is tough, durable and tasteless, and can be finished to a high polish which gives a very pleasing appearance.

Traditionally many hornworkers established themselves close by the sorting pens at the termini of the old cattle drovers' routes. In the days when meat was taken to market 'on the hoof', a number of small industries which made use of the by-products of the meat trade — leather, carpets, tallow, soap, and horn — were to be found close together at such places. Some horners were intinerant craftsmen moving from farm to farm and village to village as supply and demand required.

In the early stages of its processing, horn is a none too pleasant material, and the horner was not always a popular craftsman, despite the value of his products. His work, according to a document of 1455, created 'a Grete and corrupt Stenche to the greveous annoyance of Neighbours'. The offending smell was considered by some to be beneficial, however, and a trade journal of 1747 claimed that 'the Stenche of the Horn, which is manufactured by the heat of the Fire, keeps away the Hyp, Vapours and Lowness of Spirit, the common malady of England'.

36 Selecting ox horn in the horn store at Abbey Horn Works, Kendal. The horns are imported, mainly from Africa, though the stag antlers in the background are British

The best horns came from British breeds of cattle, especially the large horns of the ox. As the demand for horn products grew, however, home supplies became inadequate, and large quantities of raw horn were (and still are) imported from abroad. From America came buffalo horn, and from Africa and India horns and tusks from a variety of indigenous animals. The raw material – green horn, as it was called – had first to be cleaned by boiling then sorted according to its intended use. Some would be kept whole and used to make drinking horns, powder flasks, etc., while other pieces were sawn lengthways or into sections and pressed into flat plates or made into boxes. The solid tips went for button making and handles of all kinds. Roots of horns were compressed into solid cylinders and used by horn turners.

Sawing was usually done on a bow saw fixed teeth uppermost in a vice. The horn, held by the horner in both hands, was passed back and forth over the saw blade, each cut skilfully made to take advantage of any neutral shape in the piece and to avoid undue wastage.

Pieces for flattening were first heated over a flame or boiled in a copper cauldron until soft. Then, after being cut lengthways, the hollow cylinders of horn were opened out with a pair of flat-bladed tongs. Flattening was at one time accomplished simply by stamping on the still warm pieces in heavy boots and then weighting them with blocks of stone until cool. Softened again in hot water, the

158

37 Heating horn in a gas jet to make it malleable for bending

pieces were then sandwiched between iron plates and compressed even further. Later, screw presses proved more efficient, and these in turn were replaced by simple rolling mills. The last stage in the process was to clean off surface flaws with a tool not unlike a carpenter's spokeshave.

For splitting into leaves for 'glazing' purposes the horner selected horns which were light in colour and had some natural translucency. After soaking in water for a month the leaves were separated with a short, round-nosed knife called a lift which was skilfully inserted into one edge of the horn plate between its natural cleavage lines or scales. (In this respect hornworking has something in common with the splitting of slate or the cleaving of wood.) Each leaf was made as clear as possible by careful scraping and then by coating with tallow and compressing yet again, this time between hot iron plates. This produced translucent rather than transparent pieces of horn in small sheets. These made quite good windows before clear glass was available, and remained popular until the repeal of the Window Tax in the mid-nineteenth century. Being non-inflammable and difficult to break, horn leaves were well suited to use in the windows of lanterns.

The ordinary flattened pieces – horn plates, as they were called – were used by horners who specialised in making a variety of domestic and personal articles. Horn made malleable by boiling in water or by careful heating over a flame was pressed into moulds to produce a range of shaped items, including various sizes of

159

COMPLETE HORNS

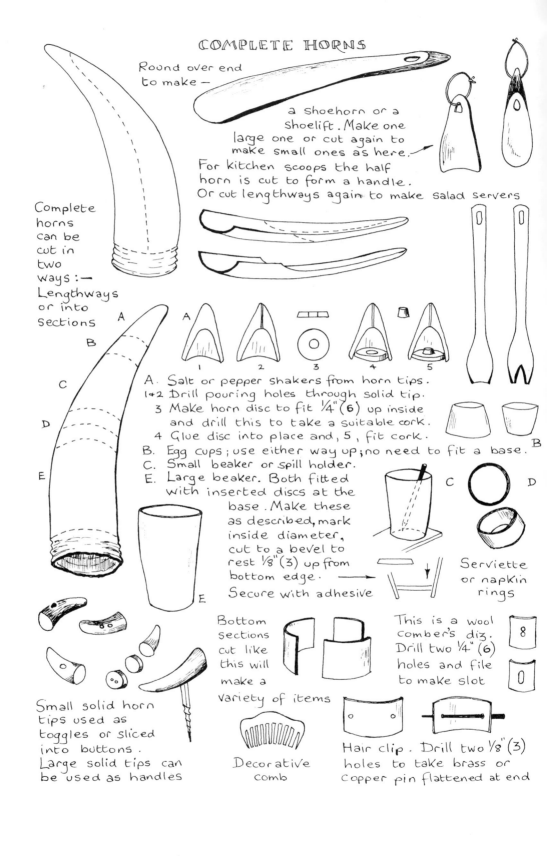

Round over end to make —

a shoehorn or a shoelift. Make one large one or cut again to make small ones as here.

For kitchen scoops the half horn is cut to form a handle. Or cut lengthways again to make salad servers

Complete horns can be cut in two ways :—
Lengthways or into Sections

A
B
C
D
E

A
1 2 3 4 5

A. Salt or pepper shakers from horn tips.
1+2 Drill pouring holes through solid tip.
 3 Make horn disc to fit ¼" (6) up inside and drill this to take a suitable cork.
 4 Glue disc into place and, 5, fit cork.
B. Egg cups; use either way up; no need to fit a base.
C. Small beaker or spill holder.
E. Large beaker. Both fitted with inserted discs at the base. Make these as described, mark inside diameter, cut to a bevel to rest ⅛" (3) up from bottom edge. ⟶
Secure with adhesive

B

C   D

Serviette or napkin rings

Bottom sections cut like this will make a variety of items

This is a wool comber's diz. Drill two ¼" (6) holes and file to make slot

8

0

Small solid horn tips used as toggles or sliced into buttons. Large solid tips can be used as handles

Decorative comb

Hair clip. Drill two ⅛" (3) holes to take brass or copper pin flattened at end spoons and ladles. Boxes and other types of container were made by folding the horn plates into the required shape and size, the joints often being 'welded' by the combined application of heat and pressure.

Pressed horn plates can still be obtained (see the chapter on materials), and are easily sawn to shape to produce 'blanks' for a wide range of work. The saw blades used in metalworking are the most suitable for this, because their teeth are closely spaced, with little set to them. A hacksaw is all that is required, or a coping saw for curved shapes, or, if available, a bandsaw fitted with a fine-toothed blade.

Further shaping is best carried out with rasps (for coarse work) and files (for fine work), or on an abrasive wheel. Holes can be drilled using standard twist drills in a hand or electric drill. Moderate pressure only should be used when drilling, otherwise the horn may splinter, especially as the drill point emerges. High-speed work produces a characteristic smell, and there is a tendency for tools to become clogged; avoid overheating, as this only aggravates the problem.

Spoon blanks were once pressed to shape in two-piece brass moulds after being softened by heating. Boiling water will do the trick, but most of the old craftsmen preferred gentle heating over a naked flame. This was often done over an oil lamp or a gas jet. A bunsen burner or a propane stove can be used. Avoid singeing the horn, especially at its edges, and watch out for your fingers too! Wrapping the workpiece in kitchen foil is a modern way of protecting the horn, while an old glove will guard the fingers. Keep the horn moving back and forth over the flame so that it is evenly heated. The temperature is right when the horn can be touched, but not held for too long, with bare hands. Overheating causes the horn to change colour and become brittle. A simple home-made spoon mould is described on p 31, and other moulds of different shape can be made on the same principle. Pressure is applied to the mould by means of a G-cramp or a vice. When the horn has cooled it will retain its new shape permanently.

Combs were made from specially selected pieces of flat plate, the teeth cut to shape with a special two-bladed saw called a stradda. This had one blade set higher than the other so that as each tooth was cut the next was partly cut, thus ensuring even spacing and uniform thickness of teeth. Many combs were made specifically as hair adornments, and these were cut to elaborate designs and decorated by carving and piercing. For work of this type the horny shell of the tortoise was frequently used.

Entire horns, and cut sections of 'round' horn, were used for a variety of purposes. From the time of the Vikings until well into the eighteenth century, complete horns of suitable size were cut to a firm rim and used as drinking horns. Many were silver-mounted and highly prized. Powder flasks, made from complete horns again and fitted with cap and spout, were once an essential piece of equipment for all gun-men, whether soldiers, pirates or noble huntsmen. Drivers of horse-drawn waggons kept horns filled with grease to lubricate their axles, and saddlers and cobblers kept them full of tallow or beeswax for their stitching thread. Horns of all shapes and sizes were used for 'blowing' or sounding. For all such work the selection of sound material was important. Similar pieces can be reproduced today when good horns are available, the work consisting mainly of cleaning and polishing.

161

Circular boxes were once popular for everything from pins to pills. They were cut from round horn, and top and bottom pieces were made to fit tightly into grooves cut inside their circumference. The old hornworkers made use of the natural springiness of their material to obtain an exact fit with these inserted discs. Lids were formed by sawing through the section once again and then attaching small hand-made hinges.

Horn beakers and tumblers for drinking purposes, or for use as spill holders, were made in this way at the beginning of the nineteenth century, many of them encircled at rim and base with inlaid bands of silver. At first horn of a semi-transparent nature was used for drinking vessels, but later black horn from Welsh cattle became more fashionable. Today modern adhesives bring work of this sort well within the scope of the amateur craftworker. Make the discs a good fit by using the horn cylinder as a template – almost certainly it won't be perfectly round. Use an epoxy resin glue and be sure to get a good seal all round if the finished article is to hold liquids.

Horns cut lengthways were used for making large kitchen spoons and scoops and for shoehorns or shoelifts. Two spoons can be made from one horn after splitting from end to end, and a matched set of spoons so made was once highly treasured. Spoons require a mould for forming, but scoops, or a very nice pair of salad servers, can be readily made by sawing, then filing or grinding to shape. Horn scoops were often made to a specified size or capacity, thus serving as handy measures. Shoelifts were also made two from a horn, and these have remained popular and are still in demand today.

For use at the table or in the kitchen horn has certain advantages over both wood and metal. Its impervious quality – it is not affected by oils or mild acids, and it does not absorb or impart flavour – makes it ideal for use with food, even over protracted periods. It is also non-conductive, which led some horn craftsmen to combine their skills with those of the cutler in the making of knives and other hand-held implements. Initially, solid ox-horn tips or sections of stag antler were used for handles, drilled through and fitted tight over the solid forged tang of the blade. Later, as demand grew and cutlery design changed, the Sheffield horners, who worked closely with the master cutlers of that town, developed another method. Flat plates of horn were moulded in matched pairs in heated steel presses to fit each side of a flattened knife handle, where they were held in place by plain or decorated rivets.

Today top-quality cutlery may still be found fitted with solid horn handles. Carving sets made in this way are always in demand, stag antler being as popular now as it always has been. Its serrated surface provides a good firm grip, and each handle is of course unique.

The old horners finished their products by hand, a laborious and complicated process involving first scraping, then rough polishing, and finally buffing to a high-gloss finish. Scraping was done with steel scrapers or a skiving knife, and for rough polishing a paste of charcoal and water was applied, first on a pad of calico, then with a piece of natural fur – part of an old beaver hat was said to be best. Final polishing was achieved with finely ground wood ash applied with the palm of a warm hand. Later, rotating wheels made the work easier, the horn

FLATTENED HORN

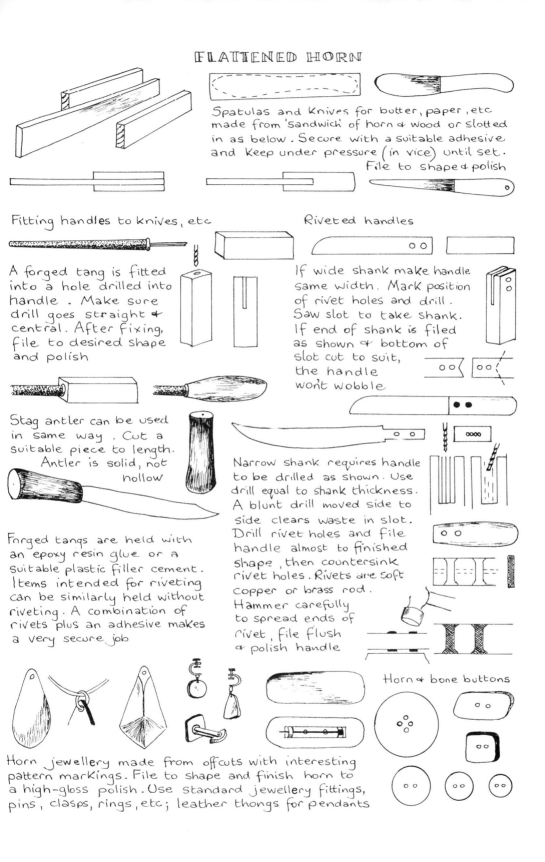

Spatulas and knives for butter, paper, etc made from 'sandwich' of horn & wood or slotted in as below. Secure with a suitable adhesive and keep under pressure (in vice) until set.
File to shape & polish

Fitting handles to knives, etc

A forged tang is fitted into a hole drilled into handle. Make sure drill goes straight & central. After fixing, file to desired shape and polish

Stag antler can be used in same way. Cut a suitable piece to length. Antler is solid, not hollow

Forged tangs are held with an epoxy resin glue or a suitable plastic filler cement. Items intended for riveting can be similarly held without riveting. A combination of rivets plus an adhesive makes a very secure job

Riveted handles

If wide shank make handle same width. Mark position of rivet holes and drill. Saw slot to take shank. If end of shank is filed as shown & bottom of slot cut to suit, the handle won't wobble

Narrow shank requires handle to be drilled as shown. Use drill equal to shank thickness. A blunt drill moved side to side clears waste in slot. Drill rivet holes and file handle almost to finished shape, then countersink rivet holes. Rivets are soft copper or brass rod. Hammer carefully to spread ends of rivet, file flush & polish handle

Horn jewellery made from offcuts with interesting pattern markings. File to shape and finish horn to a high-gloss polish. Use standard jewellery fittings, pins, clasps, rings, etc; leather thongs for pendants

Horn & bone buttons

passing from a wheel of Portland stone to various discs of calico, then of softer linen, each impregnated with an increasingly finer grade of abrasive paste. Finally, buffing wheels of finest lambswool produced the polished finish.

Polishing is certainly best done on a buffing wheel if one is available; the accessories supplied for use with portable electric drills are suitable. Various proprietary polishes can be used, including those sold for polishing jewellery and plastics. Polishing can of course be done by hand – it just takes longer. Use a soft cloth pad, and, where practical, hold this flat on a firm surface and rub the workpiece vigorously on it. Experience has shown that even with high-speed polishing, thorough scraping to remove all traces of tool marks and surface scratches before polishing is essential. Fine-grade emery cloth, steel wool or wet-and-dry abrasive paper can be used if these are more convenient.

Closely allied to horn, bone can be similarly worked, except that it is not suitable for bending or moulding. Its use by Stone Age man is well attested, and craftsmen of more recent times have used it to good effect as handles for cutlery and cupboards, as well as for making paper knives and folders, items of jewellery and, of course, napkin rings.

Raw bone, direct from the abattoir or left over from the table roast, can be made ready for use in the time-honoured way by boiling for several hours in lime or soda water, changing the water frequently during the process. Afterwards it must be left out in the sun to bleach for one to two weeks. Bleaching in a 20 per cent solution of hydrogen peroxide is a newer method which takes less time (24 to 48 hours) and gives a good, even colour.

Pieces of ivory and whales' teeth can be similarly used if obtainable. Both are now comparatively scarce, as are the animals from which they come; in spite of being the largest in size, they are now among the smallest in number on account of their indiscriminate slaughter. Intricate sculptures in ivory have long fascinated visitors to the East, while the art of carving whales' teeth was copied from the Eskimo by mariners who sailed both the northern and southern oceans. Such carvings, often incised patterns and pictures whose lines were emphasised by rubbing in ink or lampblack, are known as scrimshaw.

All these materials make pleasing ornamental goods and jewellery items. Horn especially, with its variety of subtle tones and colours, has long been fashionable for such things as brooches, pendants, scarf pins, earrings and hair slides, and also, of course, for buttons. Many of these smaller items can be made from offcuts remaining from other work.

Horn is still popular with makers of country walking sticks and shepherds' crooks, and one or two small firms in England continue to manufacture horn products on a commercial basis, mainly ornamental goods and jewellery. Infra-red heat is now used for softening, but although hydraulic presses have replaced heavy boots for pressing, and the laborious finishing is now done on electrically driven buffing wheels rather than by hand, the horn is still handled in the same time-honoured ways. As with so many other things in everyday use, however, plastic has now almost entirely taken over, some of it made to look, quite convincingly, like horn. Today too much natural horn ends up – as the waste products of the horner's craft have always done – as fertilizer.

BASKET MAKING

Seated on the floor, his work supported on a flat wooden board between his out-stretched legs, the craftsman seems hardly to be aware of us as we watch him. He is partly obscured from our view by a cage-like arrangement of upright, slender rods which constantly wave about, rotating slowly anti-clockwise as he works. His strong, nimble fingers expertly bend and weave other rods between the up-right ones, and it is clear that he is using a tough but pliant material. By his side lie more of the same slender rods. At frequent intervals, as the end of one weaving rod is reached, another is taken from the bundle by his side and woven in with the rest. Occasionally he uses a flat iron bar to beat down and firm his work. As we watch he measures its height with a curious stick marked off with shiny brass studs, counting with his fingers the number of studs to the top. Apparently satis-fied, he begins to bend over what remains of the upright rods and entwine them one with another. There is about this man an air of quiet competence, in the rapid but unhurried movements of his strong hands an obvious skill, that makes it difficult to believe at first that the basket maker we are watching cannot see.

He is one of many blind craftsmen in the basket-making industry today, help-ing, together with his sighted colleagues, to keep alive this most ancient of crafts. Although there are now perhaps only two or three men in workshops where a dozen or more would have been found a generation ago, there is still plenty of work for the really skilled basket maker who can produce top-quality work. Many professional craftsmen work alone or in small family concerns, and there has long been an amateur interest in basketwork as a leisure activity and for therapeutic purposes.

The practice of interlacing the stems of certain plants into a semi-rigid fabric is one of the most primitive and universal arts of the world. Whoever it was who first wove the branches of a tree together to provide shelter began it. The making of hurdles and wickerwork huts and the wattle-and-daub method of house con-struction which came later were extensions of these first crude attempts. In this chapter, however, we are more concerned with basketwork containers of various kinds, a basket being defined as a receptacle made of pliable materials woven to-

165

38 A blind basket maker at work. By his side is the gauge stick he uses to measure the height of the work

39 Harvesting willow using the reaping hook

166

gether and used to hold or carry a variety of commodities. Being light yet extremely strong, baskets are ideal for carrying loads as well as for storage.

Baskets were among man's earliest artefacts, apparently predating even pottery: there is evidence to suggest that baskets were lined with clay to render them watertight before it was discovered that clay pots could be made free-standing. Suitable materials for basket making could be found almost everywhere and the only tools required were hands and teeth and possibly a sharp stone for cutting and a piece of pointed bone for use as a bodkin. Perhaps a bird's nest inspired the first basket; certainly one of the earliest known examples, a grain basket of the North American Indians, is very nest-like in its construction. Early baskets were plain and functional, but their decoration became one of the early art forms, figuring prominently in the religious ceremonies of many primitive peoples. The similarity in basket construction and in the weaves used in places as far apart as Africa, China and Europe is quite remarkable; only in the design limitations of the materials used – cane, willow, rush or any other suitable stems – is there any significant difference.

Most British basket makers have traditionally used the young, pliant stems of certain species of willow known generally as basket willow or osier. Osier growing and basket making were frequently combined, for most basket makers liked to grow and prepare their own material. Otherwise it could – and still can – be bought from specialist growers.

Willows grow best in rich soil close to water. Occasional flooding is desirable, but the land must otherwise be well drained, as stagnant water at the roots ruins the crop. Somerset is now the principal growing area in Britain, but in the past osier beds were scattered throughout the country wherever conditions were suitable, often concentrated where the demand for baskets was high, for example close to fruit-and-vegetable-growing areas.

Osiers for basket work are grown in regularly spaced rows as 'stools', which at winter's end resemble rather oddly shaped, spiky stumps cut close to the ground. In early spring each of these stumps throws up dozens of quick-growing, bright yellow shoots, which in turn become tall and slender grey-green leafy wands, waving and rustling through the summer when the wind is in the willows.

Harvesting takes place each year during the winter; it is carried out by hand using a heavy sickle or reaping hook. Careful cutting can ensure a good annual crop from each stool over a period of about thirty years. Eventually the yield diminishes, the old stools are dug out and the land turned over to cattle pasture for four or five years before being replanted.

For replanting, 'sets' or cuttings taken from young rods of the required variety are cut 12–14in (300–350mm) long. These are pushed well down into the ground, right way up, by the palm of the planter's hand, which is protected by a heavy leather glove. His downward-pointing forefinger measures the 3in (75mm) or so that the set should stick up above the soil surface. In the following autumn the young shoots that have sprung from the buds of the sets are cut back to help strengthen the root and encourage new growth. The same is done the next year, and it is only after a full three years of growth that the first crop of usable rods is taken. After that, cutting can take place annually.

Some rods – the trade name for the cut stems – are used as harvested, but most are processed by the grower before use or sale. Those used as harvested are graded according to length, tied loosely into bundles and stacked in a dry, airy place in the open to season. Brown rods, as these are called, are recognisable by their rough, grey-brown bark and are used mainly in work exposed to damp, such as fish and vegetable baskets and garden furniture. Some rods, known as green rods, are cut during the summer and used unseasoned for coarse work, particularly for crab and lobster pots and, in combination with sticks and hoops of hazel, in fish traps – putchers for salmon and hives for eels.

The largest proportion of willow used is in the form of white rods. These are obtained by peeling off the bark – a job best done in the spring just as the sap is rising and the willow about to break into leaf. This normally means cutting late so that peeling can take place immediately, but in order to extend the season winter-cut rods are pitted – that is, stood upright in bundles in shallow pits of running water so that the sap continues to flow.

40 Stripping the willow – a family occupation

The peeling or stripping was traditionally carried out by women and children, the latter often given time off school in willow-growing areas to help at this busy time. They used a simple tool known as a stripping brake, consisting of two pieces of springy iron set upright and close together in a post in the ground. The stripper stood facing this and, placing a willow rod between the blades, butt end first, pulled forward from the tip to break the thin layer of bark. Then the rod was reversed and pulled right through the other way, the bark peeling off clean to fall

168

behind the brake. Machines with rotary blades are now used extensively for stripping, one operator feeding in several rods at a time at one end, another collecting the shining white rods as they emerge at the other. Afterwards the newly peeled rods are dried in the open air, resting upright against wooden posts or spread out along fences and hedgerows.

The final category of prepared willow rods are known as buffs. These too are peeled, but first they are boiled in water for several hours and then allowed to stand in the same water for some time longer, the actual time varying from grower to grower. Tannin in the bark stains the rods to a warm, red-brown colour which is revealed when the bark is stripped. After being allowed to dry out in the open the buff rods are ready for use. Many growers claim that buffs are more durable than whites and less susceptible to rot, the boiling process having killed off any lurking insects or fungal growth and the presence of the tannin protecting them from subsequent attack.

Willow rods are still sold under these names – browns, whites and buffs – and very little has changed about them in hundreds of years. They are still graded according to length (not by thickness as cane is), in foot lengths from 3ft (900mm) upwards and sold by the bundle or bolt, the standard girth of which is 37in or just under a metre at the base. Smaller quantities are now also sold by weight.

Willow skeins are also obtainable. These are thin strips split off from either white or buff rods using a small cleaver or cleave. This is an egg-shaped tool of wood, bone or metal, about 3in (75mm) long, with three or four fins at one end. Slits are started at one end of a dry willow rod with a sharp knife; the cleave is set into these and pushed along with the right hand, while the left holds the rod below and moves downward in front of the cleave. The three or four strips, triangular in section, are then drawn in turn through a tool called a shave which removes the unwanted inner pith. The shave is rather like a small plane and is normally held in the left hand, resting against the left knee. An easier way to use it, however, is to hold the shave in a vice or fix it to a table-top. The cleft strip can then be drawn through with the right hand, pith side (point of triangle) uppermost, while the left thumb, protected by a glove or leather thumbstall, holds it down on the far side of the blade. A short part of the butt end is shaved first, then the strip is reversed and the remainder of the rod drawn through. Skeins can also be made uniform in width if required by being drawn through yet another shaving tool, the twin-bladed upright.

All willow must be stored dry, otherwise it becomes mildewed and mottled. When it is required for use its pliability is restored by soaking under water – cold or warm, but never hot. Periods of soaking vary according to the thickness and type of the rods being used, and experience is the best guide. On average, though, white and buff rods need about half an hour for 3ft (900mm) lengths, rising to three to four hours for 6ft (1.8m) rods, in cold water; warm water will speed up the process. Brown rods need several hours, while skeins are merely dipped into water before use.

After soaking, rods should be stood on their butt ends to drain, the thicker butts taking up more of the moisture in the process. The rods should then be laid down in a draught-free, unheated place and covered with damp sacking or a piece

169

of old blanket to mellow. This may take as little as an hour or so, depending on their size, though they can safely be left overnight. Only just enough material should be prepared at one time to provide for the work being done.

Professional basket makers usually prepare enough to last for about two days' work at a time. Before beginning they sort out their 'stuff', as it is called, into sizes suitable for each part of the article being made: bottom sticks thicker than side stakes, waling rods a little thinner and weavers thinner still – about half the thickness of stakes. This avoids wasting time and effort later in picking over the whole bundle to find the right rod. For small-scale work it is advisable to sort out before soaking, tying each bundle loosely with string.

Old basket makers use many quaint yet very descriptive terms, among which 'nature', 'kindness' and 'greasiness' are relevant here. The first two refer to the workability of the willow, its nature being its strength and pliability, while kindness may best be described as its co-operation in doing what the basket maker wishes it to do. Greasy is how willow should not feel after it has mellowed properly. Greasiness is caused by sweating, and if this should occur each rod must be washed in clean, cold water, drawn between finger and thumb along its length, then allowed to drain until no longer wet on the outside. Only then can it be used.

The willow basket maker's tools are few and simple, the most important – perhaps more so than in any other craft – being his own hands. A pair of sharp shears or garden secateurs is wanted for cutting, and a sharp knife for cutting and trimming, and the craftsman will also need a steel bodkin for opening up the work when necessary, an iron or wooden beater for closing up large work, and a pair of pliers for pulling rods through as required.

There are literally hundreds of different types of basket, but whatever their shape or size the process of weaving does not vary greatly. A number of basic weaves or strokes are used and, with one or two exceptions, all work is started base first. In the following instructions constant reference should be made to the diagrams, ideally with a piece of work in hand.

Round baskets are the easiest to make; the basket maker begins by making a slath, which is basically an overlapping crosswork of stout rods. Called bottom sticks, these are best cut from the butt end of the rods; half are pierced by cutting through with the sharp point of a knife, and the other half threaded through them. The basket maker then begins weaving, binding together the cross with thinner rods called weavers, gradually opening up the bottom sticks as he does so until they resemble the evenly spaced spokes of a wheel.

This is done using the method of weaving known as pairing. A single long weaver is bent round one arm of the slath cross and twisted left over right, and the ends are passed in front of and behind the next arm lying clockwise. The cross is then turned ninety degrees to the left (anti-clockwise) and the process repeated. After two or three complete rounds the bottom sticks are separated, first into pairs for one or two rounds and then individually, and the weaving is continued. The separation is started by pulling the bottom sticks or stick to the left and taking the weaver right down behind the next, holding it there with the left hand. The next space is opened up with the right hand and the weaver brought through to the front with the same hand. The work is kept tight and the spaces are

BASKETRY 1

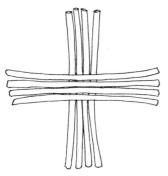

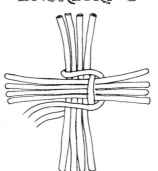

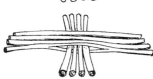

Slath started by
making interlaced
cross as shown here

Weavers bent
round & paired
for two rounds.
Bottom sticks
are then, as
shown, separated
& pairing is
continued

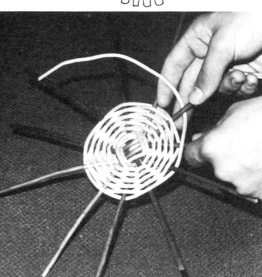

Two decorative centres. Both begin with
a cross, this one
worked with two
weavers interlaced

This is worked
with one weaver.
Suitable for skein

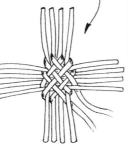

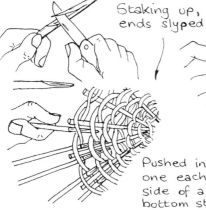

Staking up,
ends slyped

Pricking up.
Stakes kinked
up over the
point of a knife

Pushed in,
one each
side of a
bottom stick

Basket staked up and
ready for weaving. The
stakes are held upright
with a temporary hoop

BASKETRY 2

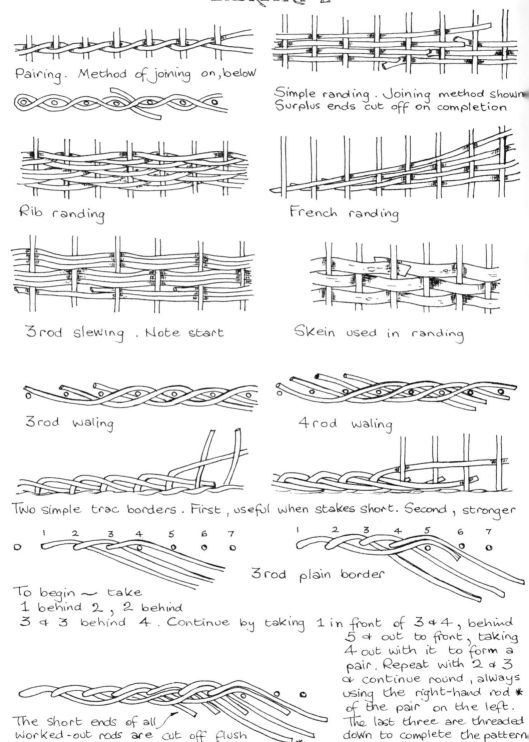

Pairing. Method of joining on, below

Simple randing. Joining method shown
Surplus ends cut off on completion

Rib randing

French randing

3 rod slewing. Note start

Skein used in randing

3 rod waling

4 rod waling

Two simple trac borders. First, useful when stakes short. Second, stronger

1 2 3 4 5 6 7   1 2 3 4 5 6 7

3 rod plain border

To begin ~ take
1 behind 2, 2 behind
3 & 3 behind 4. Continue by taking 1 in front of 3 & 4, behind
5 & out to front, taking
4 out with it to form a
pair. Repeat with 2 & 3
& continue round, always
using the right-hand rod *
of the pair on the left.
The last three are threaded
down to complete the pattern

The short ends of all
worked-out rods are cut off flush

evened out at an early stage to get the spoked wheel appearance. As the weaving proceeds the base is moulded into a 'dished' shape, the convex side being inside the completed basket, for stability.

Opening up the slath as just described is one of the most difficult operations in basketwork, and requires practice. It is for this reason that many amateur basket makers, especially those working in cane, use wooden bases for this stage of their work. These are usually made of plywood, drilled through at the edge to take the side stakes of the basket. Woven bases seem more honest, however, and should be the ultimate aim of the sincere craftworker. Willow bottom sticks with cane weavers in combination make a more easily worked compromise and are excellent for practice work. Willow skeins may also be used for making bases.

Weavers are joined up butt to butt and tip to tip so that there is no abrupt change of thickness. As the end of one weaver is reached a new one is pushed in behind the old one and woven in. When the required diameter is reached the ends of the weavers are slyped and pushed through the previous complete round to secure them. Bottom sticks are trimmed to length with shears and the bottom picked over. The term 'slype' refers to a slanting cut made at the end of a rod, while 'picking' or 'picking over' means trimming off the projecting ends of weavers so that they lie neatly in with the weaving.

Side stakes are now inserted, usually one each side of a bottom stick, thus doubling the number. For some side weaves an uneven number of side stakes is required, and this should be allowed for at this stage. Adding an extra stake is the preferred method, the additional one being inserted alongside one of the regular stakes and spaced out as the weaving begins. The butt end of each side stake is slyped to make insertion easier, and they are pushed about 2in (50mm) into the weave of the base all round its edge. Next the stakes are bent sharply upwards over the point of a knife so that they kink and do not crack. The use of the knife gives the name 'pricking up' to this operation, and when all the stakes are up they are held temporarily in place with a loosely coiled hoop or frame.

'Upsetting' is the name given to the next stage, which is an important one, since it sets up the basket's final shape. Well done, it also contributes a great deal to the strength of the finished article. The weaving method used is known as waling and may be done with three, four, five or six rods which should be almost as stout as the side stakes themselves. It is easiest to start with tops, but a stronger edge to the basket is produced by starting with butts. To start, ends should be slyped and pushed into the base close to adjacent stakes. A four-rod wale is a good one to start with, working round, left to right, in front of two stakes and then behind the next two with each weaving rod in sequence. The first round should be very firm and worked well down over the angles of the upset stakes to give the basket a strong bottom rim on which to stand. When working the second round, consideration should be given to the shaping of the basket, and as the tendency is to allow the stakes to splay out too much at this stage, this should be corrected by keeping the work a little tighter than may seem necessary. Three rounds of waling are usually sufficient on the average basket.

The choice of weave with which to complete the basket is a wide one. Pairing as for the base, using an even number of stakes, is one possibility, but there are in addition various forms of two other basic weaves known as randing and slewing.

Simple randing, with willow, involves weaving single rods of similar length in and out between an even number of stakes. To start, a butt is laid inside between two stakes and the weaving rod worked in and out the stakes to make one complete round without overlapping. The second weaving rod goes butt first in between the next two stakes to the right and finishes as before, the third rod the same and so on. Butts always lie to the inside, tips to the outside, and surplus ends are trimmed off when the basket is picked over.

A variation is rib randing, where the weaving rod is taken in front of two stakes, then behind one, in front of two again, behind one and so on. This produces a close, interesting weave but can only be done when the number of stakes is not divisible by three. In French randing the butt of a weaving rod is laid in and worked one normal (simple) randing stroke. A second weaving rod is now laid in to the left of the previous one and this too is worked one stroke, new rods being added and worked in this same way right around the base. Moving to the left, each weaver is worked to the right one stroke at a time until all the rods are worked out. French randing may be done on any number of stakes, with weaving rods of equal length and thickness.

Slewing is worked over an uneven number of stakes using two or more weavers at a time. Start and finish are graded so that there is no abrupt change. Two-rod slewing is started with a single weaver as in randing, but when this has been worked for about half its length a second weaver is laid in above it. The two are then worked together as a flat pair and when the first rod runs out its tip is left outside and another is laid in above the second to make up the pair again. A three-rod slew is started in the same way, second and third rods being added when a third of the previous one has been worked. New rods are added in the same way so that there are no gaps in the weave.

The finished top edge to a basket is known as the border, and there are many of these, some more pretty than practical. The aim here should be firmness and strength combined with neatness. Before a border is begun, two or three rounds of waling should be worked to complete the side weave. This firms the basket and helps keep it in shape. Borders are worked with what remains of the upright stakes after the side weaving of a basket is completed, and the required length should be taken into account when measuring and cutting the side stakes. Before starting the border, make sure that the stakes are still damp and pliant. If not, they must be soaked in water again, otherwise they will surely break.

Trac or track and plain borders are the ones most commonly used in willow basketwork, and there are several variations of each. In a simple trac border each stake is bent over in turn, taken behind the next on its right and in front of the next two, and left behind the next. Plain borders can be of the 'behind one' or 'behind two' variety and may be worked with two, three, four, five or six rods. A three-rod plain border is described in the diagrams.

Not all baskets are made with woven willow rods. Mention has already been made of the use of cane. This is rattan cane and comes from a tropical jungle plant which produces trailing stems up to 50ft (15m) in length. These are split to produce two kinds of cane, the flat glossy cane used in chair seating, which

174

comes from the outer surface, and centre cane, used in basketwork, which comes from the centre or core of the rattan stems. In the East, bamboo is split to make fine baskets and woven work, while in other areas palm leaves provide excellent material.

The pliable stems of many other plants have been employed in basket making, country folk in some parts of Britain being quite expert at making these 'hedgerow baskets', as they are often called. Split hazel, stems of the rowan or mountain ash and some species of poplar have all been utilised, as have strips of bramble after removal of the thorns.

A rather different type of basket which was once widely used, particularly in the north of England, is made by interweaving lengths of thinly cleft oak. Variously known as spales, spelks, swills, scuttles, skeps, slops or wiskets, these baskets are more or less oval and bowl-like in shape, bearing a close resemblance to the framework of the primitive coracle type of boat. Very strong and quite durable when well made, they were used at one time to carry all manner of things, from potatoes and feedstuffs on the farm to bobbins and waste in textile mills. Specially shaped ones were adopted for seed sowing in the days when seed was broadcast by hand, and extra strong ones were made for carrying coal. They made excellent cribs for babies, being light to carry about and easy to rock gently on account of the slightly curving base. Those few which are still being made now do service most often as log baskets.

SPALE BASKETS

Oak strips 1" to 2" (25–50) wide cleft for the weaving

Hoops are steam-bent & secured with clenched nails using a splice joint

Spells secured to hoop by either of two methods shown below

Shaved with a drawknife, taws are further thinned as shown

1 & 2. Start of spale weaving, bottom spells in place   3. All spells in place
4. Continuation of weaving with taws   5. Completed; note hand holes

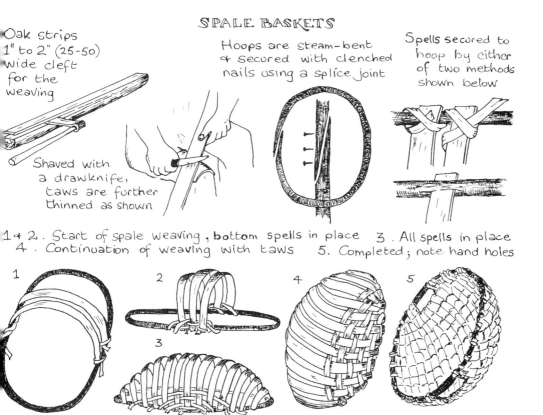

1   2   3   4   5

41 A spale basket maker at work. Note the chopping block used to cut pieces to length

Unlike most other baskets, spales are started by making the rim first. Known as the bool, this is usually a hoop of hazel an inch or so (approximately 25mm) thick. Ash or birch may also be used. The hoops are shaped by being bent round a frame after steaming or boiling to make them pliable. The overlapping ends, suitably trimmed to lie together, are secured by clenched nails.

Strips for weaving are cleft from poles of coppiced oak about 6in (150mm) in diameter. These must be straight-grained and free from knots. When they are needed for use the bark, which was once used in the tanning of leather, is removed and the poles are sawn into lengths of 4–5ft (1.2–1.5m). They are quartered by means of a beetle and wedge and then placed in water in a large tank and boiled for several hours. This is done to loosen the fibres of the wood, making it more easily worked in the next process. While still warm from the water tank each quarter is carefully cleft into strips 1–3in (25–75mm) wide and a little less than $\frac{1}{4}$in (6 mm) in thickness. A short-handled froe, which is sometimes called a lathe axe in spale-making districts, is used for this.

A start is made by striking the back of the tool with a wooden mallet, after which the thin boards are split off with a levering action. These are then shaved more thinly on the familiar shaving horse with a drawknife. Two thicknesses are required – spells or spalles, which are fixed across the basket, and taws or tahs (sometimes tyres), which run the length of the basket and are woven through the

176

spells. Taws are pared more thinly so that they are more flexible. Some makers did this fine paring with a sharp hand knife, drawing the taw against the knife across a leather pad fixed above the right knee. Alternatively, in more recent years a type of planing machine has been available for this final trimming.

When enough strips have been prepared the actual weaving can begin, methods varying slightly from place to place. As in other basketwork the strips must be kept moist so that they remain pliant. The craftsman, seated on a stool, takes the prepared rim across his knee and, starting in the middle, begins fixing the widest strips across from one side to the other. These are the spells or ribs of the basket and they form the warp of the weave. Some fix them in place by inserting their ends into slits made in the bool or rim with the blade of a knife, while others rely on a clever twist which binds the strip to the bool. Whichever method is used, they are further secured by subsequent weaving.

Then, starting with narrow bands at two points on opposite sides of the rim, the taws which form the weft of the basket are woven in. These are woven in an increasing semicircle; at the start, and when the rim is reached again, the ends are wound once round the rim and pushed down securely behind a rib. Several rows are woven on one side, then several on the other, so that the last part to be done is the middle section. Wider bands are used as the work progresses so that the base is made more sturdy than the sides. Spaces are left at each end below the rim to serve as carrying handles. As the softened wooden strips dry out and set to their new curved shape they gain in strength, making this type of basket ideally suited to heavy agricultural and industrial use.

TRUGS

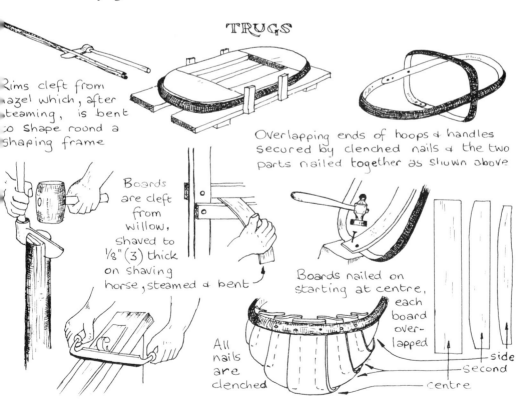

Rims cleft from hazel which, after steaming, is bent to shape round a shaping frame

Overlapping ends of hoops & handles secured by clenched nails & the two parts nailed together as shown above

Boards are cleft from willow, shaved to 1/8" (3) thick on shaving horse, steamed & bent

Boards nailed on starting at centre, each board overlapped

All nails are clenched

side
second
centre

Smaller baskets of woven wood were popular at one time for packing soft fruit such as strawberries and blackcurrants. Known as chip baskets or punnets, these were made from thin strips of cleft willow, poplar or alder. Later these baskets were replaced by mass-produced containers using machine-cut wood veneers simply overlapped and held together with metal staples.

One type of basket which is not woven is the trug. Still available and popular as garden baskets, these were being made in the sixteenth century, and although the name trug could be a variant of 'trough' it is thought to go back even further and to derive from the Anglo-Saxon word *trog*, meaning a boat. Trugs certainly resemble boats in shape, and to some extent in construction too, for they are 'clinker-built' of overlapping boards.

The trug has a hooped rim of cleft ash, hazel or chestnut, usually with a handle and sometimes with bracing pieces of the same material attached crosswise to it. Within this framework thin curved boards of willow are arranged to form a shallow, concave receptacle. Work begins with the making of the rim or hoop. Coppice-cut rods about 1in (25mmm) in diameter are split into two halves and shaved smooth on their inner surface, leaving the bark intact on the outside. Cut to length, these are then placed in a steam chest until pliable. Some shape the hoops by rolling them on a home-made contraption, but usually a setting frame is used to hold the hoop until cold and permanently set. Then the overlapping ends are trimmed and clench-nailed together. Different sizes of setting frame are used to suit the various sizes of trug made. Rims are rectangular with rounded corners and so are handles, for these completely encircle the trug, passing underneath it to give strength where it is most needed. These two hoops, which together form the main framework, intersect at right angles and are clench-nailed together where they cross.

The boards which form the body of the trug are cut from pollarded white willow, although other timbers are sometimes used instead. After being cross-cut to length these are cleft with a froe into strips no more than $\frac{1}{8}$in (3mm) in thickness and in widths from about 1in to 3in (25mm to 75mm). Power-driven circular saws are now used, fitted with a thin, fine-toothed blade to reduce wastage in the kerf or saw-cut.

Next, each board is shaved smooth with a well-sharpened drawknife while held in the jaws of a shaving horse. The boards are then sorted according to size and finished to suit the curve of the trug. Three kinds of board are made for each size of trug, each kind occupying a different position in the completed basket. The longest, with ends cut almost straight, is known as a centre board and occupies the centres of the trug; shorter ones with slightly tapered ends are seconds and go either side of the centre board, while those with most taper are sides and fit up under the side rim of the trug.

The boards are steamed in the same way as frames and bent to the required curve while pliant by levering between two fixed wooden bars. While still damp – or, if they have been allowed to dry out, after dipping in water – the boards are bent inside the framework and fixed there with nails. The centre board goes in first and is nailed to the rim from the inside. This is followed by the seconds and finally the sides, each board overlapping the previous one. All the nailing takes

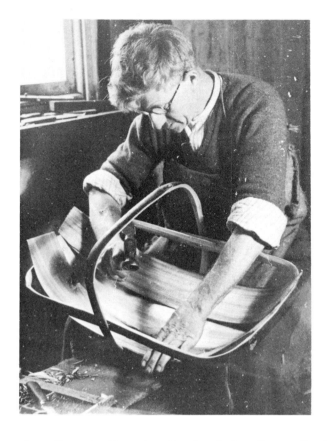

42 Nailing up a trug

place from inside using flat-headed nails, preferably of copper. A heavy, flat-headed hammer is employed, and each nail is clenched as necessary on a suitable anvil, usually a piece of iron bar fitted to the bench. When all the boards are in place, protruding ends are trimmed flush with the rim of the frame.

Small to medium trugs have one centre board, two pairs of seconds and one pair of sides, making seven boards in all. These trugs range in length from 12in (300mm) to 24in (600mm) and are sold now for general garden use. Most are fitted with small blocks of wood below which act as supporting feet when the otherwise round-bottomed basket is placed on the ground. The largest trug is the bushel trug, some 30in (750mm) long. It has a centre board, three pairs of seconds and two sides, making nine boards altogether. Too big to lift with one hand when full, it has no central handle, an opening being left below the rim at each end for carrying purposes. Large trugs are braced for additional strength.

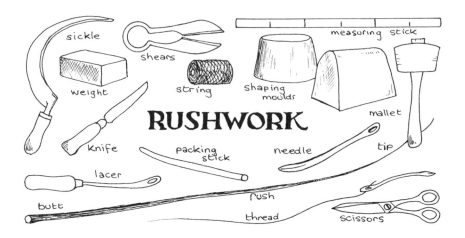

RUSHWORK

Since the dawn of civilisation rushes have been woven into the very fabric of man's history. Archaeological evidence suggests that rush mats were in use in Palestine and Jordan over eight thousand years ago; Egyptian Pharaohs lounged in chairs of woven rushes, while Moses, as a baby, lay safely concealed by them. Before carpets were introduced from the East by returning Crusaders, rushes were strewn thickly upon the floors of European dwelling houses. Not only humble folk but also the rich used them in this way as a means of protection against the cold and damp of earth or stone-flagged floors. In churches too rushes were used for this purpose. Rushlights were made by dipping the centre pith of the rush, cut with a strip of the outer rind remaining, into hog's fat to produce a cheap form of candle. Dipped in rancid butter, rushes were used as a form of lighting by Irish crofters earlier this century, a 2ft (600mm) length burning for about one hour.

Rushes were also used for thatching, for strengthening the plasterwork applied to house walls and, tied in bundles, for the foundation of pack-horse trails through swampy ground. Later they were used for bedding and seating, mat making, bags, hats and horse collars, and for wrapping cheese. Coopers used them to caulk their barrels, and people knelt on rush hassocks in church. They have been used to protect plants and bulbs from the harmful effects of frost, and to make tradesmen's bags, shopping baskets, table mats and fancy goods of all kinds.

The rush-bearing ceremonies held each year at Ambleside, in the English Lake District, and elsewhere commemorate the practice of changing the rushes used for floor covering. During the Middle Ages, when large quantities of rushes were used for this purpose, they were rarely changed; owing to the social habits of the time, they became not unlike the deep litter on which some farm livestock is kept today. 'Nose herbs' – sage, mint and lavender – were added in an attempt to sweeten the offensive smell, but these crude carpets were often a source of disease. Regular changing – at least annually – partly solved this problem, and later the introduction of plaited and woven rush mats made the task much easier. Coil mats were the first to be used, consisting of a long plait of rushes coiled and sewn together until the required diameter was reached. Perhaps it was a few strands of rush idly twisted together by someone lounging among the loose rush litter on a cottage floor which led to the making of the first plaited mat. Whatever its origin, most ordinary rushwork, especially large work, is still done in this way.

Attention has already been drawn, in the chapter on materials, to the variety of plants known as rush. It is the large fresh-water rush *Scirpus lacustris*, with its spongy, cylindrical green stems, which is best for plaiting. These rushes require no cultivation, but only protection, growing naturally in rivers and along the margins of some lakes. Normal practice is to harvest every two years during July and early August when the rushes have attained a height of about 6ft (1.8m) above water level. They are cut below water level, as close to the river bed as possible, the cutters either working from punts or wading waist-deep to cut an armful at a time with a curved reaping hook. Care must be taken that the rushes are not bent at this stage, otherwise they will break at that point after drying.

After cutting and collecting at the river bank the rushes are washed clean of mud and weeds and spread out on the ground to dry. Sometimes they are stacked in loose bundles or leant against wire fences. Drying is best done in partial shade rather than in full sun, which causes the rushes to bleach and lose strength.

Careful drying, or curing, is important for good rushwork. If the rushes are not cured for long enough they dry out at a later stage and shrink, so that the finished work becomes loose and open. If too dry they become brittle and break easily. Rain causes mottling, and if they get too wet they can become mouldy and

43 Harvesting rushes in the traditional way

rot. Opinions vary as to the time required for curing, from several days to several weeks, depending largely on weather conditions. Quick curing preserves most of the green colour of the rushes, which fade over a longer period to tones of brown and yellow.

About three big armfuls of fresh green rushes shrink when cured to make a bolt — the traditional unit of measure — which should be 40in (1m) in circumference at the butt end. Nowadays they are more likely to be sold by weight, in bundles weighing between 5lb and 6lb (2.3–2.7kg). These should be stored in a dry, airy place until ready for use.

Before use the rushes are dampened to make them pliable enough to manipulate without breaking. Two or three minutes in a trough or bath of cold water is sufficient, after which they are wrapped in a damp sack or a piece of old blanket and left for two or three hours to mellow. Alternatively, they can be sprinkled with water from a watering can, wrapped up and left overnight. Only the amount required for the job in hand is prepared at one time, and the rush should remain slightly damp throughout the work.

Simple plaiting requires little skill, especially for the simple three-strand plait, the knack lying mainly in the ability to produce a tidy plait of even thickness and tension, and in knowing when and how to insert a new length of rush. The longest rushes are selected, and the butt ends — that is the thicker, lower ends — of three are tied tightly together. This tied end is then fixed to a convenient hook or door handle so that the material can be kept under tension while the plaiting takes place. If the rushes are thin, or if a very thick plait is required, tie six or even nine together and work two or three together in each strand. The plait is worked by taking strands alternately over and under each other in a regular pattern. In a complete set of movements each side strand goes to the opposite side and back again, while the centre strand goes to both sides. Five-, seven-, nine- and eleven-strand plaits are worked on the same principle to produce a wider plait. The uneven number of strands ensures an even selvedge on either side.

Strands should be of uneven length so that new rushes are not all joined in at the same place. When 6in (150mm) or so of a strand remains a new one is added, butt first, and twisted in as the plait proceeds. Care should be taken not to work right to the end of a tip which is brittle. Such tips are best broken off before use.

To make an oval mat using plaited rush, double back the first 12in (300mm) and stitch the two lengths together, edge up, to form a double row. Then wind the remainder of the plait round and round this central core, stitching as you go. Make enough plait to complete the mat before starting the stitching if possible, or continue plaiting as the work progresses. Short lengths of plait can be joined by overlapping at the joint, but it is difficult to do this really neatly. To finish off properly, end the plait with uneven strands and tuck each one as it is reached into the mat to give a gradual finish to the edge. Use strong thread or fine string in a natural colour for the stitching.

Mats of all sizes and shapes can be made in this way, from table mats to floor coverings, depending only on the size and quantity of the plait. Round shapes are coiled, snail-like, around a central point, while squares and rectangles are started by bending the plait several times, concertina fashion, to make a suitable core.

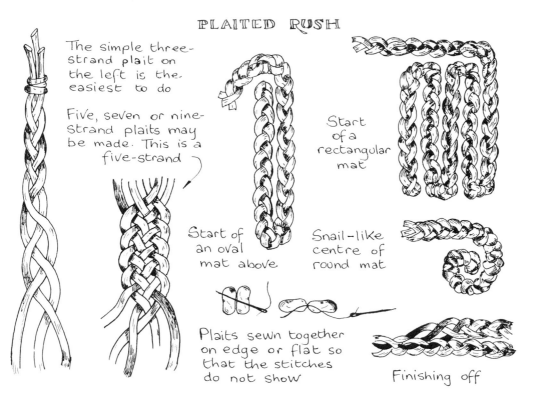

The simple three-strand plait on the left is the easiest to do

Five, seven or nine-strand plaits may be made. This is a five-strand

Start of a rectangular mat

Start of an oval mat above

Snail-like centre of round mat

Plaits sewn together on edge or flat so that the stitches do not show

Finishing off

Small squares and other shapes, of similar or different sizes, can be stitched together to make larger mats.

Rushes plaited and sewn together in this way have been used in many ways other than in mat making. Large baskets known as skips, used for carrying and storing all manner of things, were made from plaited and coiled rush or straw, and a warm and very comfortable chair used to be made in the same way. Known as a beehive chair, it was similar in construction to the once popular straw beehive or skelp; some chairs had hoods to ward off draughts, and in Wales these were known as harp chairs. A similarly hooded chair of coiled straw and reed rope, traditionally associated with the crofting communities of the Orkney Islands, was made on a simple wooden framework, often of driftwood. Truckle beds, temporary affairs of coiled straw or plaited rush which could be tucked away under a main bed when not needed, were often used in inns, and were also made and used by shepherds sleeping out in the fields. For carrying their tools and midday meals workmen used plaited rush bags known as frails, some having webbing handles running right round and underneath the bag for added strength. The weak spot of any rush bag or basket tends to be the handle with which it is carried. Rushes are still used today in the making of domestic linen baskets.

Many articles are woven with single rushes rather than plaited, using techniques not unlike some of those used by willow and cane basket makers. Small

183

WEAVING RUSH

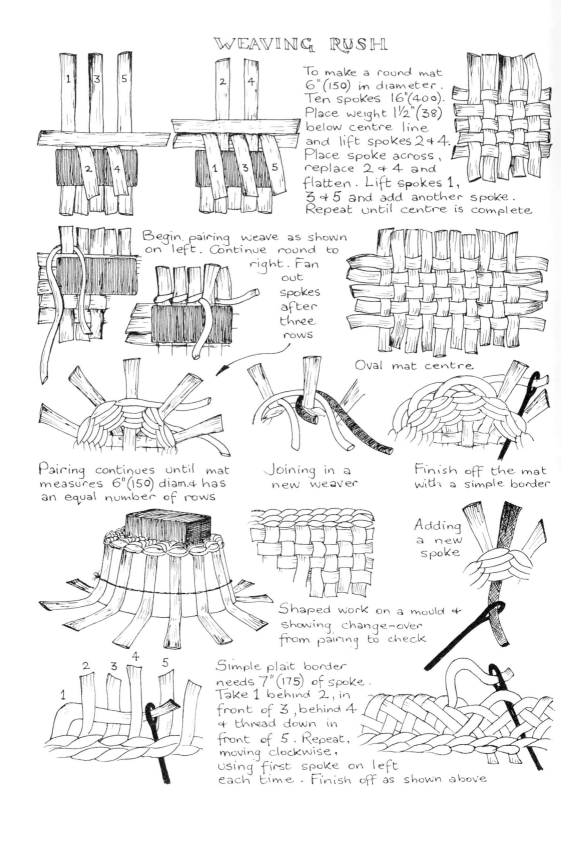

To make a round mat 6"(150) in diameter. Ten spokes 16"(400). Place weight 1½"(38) below centre line and lift spokes 2&4. Place spoke across, replace 2&4 and flatten. Lift spokes 1, 3&5 and add another spoke. Repeat until centre is complete

Begin pairing weave as shown on left. Continue round to right. Fan out spokes after three rows

Oval mat centre.

Pairing continues until mat measures 6"(150) diam.& has an equal number of rows

Joining in a new weaver

Finish off the mat with a simple border

Adding a new spoke

Shaped work on a mould & showing change-over from pairing to check

Simple plait border needs 7"(175) of spoke. Take 1 behind 2, in front of 3, behind 4 & thread down in front of 5. Repeat, moving clockwise, using first spoke on left each time. Finish off as shown above round or oval mats suitable for use at the table are quite simple to make. Both shapes are started with a checked pattern of flattened, interwoven rushes, the round mats having a square centre pattern and the oval mats a rectangular one. The only tools required are a needle with an eye large enough to take a small end or tip of rush – a sack needle is the type usually used – a pair of scissors and a cloth-covered flat stone or brick to act as a weight.

The rushes used to start the work are known as spokes. Butts are selected for this, and after cutting to the required length are squeezed out flat between finger and thumb, starting at the thick end of the butt. For a round mat half the spokes are laid on a flat surface, thick end to thin end, and weighted, while the other half are systematically woven through them to form a square centre of checked weave. Then, after making sure that the ends of the spokes are all lying even, one-third of a long, thin weaving rush is looped round one of the spokes and both ends are woven to the right, in and out of the spokes, in the manner of the basket makers's pairing weave. The spokes are opened out fanwise as the work proceeds. A new weaver is joined in, tip to butt, when about 4in (100mm) of the old one remains, and the two are woven together, the loose ends being left on the under-side of the mat and trimmed off closely on completion. The mat is kept flat and weighted, both mat and weight being turned anti-clockwise as the weaving continues to the right.

As work progresses the weight is removed, and when the required diameter or width is reached the end of the weaver is threaded down alongside the nearest spoke and under four rows of weaving to secure it. This is done with the aid of the needle, which is pushed, eye first, under the weavers and out to the edge. Then the end of the finishing weaver is threaded through the eye and the needle is with-drawn, pulling the weaver down with it, the loose end being brought to the underside of the mat and trimmed off.

Mats are completed by working a simple border all round, using the ends of the spokes left for the purpose. Working from the underside the needle is pushed, eye first, under four rows of weaving alongside a spoke. The spoke lying second on the left from the needle is brought behind the intermediate spoke, threaded through the eye of the needle and pulled firmly down into the weaving. This movement is continued, working round to the right until all the spokes are neatly tucked away. Finish off by closely trimming all the loose ends with a pair of scissors.

To make oval mats, two-thirds of the spokes are laid flat and the remaining third woven through them at right angles to form a rectangular checked centre. Weaving and finishing is continued as for the round mats. Making small mats suitable for the table is good practice for anyone using rush for the first time.

Shaped work can be woven using similar techniques, and is done over a block of some kind which acts as a mould for the required shape. A box, tin or flower pot of the required size and shape may be used to provide this firm foundation. In this work the spokes must be long enough to go across the base and down both sides of the mould and still have enough left at each end – about 6in (150mm) – to form a woven border. Start by laying the spokes flat on the table-top in order to work the checked weave base as if making a table mat. The shape should

185

match that of the mould base, of course. Weave two or three rows of pairing weave to secure the centre, then tie firmly to the mould, base uppermost. Continue pairing until the weave just covers the base of the mould, shaping the work as required.

Sides may be continued in pairing weave or in a simple but effective checked weave using a single rush weaver. Rushes for the latter should be about the same size as those used for spokes and are squeezed out to form a wide, flat weave. One extra spoke must be added to give an odd number for this particular weave: it is threaded down, with the needle, alongside an existing spoke and passed under several rows of weaving to secure it. Side patterns may be changed as the work goes on by dropping a weaver to go from pairing to check and adding one as described to return to pairing. Work should always finish with a few rows of pairing.

During weaving, side spokes tend to get pulled over to one side, usually the left. Keep them straight by pulling firmly towards the right, especially during the first few rows of side weaving. Should a weaver break in use, simply join in a new one and continue. For a broken spoke the method described for adding an extra spoke should be followed, threading the replacement down alongside the broken end. It may be necessary to secure this replacement with a small knot.

The simple border described for mats can also be used for shaped work, but there are a number of alternative borders, some quite elaborate. One suitable for both larger mats and shaped work is the simple plait border in the diagrams.

Shaped work can also be made by winding plaited rush round a mould. The plaits are stitched into place as the work proceeds. This method is particularly suitable for heavy-duty items such as log baskets.

The weaving of chair and stool seats from rushes is another form of work which uses a different technique altogether. The method seems to have become popular in Britain during the early part of the eighteenth century, and is associated mainly with simple cottage chairs, principally those made in the so-called ladder-back style of the period. Most seat rushers, or matters as they were known in the early chair industry, were women who often did the work in their own cottages. It was dirty, unpleasant and unhealthy when done on a large scale, the rushes being dusty when dry and muddy when wet. Itinerant rush bottomers were once a familiar sight too, calling to collect chairs for re-rushing and often carrying out the work while sitting at the roadside. Rush-bottom chairs are now popular again for use in dining room and kitchen, and there is a steady demand for new chairs in this style, while large numbers of old chairs are being re-rushed and given a new lease of life.

Basically, rush bottoming or matting is done by taking two rushes of similar size, placing them alongside each other, butt to tip, and twisting them together to form a strong, smooth coil of even thickness. This rush coil is woven over and round the frame of the chair or stool. The twisting or coiling, which is all-important, takes place as the work proceeds and is done only on the top of the seat and around the framework where it will show; underneath the rush is not coiled. The frame of the chair or stool must be specially made either for rushing or for matting in a similar way, using some other suitable material such as cord or sea

186

RUSH SEATING

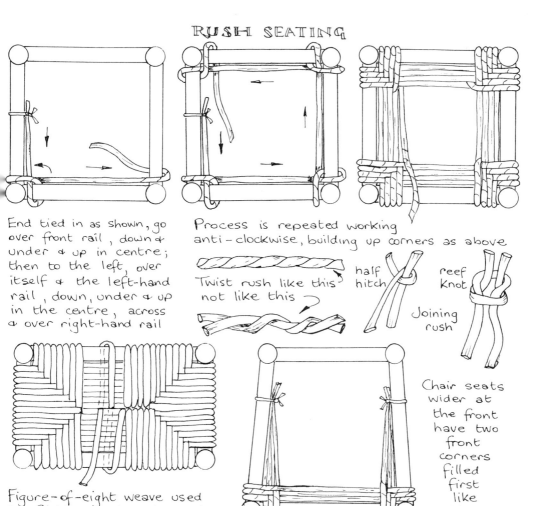

End tied in as shown, go over front rail, down & under & up in centre; then to the left, over itself & the left-hand rail, down, under & up in the centre, across & over right-hand rail

Process is repeated working anti-clockwise, building up corners as above

Twist rush like this not like this

half hitch

reef knot

Joining rush

Figure-of-eight weave used to finish a rectangular seat

Chair seats wider at the front have two front corners filled first like this

Top of seat being worked. Note twist

Corner pockets are stuffed from below

grass. The horizontal members of the frame should be nicely rounded so as not to cut the rush, and the four corners should normally be raised to hold the weaving in place.

Good work is characterised by having coils of even thickness throughout, worked to a covering of five or six coils to the inch (25mm). A single rush is used if thick enough, or three or even four can be used together if they are very thin. The rushes should be twisted together between finger and thumb and not coiled loosely around each other. It is a good idea to practise twisting coils before beginning an actual job in order to get the feel of the correct movement.

The plaiting rush, *Scirpus lacustris*, is suitable for seating, and is the one normally used in traditional English chairs. Imported rushes coming mainly from Holland are often used nowadays for seating, one particular species, which is probably *Juncus acutus*, growing well in the salt-water polders of that country. Variously known as the Great Sea rush, Sharp's, salt or golden rush, it has less pith, and although it does not grow quite so tall or so thickly it is stronger and more hard-wearing than the fresh-water varieties. It cures to a rich golden colour.

An average-sized chair or stool requires about $1\frac{1}{2}$lb (0.7kg) of dry rush. Preparation for seating is the same as for plaiting and weaving. The damp, mellowed rushes are wiped clean with a cloth and squeezed between finger and thumb from tip to butt, breaking off any brittle tip. The start is made by tying the first ends of rush tightly together with string. For a square or rectangular seat (usually only stools have this shape) the string is then tied to the inside of the left-hand rail of the stool frame, about halfway along. The rushes, brought over the top of the front rail, are held in the left hand (of a right-handed person) while the right hand begins the twisting, the twist being made away from the corner. The coil then goes below the front rail, up behind it on the inside of the frame and then, twisted again, to the left, over itself and round and under the left-hand rail. Then, without twisting, it comes up on the inside again and goes across to the opposite front corner where, twisted again, it goes over the rail and the whole process is repeated. (See diagram for weaving sequence.) The rush is pulled quite tightly across, and care has to be taken to ensure that the cross-over which forms at the corners as the work proceeds is kept square.

New rushes are joined on as old ones run out by tying in with a reef knot, or an extra rush can be added to one that has become too thin by means of a half hitch. Joins are made underneath and clear of the corners. Some professional bottomers work with pairs of rushes of uneven length and simply twist in a new length of rush as necessary, but coils must be well made for this, and knotting, although it takes a little longer, is recommended to begin with.

Rush seats are padded in order to firm the centre and raise it slightly above the edges of the chair frame. Padding also tightens up the weaving and makes the seat stronger and therefore more hard-wearing. Short ends and broken pieces of rush can be used for this, but they must be thoroughly dry. Clean straw is also suitable for use as a padding material. The padding is built up gradually, usually working from the underside of the seat, by using the fingers to push handfuls of material into the pockets of rush which form at the corners. This is done after every ten or eleven rounds of weaving, and a packing stick is used to push the padding firmly in as the pockets get deeper and the space between them smaller.

The coiled rushes shrink a little as they dry out, and for this reason a seat is best made in two or three stages, leaving it at least overnight between each stage. After this the coils can be pushed closer together, resulting ultimately in a much firmer finish. The final coils should be worked as close together as possible.

When a seat is rectangular rather than square, the corners are woven as described above and the remaining centre portion is completed with what is known as the figure-of-eight weave. In this the rush coil is worked over the front rail, underneath and up in the centre, over the back rail, underneath and up in the centre, then over the front rail again, and so on. This weave is worked right across the space, but from the centre line – measured and marked before the work begins – the coiling is reversed so that it matches up with the coils already worked at the corners on the other side.

Chair seats are often wider at the front than at the back. The difference is usually only a few inches, but it is enough to require a slightly different technique, for square corners are essential when rushing, and the extra space on the front rail must first be filled and squared off. After this the sequence for square or rectangular seats can be followed. There are several ways of filling the extra space, but only one need be described here.

First the length of the back rail is measured and this distance is marked in pencil on the front rail, leaving an equal space at each end. These are the spaces which have to be filled to square off the seat. The weaving rushes are tied in to the left-hand rail as before, worked normally over the first corner, taken across to the opposite front corner and again worked over in the normal way. Instead of continuing to the back corner, however, the rushes are cut and tied in to the right-hand rail halfway along, as shown in the diagram. New rushes are tied in each time and worked over the front two corners only until the marks on the front rail are reached. After this the weaving is continued round all four corners in the normal way. Again the work is best done in stages and padded as it proceeds. If a centre space remains it is filled with the figure-of-eight weave.

All seats are completed by tying the final end of the rush to the last coil opposite to it underneath the seat. Neatness on the underside is a mark of good craftsmanship, all loose ends and knots being tucked away out of sight and the rushes bedded in close to one another as the work progresses.

Some chairs have wooden edging pieces fitted after the rushing is completed – thin fillets of wood pinned on to the edge of the seat, partly to protect the rush, but mostly for appearance. These are not really essential and are now rarely fitted, but if you are renovating an old chair which has them, it is perhaps as well to replace them for the sake of authenticity. A rush seat requires no further finish, and with normal use and wear should last ten to fifteen years; many last much longer.

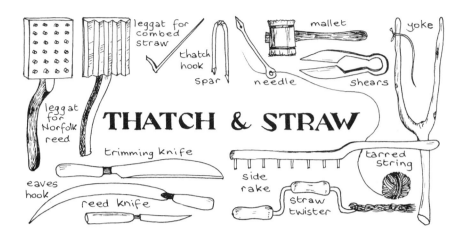

THATCH & STRAW

leggat for combed straw · thatch hook · spar · mallet · needle · shears · yoke · leggat for Norfolk reed · trimming knife · side rake · tarred string · eaves hook · reed knife · straw twister

Thatched cottages are universally admired for their picturesque qualities, epitomising the rural way of life of a bygone age. Thatch has certainly been used as a roofing material for a very long time – since people first moved out of their caves and lived in huts – but its rural status is of comparatively recent origin. Once it was as common in towns and cities as in the country, and not only cottages and farm buildings but bigger buildings, including churches and medieval manors, had roofs of thatch. Superseded by tiles and slate during the eighteenth century, thatch was relegated to the humblest cottages and to farm use. By the middle of the nineteenth century only farm labourers and livestock slept under the protection of straw, wealthier folk regarding thatch as being beneath them, rather than as something to have over them.

During the centuries when thatching was widespread there was always a ready supply of thatching material, mainly as the by-product of cereal crops reaped and threshed by hand. Even after the introduction of the binder and the threshing machine the supply continued well into the present century. It was the advent of the combine harvester, and later the development of shorter-stalked varieties of wheat, that changed the situation. With the decline in the supply and use of thatch for houses – though it continued to be used, as it had always been, to give temporary cover to annual ricks or stacks of hay and straw – the number of men skilled in thatching also declined. Consequently, when it later became fashionable to own a thatched house, and when their preservation became a matter almost of national concern, thatching materials – and, more important still, the thatchers themselves – were difficult to find. The few old thatchers who had 'kept their hand in' were in great demand, and had more work than they could cope with. Training schemes soon solved that problem, however, and today about nine hundred thatchers are kept busy throughout the British Isles.

The demand for materials has also been met, partly by imports, but increasingly by a return to older, long-straw varieties of wheat and to traditional methods of harvesting. The grain yield from such crops, grown primarily for thatching, is of secondary importance.

190

Wheat straw is by no means the only material which the thatcher uses. The straw from rye is said to be good, and in some regions heather and bracken have been utilised. Rushes and reeds are also employed, the so-called 'Norfolk reed', which may come from a number of other places including Holland, being widely used again today. Considered by many people to be far superior to straw, it can be expected to last two or three times as long.

Wheat straw is used in thatching in two quite distinct ways, either as long straw or as combed wheat reed. Sometimes known as 'Devon reed', the latter should not be confused with the reed plant, *Pragmitis communis*, mentioned above as Norfolk reed. Superficially, combed wheat reed does resemble Norfolk reed in texture when laid on a roof, both having a close-cropped, brush-like appearance which is caused by the exposed ends of their stalks.

Thatching, like so many other crafts, varies regionally. In addition, generations of thatchers have brought their own individual methods and language to the craft, and every thatcher seems to have his own way of doing things and his own way of describing it. Working methods vary only in detail, however, and one soon learns that a thatching fork, a hoc, a bow and a jack, yack or yoke are all the same thing – a forked branch used to carry material up on to a roof – and that similarly spicks, spics, spears, specs, spars, sprindles, pegs, pins, botches and broaches are all different names for the cleft hazel or willow sticks bent hairpin fashion and used to secure the thatch in place.

Most of the thatcher's work consists of repairs – either complete re-thatching, or patching, or re-covering – although occasionally a new building or a renovated building with new roof timbers is given a wholly new covering of thatch. For complete re-thatching all the old thatch has first to be removed and the woodwork of the roof beneath made good before the new thatch can be laid. In patching the portion of poor thatch is removed to leave, if possible, a foundation of old but sound material, and the new stuff is laid over this, pinned to it with spars or spics. Sometimes a thatch may be completely re-covered in this way.

For long-straw thatching the material is first spread out in a loose line on the ground, damped all over with water, then drawn out in handfuls, butts first, and gathered into compact bundles, each measuring about 18in × 4in (450mm × 100mm). Depending on locality these may be known as yealms, yelms, yolms, holms or hclcms.

Laying thatch begins at the bottom right-hand corner of a roof and to the right of the thatcher's ladder, long straw being laid in arm's-stretch courses about 30in (750mm) wide, worked upwards from eaves to ridge. On completion of one course, the ladder is rolled twice to the left and another course is laid on, and so on across the roof from right to left. The first layer of straw usually consists of 'bottles' or 'dollies', which are yealms doubled up and tightly tied before being placed, butts down, right on and overhanging the edge of the eaves and over any gable end. The object of this is to thicken the outer edge of the thatch and so keep rainwater run-off well away from the wall below. Subsequent yealms are laid on, the first with butts down to the ends of the bottles, overlapping them completely, all others up to the ridge with tops down, and each overlapping the one below by at least half its length.

THATCHING

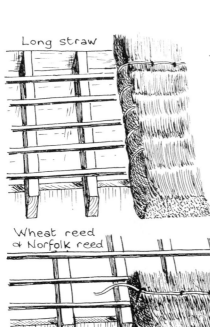

Long straw

Thatching started at bottom right-hand corner ~ see photo, and fixed securely to roof rafters. Straw is worked up in courses from eaves to ridge but reed moves across from right to left as shown below

Wheat reed & Norfolk reed

Stitching with twine

Straw rope & hazel spic

Hazel sway & iron hook

Three different methods of fixing thatch; used separately or in combination

Section thro' a half-completed roof, below, shows thickness of thatch & method of fixing

Finishing at the ridge

Rolls are laid on lengthways. Straw is bent over from either side but reed will not bend & is covered with straw or rush. Held in place & finished as shown

Methods of fixing vary, and some thatchers may use a combination of different methods as occasion demands. The bent wooden spars or spics traditionally used for pinning one layer of thatch to another are most frequently used in rick thatching and in repair work, spars for the former purpose being made longer than those used for house work. Iron thatching hooks are also used; these are long iron pins, one end cranked over like a figure seven, the other sharply pointed so that it can be driven into the wooden rafters of the roof. Both wooden spars and iron hooks may be used to hold the long lengths of split hazel, known by most thatchers as sways, which are laid across the lie of the straw. Sometimes the sways are fixed in such a way that they are subsequently covered with thatch; others are left visible and made decorative, as well as highly functional, with a pattern of cross-pieces. Twisted ropes of straw may sometimes be used in this way, again held in place by spars or hooks.

Very often tarred string is used to hold thatch in place, stitched in and out among the thatch and right round the roof rafters below, or secured with staples. A lot of present-day thatching is fixed by this method, the tying material most frequently used today being binder twine. Fixing with string or twine usually requires an assistant inside the roof, whose job it is to check the ties and pass the long steel needle threaded with the stitching material back to the thatcher on the outside. Occasionally a special needle is employed which can be handled by one man alone.

Treatment at the ridge or apex of a roof generally follows a set pattern. Yealms are laid right up to the ridge line, and a final row is then laid on thickly and bent over the top, to be held firmly on either side by sways and a pattern of cross-pieces, or liggers and cross-rods, as long-straw thatchers prefer to call them. Thus fixed, this final layer forms an effective ridge covering.

As work progresses across the roof the thatching straw is frequently combed with a side-handled rake so that the straw lies evenly. This treatment produces in the finished roof those graceful, flowing lines which, together with the pattern of liggers and cross-rods, give long-straw thatch its distinctive appearance.

Combed wheat reed is obtained by passing handfuls of wheat straw through a combing machine which, instead of threshing it in the usual way, strips the loose flag or side leaves from the stalks and at the same time threshes the grain from the ears without the stalks themselves passing through the threshing drum. The straw, or wheat reed as it is now known, comes from the machine on a conveyer belt, butt ends all lying in one direction, and is then collected and gathered into bundles weighing between 28lb and 30lb (12.7–13.6kg). These bundles – known in Devon as nitches – are tied twice with twine and then bumped, butts down, on a wooden board to level the ends and drive the layers of reed into a tight mass.

The material is stored and transported in this form, and when required for use the nitches are untied, spread out on the ground and damped down with water. This damping helps to make the straw more pliable and easier to handle, especially during dry weather, and particularly when there is any wind. Then it is gathered again into good double handfuls known as wadds, tied and compacted by bumping as before.

Wheat reed and Norfolk reed are both laid in similar fashion on to a roof, the

44 Using the leggat to beat the thatch firm and even

object with each type of material being to obtain a neat, hedgehog-like finish of exposed butt ends all over the roof. With well-laid reed of both kinds, rainwater can be seen to drip from stalk to stalk down the slope or pitch of the roof, which should be in the region of 50 degrees. In laying reed there are again some differences in method, particularly in the way in which a ridge is finished, and it should also be noted that the genuine reed is usually at least twice the length of any wheat reed.

Norfolk reed (*Pragmitis communis*) is an aquatic or semi-aquatic plant and is harvested annually or biennially in December after its long leaves have been stripped off by frost. Regular cutting ensures straight, clean material. Some reed beds contain in addition other plants such as reed mace (*Typha latifolia*) and wild iris (*Iris pseudacorour*); this material is sold as mixed reed and is said to be even more durable than reed alone. Supplies of reed are by no means confined to

194

Norfolk; it grows in many areas, and some is imported from Europe. It is graded according to length and made up into bundles measuring about 12in (300mm) in diameter at the base. These are bumped, butts down, to level and compress the stalks. Traditionally reed has always been sold by the fathom – a number of bundles tied together and measuring 6ft (1.8m) in circumference at the butt end.

Bundles or wadds of reed are laid on a roof, not in ascending courses as with long straw, but in regular layers extending from right to left across the whole of the roof, or across a section at a time if it is a large area. They are laid to the right of the ladder, the first layers beginning fanwise at the corner of the roof and up over the gable so that butt ends are presented outwards all the way round. As each new bundle is laid on along the eaves, the angle is brought gradually up to the vertical. This first row is tied securely to the rafters and just behind the barge boards with tarred string or binder twine, and a second layer, known to some thatchers as the brow layer, is laid directly on top to thicken up the edge of the eaves. This and subsequent layers are held with hazel sways which are either fixed with iron hooks or stitched into place with cord. In some cases sways may be dispensed with altogether and the bunches tied directly to the rafters. Layers are added with an overlap of about half their length, each succeeding layer covering the sway or cords holding the layer below it.

As the work proceeds a tool known as a leggat is used to dress the ends of the reed stalks level and force them down tightly. This tool consists of a flat piece of wood, 8in to 10in (200mm to 250mm) square, fitted with a handle. For wheat reed the face of the tool is grooved, but for Norfolk reed it has short studs – often horseshoe-nail heads – all over its surface. The leggat is used with a beating action against the ends of the thatch stalks, pushing them down into the roof to leave only a few inches of their ends exposed and lying more or less parallel to the pitch of the roof.

Bundles of reed are laid right up to the ridge line, where rolls of tightly tied reeds are laid and tied down along the apex in order to firm up the peak of the roof. With wheat reed the ends of the last wadds from each side are bent over the ridge and twisted in, and a second roll may then be put on. Yealms of straw are next bent right over the ridge, as in long-straw thatching, and secured with sways or liggers on each side. Norfolk reed will not bend without breaking and so cannot be finished in this way. Instead sedge (*Cladium nariscus*) or rush (*Scirpus lacustris*), or occasionally straw, is used for ridging purposes. Two or three layers may be bent over, each laid over ridge rolls of reed and again held on either side by sways. On completion the thicker ridge covering is often cut to a scalloped or wavy edge.

Where there are dormer windows or valleys, producing a change in the roof line, great skill is needed to lay the thatch so that it flows correctly, directing rainwater away from awkward corners rather than towards them. Thatched valleys must be rounded off by being padded out with extra material, unless they are to be tiled and to have the rainwater directed into them as into a gutter. In some places, especially around chimneys, a flashing of lead or other material is laid on for added protection.

Finally the thatch is neatly trimmed all over with shears, some thatchers doing

STRAW DECORATIONS

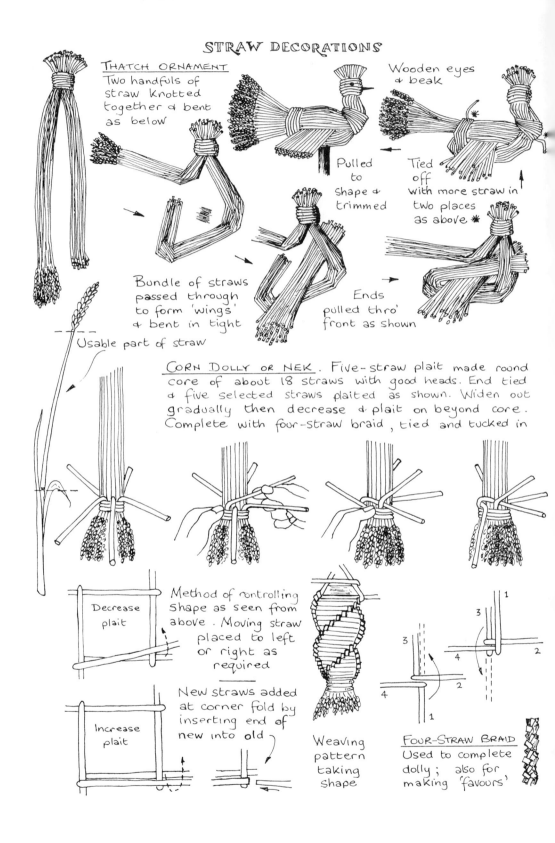

THATCH ORNAMENT
Two handfuls of
straw knotted
together & bent
as below

Wooden eyes
& beak

Pulled
to
Shape &
trimmed

Tied
off
with more straw in
two places
as above *

Bundle of straws
passed through
to form 'wings'
& bent in tight

Ends
pulled thro'
front as shown

Usable part of straw

CORN DOLLY OR NEK. Five-straw plait made roond
core of about 18 straws with good heads. End tied
& five selected straws plaited as shown. Widen out
gradually then decrease & plait on beyond core.
Complete with four-straw braid, tied and tucked in

Decrease
plait

Method of controlling
Shape as seen from
above. Moving straw
placed to left
or right as
required

New straws added
at corner fold by
inserting end of
new into old

Increase
plait

Weaving
pattern
taking
shape

FOUR-STRAW BRAID
Used to complete
dolly; also for
making 'favours'

3

1

4

2

3

2

4

1

this as the work proceeds, others leaving it until last, and the eaves are cut square all round with the eaves knife or hook.

To prevent damage by birds, thatch is often covered, or partly covered, with fine wire netting or tarred string net. An inconspicuous nylon netting is used for this purpose by some modern thatchers. Long-straw thatch requires netting much more than does reed thatch which, when done well, should be bristly enough to keep the birds out. Other additions, more ornamental than netting and said to keep away both birds and witches, are the straw figures of pheasants, foxes and so on which some thatchers use as a finishing signature to their work. Some people say that the makers of such devices have more time than sense, but others believe it to be 'proper'.

Some of these figures, though different in purpose, are similar in appearance to corn dollies, those intricate straw shapes, beloved as domestic ornaments, whose violent, pagan ancestry has long been forgotten. These woven or plaited decorations have their origins in the belief that to preserve the last sheaf of corn taken at harvest time was to keep alive the spirit of the corn goddess or earth mother and thus ensure the fertility of the land for next year's crop. In some societies the ritual which surrounded this ceremony was quite savage, involving the spilling of human blood in a kind of religious, sacrificial orgy. The name dolly is thought to be a corruption of the word idol. In Britain the making of corn dollies died out with the arrival of the combine harvester, but in recent years there has been a renewed interest in the craft.

Corn-dolly making requires the same varieties of wheat as are used by thatchers (see the chapter on materials), harvested in a similar way. The straw is best used

45 A traditional corn dolly

soon after cutting, but if allowed to become dry it can be damped to make it pliable and workable again. It is first cut to length, above the first joint and below the ear for weaving, some being left with ears intact for certain types of work. Side leaves (flag) are stripped off to leave the clean, glossy stalks. Rye or oat straw, if long enough, can be used, but barley is less suitable. After cutting, the straw is graded according to thickness into fine, medium and thick and kept separate for different kinds of work.

Damping, or tempering as it is sometimes called, is done either by soaking in cold or warm water or by pouring really hot water over the upright stalks. After wetting, the straw is stood on end so that surplus water is able to drain away. Only a sufficient quantity for the job in hand should be tempered at one time, and spare material should be kept wrapped in a damp cloth while work is in progress.

A plait using five straws is the easiest shape to begin with, this number of straws producing a four-sided or square figure which forms the basis for a number of different designs. The attractive spiral pattern arises naturally from the nature of the weave. Five straws are tied tightly together at the ear end (the ears themselves may be cut off or left on, depending on the particular design). Then, with the short end held between finger and thumb of the left hand, the right hand is used to bend the straws down at right angles and outwards in the manner of a fan. Working anti-clockwise, and mentally or actually numbering the straws one to five, take straw number one and lay it over two and three to lie between three and four. Turn the straws a quarter-turn clockwise, then lay number three over numbers one and four to lie between four and five; take four over three and five, and five over four and two, turning a quarter-turn clockwise each time. This will give a tight round to start with and may be continued in the same sequence, beginning with straw number two, to produce a straight shape. To widen out the dolly proceed from this stage as follows: lay straw number two over number five to lie parallel to number one, then bring one under and over two so that it lies parallel to three and continue in this way, the weaving straw, seen from above, always lying to the right of the top straw. To reduce the width of the plait follow the same sequence but lay the weaving straw to the left of the top straw. Care should be taken not to widen out or to reduce too quickly, or gaps will be left in the weaving. These instructions should be read with reference to the diagrams and preferably with a piece of work in the hands.

New weaving straws are added when the old ones become too short or get kinked. The old straw is cut off just before making a corner fold, and the thin end of a new straw is inserted and pushed in firmly but without splitting the old one. The joint will be hidden in the corner fold when it is made.

Straight plaits can be made round a pencil or a longer piece of wooden rod which is removed on completion. If the plait is not opened out, woven tubes are produced which can then be bent to almost any shape and tied in place. Plaits may be made using any number of straws, more straws having the effect of bringing the corner folds closer together. Work is usually started and finished off by tying, using either buff-coloured thread or raffia, both of which obviously blend well with the straw. By contrast, dollies are often tied off and decorated with ribbon, usually red in colour.

198

The traditional corn neck or nek is a simple plaited column, usually made on a solid core of straw complete with the ears or head. This core is made by tying together a bunch of straws bearing good heads, the first tie being made just below these heads. Five straws, evenly spaced around the bunch, are then selected and bent outwards to be used as weavers, the remainder of the bunch being tied in one or two more places to form the core. The five weavers are plaited as in the basic plait described above. The plaiting is continued to the end of the core and then on beyond it, gradually reducing the plait until it is closed up. When this stage is reached the neck is finished off by working a length of four-straw braid and tucking the end in to form a loop.

The four-straw braid is made by tying off the plait and using the four longest straws remaining – new straws being difficult to add while braiding. The four straws are worked as shown in the diagram, straw number one being kinked over number two to lie beside number three. Straw number three is then kinked over number four to occupy the quadrant left empty by number one. The work is turned a quarter-circle clockwise, the movement repeated with straws four and two, the work turned again and the movement repeated, and so on. If opposite straws are kept parallel and do not overlap, an attractive zig-zag pattern is achieved.

There is a variety of other braids which can be worked with two, three or four straws, all of them being used at one time to fashion what were generally known as favours. These were plaited by young men out walking with their sweethearts at harvest time. The braids were twisted into loops and lovers' knots and worn as brooch or buttonhole decorations.

SPINNING & WEAVING

The spinning of fibres and the weaving of fabrics constitute one of the most wide-spread of craft industries. In some parts of the world quite primitive methods continue to be used, while in others high levels of sophistication have been achieved, both in the fabrics made and in the means of production. In the Middle Ages spinning and weaving were the foundation of Britain's wealth, establishing her as an important exporting nation and ultimately giving rise to the formation of a major industry. To a large extent it was the growth of this industry which led to the Industrial Revolution. Until this traumatic upheaval the processes of spin-ning and weaving were essentially rural, carried out not mechanically, in factor-ies, but by hand, mainly in the country folk's own cottages.

Generally the women spun while the men wove, and often whole families would take part in the range of processes involved. These varied according to the materials being used. The fibres of the flax plant were among the first to be used; these, when spun, produce a strong thread from which is woven the material known as linen. Flax is harvested at intervals throughout the summer months by pulling rather than cutting. Then, after removing the seed heads, the stalks are retted, which involves immersing the flax in water, preferably a running stream, for several days. Retting rots away the vegetable matter of the stalks to leave the required fibrous material. This is then dried and scrutched – which means that what is left of the remaining unwanted parts of the plant are removed by beating – and then heckled. In this last process the short pieces are removed by combing through metal-toothed combs to leave the long fibres ready for spinning.

Other plant fibres have been, and still are, used, but it was wool which was once the dominant fibre throughout most of Britain. Indeed there are still places where, if you speak of weaving, people think only of wool. The British climate, and much of the countryside, are particularly suitable for raising sheep, and sheep farming has long been an integral part of agricultural practice in many re-gions. Until the eighteenth century sheep were bred mainly for their wool, mutton being considered a very inferior meat, and the combination of selective breeding and the remarkable variations in soil, grass conditions and altitude throughout the country gave rise to a large number of different breeds of sheep and a considerable variety of wool types.

Briefly, the forty or so breeds of British sheep are classified into three groups – long wool, short wool or Downs, and mountain sheep – and the character of the fleece of each breed is directly related to environmental factors. Long wools are the breeds of the rich, grassy lowlands, and their wool is long, lustrous and somewhat coarse. The Downs breeds are native to the low hills and downland areas and have a fine, short wool, while the mountain breeds are those sheep which live above the 1000ft (300m) line. Their wool is strong and coarse and often contains a high proportion of hair. There are many variations within these three broad categories, each producing subtle differences in wool quality, texture, colour and workability. Fibres of medium staple – as their length is called – are the easiest to work with.

Sheep are sheared during early summer, the precise time varying geographically. Formerly all shearing was done with hand clippers by the men who raised the sheep, but the modern practice is machine shearing, usually performed by specialists who travel from farm to farm with their equipment. Here and there, however, one can still see sheep being sheared by hand. The fleece is clipped close to the underskin – except with mountain breeds, where about 1-in (25mm) of wool is usually left on – and when the work is well done the wool holds together so that it resembles a complete pelt. Expertly rolled and tied, each fleece is then sent off for sale.

Before the raw fleece can be spun into wool it must first be sorted. Not only do fleeces vary from breed to breed, but single fleeces will produce several different grades or qualities of wool. The best, or fine, as it is usually called, comes from the shoulders, while that from the legs and haunches and around the tail, known as the britch, is much coarser and of poorer quality. At some stage the wool has to be cleaned, too, for as it comes from the sheep it is greasy and may also be dirty. It may be washed and dried, and sometimes dyed and dried again, at this stage, but more often this is done later. Some people wash it after spinning, since the natural oil in the wool aids the spinning process; sometimes, as in the case of close-textured cloths such as tweed, it is best to weave the cloth with the grease intact and clean it afterwards.

Now comes the task of preparing the tangled mass of wool for spinning. First the matted fibres are gently pulled apart by hand, taking care not to break the fibres but only to separate them and remove coarse lumps, seeds and other foreign material. This is continued until a soft, downy mass is obtained, the process often being aided by the addition of a few drops of clean vegetable oil.

Next comes carding, which used to be done between two boards covered with the prickly heads of the teasel plant – *la cardène* in French, hence the term carding. The teasels were superseded by carding cloth, which is leather or some other heavy material inset with fine steel wire hooks. Pieces of this cloth are mounted on a pair of boards with handles. A small quantity of wool fibre is placed on one board, and then the other is placed on top and drawn lightly but firmly across it. This is repeated several times, transferring the fibres from one board to the other at intervals until they are spread out evenly across one of the boards. Then, with

46 Carding and spinning in a garden early this century

the back of the other board, they are collected as a feather-light fluffy roll and put aside. 'Air rolled in wool' is how the finished product is described. A large number of these rolls are made at one time so that the spinning can continue without interruption.

For the long-stapled silky wools used in fine worsted cloths, carding boards are not so suitable, and instead the wool is combed, using steel-toothed combs which at one time used to be heated. Again a little oil aids the work – a drop of olive oil is placed in the palm of the hand and the wool is rolled gently in it.

The main reason for carding or combing is not to lay the fibres parallel, as is so often supposed, but to form a sort of fluffy, hollow tube consisting of evenly spaced fibres lying at right angles to the length of the tube. Wool binds together naturally by means of tiny scales on its fibres which overlap from root to tip. In addition the fibres are crimped along their length, and it is these two factors which enable a good yarn to be readily made from wool. By arranging the fibres in such a way that, when several are drawn past one another, they cling together, a continuous strand may be formed. If at the same time the strand is twisted, it gains considerably in strength. It is the drawing out and twisting of the wool fibres which forms the basis of the next important process, that of spinning.

Before the invention of the spinning wheel, spinning was done with a simple spindle held in the hand. It may still be done in this way, and indeed some prefer

202

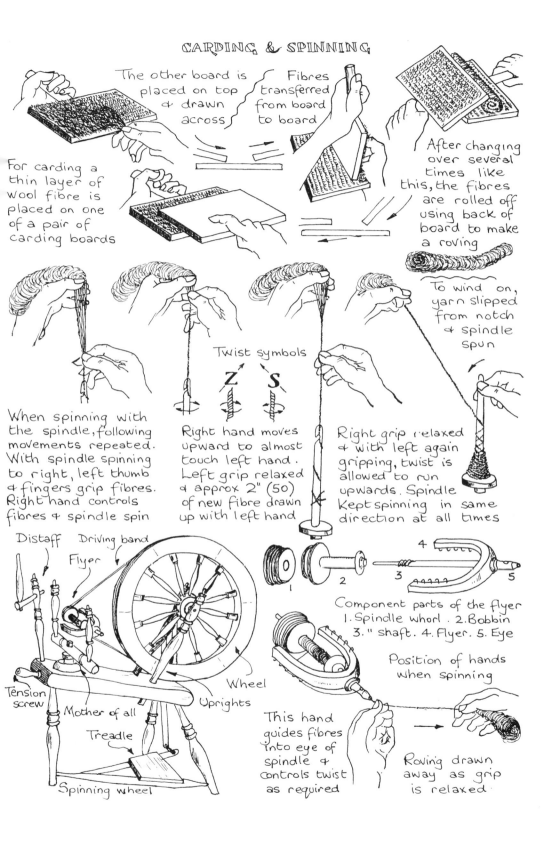

CARDING & SPINNING

The other board is placed on top & drawn across { Fibres transferred from board to board

For carding a thin layer of wool fibre is placed on one of a pair of carding boards

After changing over several times like this, the fibres are rolled off using back of board to make a roving

To wind on, yarn slipped from notch & spindle spun

Twist symbols

Z   S

When spinning with the spindle, following movements repeated. With spindle spinning to right, left thumb & fingers grip fibres. Right hand controls fibres & spindle spin

Right hand moves upward to almost touch left hand. Left grip relaxed & approx 2" (50) of new fibre drawn up with left hand

Right grip relaxed & with left again gripping, twist is allowed to run upwards. Spindle kept spinning in same direction at all times

Distaff   Driving band
Flyer

Tension screw   Mother of all
Treadle

Wheel
Uprights

Spinning wheel

Component parts of the flyer
1. Spindle whorl. 2. Bobbin
3. " shaft. 4. Flyer. 5. Eye

Position of hands when spinning

This hand guides fibres into eye of spindle & controls twist as required

Roving drawn away as grip is relaxed

spindle-spun yarn, the main advantage of the spinning wheel being its increased rate of work.

The spindle consists of a slightly tapered stick several inches in length and notched at the top. It has a circular whorl weighing about 1oz (28g) at the bottom which is free to slip easily on and off. A length of coarse spun thread is attached to the spindle to provide a start to the spinning. Then, with a roll of the carded wool held in the left hand, and several inches of the yarn with the spindle dangling from it between finger and thumb of the right hand, a little of the wool fibre is drawn out and twisted in to the end of the yarn. This is done by setting the spindle spinning in a clockwise direction while the finger and thumb of the left hand grip the yarn and fibres together just above it to contain the twist. With the spindle still spinning, the right hand is moved up closer to the left, and the left hand relaxes its pressure and moves upwards sufficiently to allow about 2in (50mm) of fibre to be drawn down. Then, with the left thumb and finger again gripping the yarn and fibres together, the grip of the right hand is released and the twist from the revolving spindle allowed to run upwards.

This process is repeated over and over again, the hands allowing a few inches of fibre to be drawn out each time, and at the same time controlling the twist set up by the spindle, which must be kept revolving in the right direction. (Spinners use the symbols 'Z' and 'S' to indicate clockwise and anti-clockwise twists respectively.) Just before the spindle reaches the floor the spinning is stopped, the spun fibres are slipped from the spindle notch and the yarn – for this is what the fibres have now become – is wound on to the spindle. Enough is left to slip under the notch and hold in the hand, and spinning is commenced once again. As the handful of combed wool is used up, the drawn-out ends of a new piece are intermingled with the last of the old. The skilled spindle spinner puts several together at the start into a continuous roving which is then lightly wound on to a stick known as a distaff.

Spinning with the spindle is not easy at first – the beginner is likely either to draw out too much fibre and make a slub (a thickening of the yarn), or to draw out insufficient, in which case the yarn will break. A perfectly even yarn is not essential, as some unevenness is part of the appeal of hand spinning, but practice and patience are necessary to obtain a good, continuous length of yarn.

Cotton, the fibres of which are both shorter and finer than those of wool, cannot be spun with the heavy hanging spindle, and in India, where cotton has been grown and used in weaving for centuries, a different method of spinning was developed. There a primitive spool was revolved by hand in a vertical position, its lower end supported in a bowl on the ground. At some unspecified time this was attached to a wheel and revolved horizontally and the first crude spinning wheel was evolved. Not until early in the fourteenth century, however, was this idea brought to Europe, where it was readily adopted.

The people of India knelt at their spinning wheels, but Europeans found it more convenient to place them on benches, and eventually fitted them with legs. Three legs were usual in early models so that, like the three-legged stool, they stood firmly on uneven floors, without rocking. They were of simple construction, consisting of a large wheel which, by means of a cord, was made to drive a much smaller wheel attached to a horizontal, pointed spindle. The difference in the relative sizes of the two wheels caused the spindle to revolve at great speed. The wheel was at first turned by hand, either by means of its spokes or by pushing on its rim. Later a cranked handle was fitted to some models.

One end of a roving of carded fibre was twisted between finger and thumb and attached to the very point of the spindle. The roving was held by the left hand at a slight angle to the spindle, finger and thumb regulating the amount of fibre released and the degree of tension. During spinning the angle of the yarn caused it to slip off the spindle rather than be coiled on to it, each revolution thus adding one turn of twist to the yarn. As twist was added, more fibres were drawn out from the left hand, until the twisted yarn became too long to be held at arm's length by the spinner. Then the yarn was held at right angles to the spindle and wound on to it. Spinning and winding continued alternately in this fashion until the spindle was full, when the yarn was transferred to a spool.

These two actions were combined into a simultaneous process sometime in the early sixteenth century by the introduction of the flyer and bobbin, and the process was further speeded up by driving the wheel with a foot-operated treadle. The large wheel is now smaller and has two grooves in its rim to accommodate two driving cords, one running as before to the spindle, to which is now attached the 'U'-shaped flyer that revolves with it, and the other to a bobbin free to revolve on the spindle within the arms of the flyer. By virtue of a slightly larger pulley, the flier revolves at a slower speed than does the bobbin. The spindle has a hollow point and the fibres, regulated still by the hand of the spinner, pass through this opening or eye and out again a short distance along. The yarn is then taken up to the arm of the flyer, where it is guided by hooks, or hecks as they are called, and wound on to the bobbin directly underneath. The difference in speed between the flyer and the bobbin causes the yarn to twist as it passes from one to the other. Spinning and winding are therefore a continuous process, and stops have only to be made at intervals to move the yarn from heck to heck as the bobbin fills up.

Some of the earlier 'great wheel' spinning wheels continued in use for bobbin-winding purposes, and one of the easiest ways to learn how to use either this type or the flyer or bobbin wheel is not to spin with it at first but to use it initially for winding, and then to practise by twisting together two or more ready-spun yarns. By this means one can come to terms with the working action of the wheel, which can be quite subtle, varying from one wheel to another, without having to pay too much attention to the drawing out of unspun fibres. Two balls of old knitting wool winding out of two separate plant pots will suffice to begin with.

After the wheel has been checked to see that it is working properly, with the driving band in place and so on, one end of a length of yarn is tied tightly round the bobbin, brought over the guide hooks on the flyer, and threaded down and out through the eye of the hollow spindle. To this the yarns to be plied are tied. The wheel is started by hand in a clockwise direction and kept turning by treadling slowly, leaving the hands free to guide the yarns through the eye of the spindle. It will be seen that as they are taken up by the bobbin they are also being twisted together.

When the student is ready to begin spinning properly, a roving of combed wool is twisted on to a short length of yarn left hanging from the spindle eye. Then one hand is held directly in front of, and close up to, the eye, thumb and first finger gripping the end of the twisted fibre, while the other hand holds the roving. (Some spinners work left-handed, others right-handed.) While the spinner treadles steadily, some twist is allowed to form in the spindle eye for a second or two, then the thumb and finger are relaxed and at the same time the roving is drawn away, to left or right as the case may be. The twist will run up the fibres, and there should be a definite pull on the yarn as the twist is formed, sufficient to prevent it winding on to the bobbin. The thumb and finger regulate the twisting movement. When sufficient yarn has been drawn out – an arm's length for the experienced spinner – it is allowed to wind on, the roving being brought back close to the eye again as it does so. The end of the spun fibres is again gripped and the complete movement is repeated. Steady, rhythmic movements of feet and hands are necessary to spin well and, again, practice is required. Spun yarn is usually wound off and stored on spools.

If the yarn is to be washed or dyed at this stage it has to be skeined, that is rewound and tied into loose hanks. Washing is done in soft, mild soapy water at about 50°C. The skeins are allowed to soak until the water is cold, then rinsed thoroughly in tepid water. Dyeing has long been a separate craft industry involving a great deal of 'chemistry', but some of the old spinners dyed their own yarn using simple, natural ingredients, obtaining a wide range of colours from such things as onion skins, elderberries, dandelion roots, lichens and the bark of trees. To 'fix' these dyes substances known as mordants are used, alum being a fairly common one.

It will by now be realised that the preparation of yarn for weaving can be a series of lengthy and laborious processes. Often it took several people to keep one weaver supplied with yarn, particularly after Kay's invention of the flying shuttle, which greatly speeded up the weaver's work rate. Yet all these processes continued mainly as domestic activities until the end of the eighteenth century. The typical weaver's cottage was a three-storeyed dwelling, with living room and kitchen at ground level, bedrooms above, and on the top floor the workshop, recognisable today in the many renovated cottages which still exist by the large upper windows designed to shed the maximum amount of light on the work. Some of the earliest 'factories' were created when a group of weavers joined up their separate attic workshops simply by removing parts of the internal walls between several cottages.

Not until James Hargreaves invented his spinning jenny and Richard Arkwright his water frame, however, did the pattern of work greatly change. The spinning jenny, which could spin six threads at once, was hand-operated to begin with, and was used in the cottages as before, as was Compton's more successful spinning mule introduced some fifteen years later. It was the so-called water frame which brought about most change, for it needed power to drive it – water power at first, hence its name, and then steam – and it was this more than anything else which led to the system of spinning yarn in mills. It was the growing cotton industry which was the first to take advantage of this new mechanisation of spinning. The wool trade followed, slowly at first, it is true, but by the end of

206

the eighteenth century machine-spun wool was available to the hand-loom wea-vers, and many began to make use of it. Quite a number of the craftsmen and women weaving by hand today use machine-spun wool.

Mechanisation came to weaving at a much later date, and even after its arrival the factory system and the cottage system continued to exist side by side, power looms not coming into widespread use until well into the nineteenth century.

From primitive beginnings – the first looms had been known as ground looms, with strands of yarn being stretched out between pegs driven into the ground or between the weaver's waist and a handy tree – looms had developed into both horizontal and vertical types. Now one set of threads, the warp, was stretched be-tween two beams, the weaver passing other threads across, one at a time, to form the cross-threads or weft, which passed through the warp in an alternate under-and-over pattern. Each weft thread was beaten in close to the previous one by means of a wooden stick known as a beater or sword.

During the Middle Ages, except for some tapestry and carpet weaving, the horizontal loom had been widely adopted in Europe. Its beams were mounted on legs, and it had a system of hand- or treadle-operated devices for lifting the warp strands to form an opening through which the weft, now wound on to a spool, could be passed across with ease. This opening was, and still is, known as the shed, and the device which formed the shed was known as a heddle, this being a rod placed across the warp and having every alternate warp thread attached to it by means of loops or leashes. When lifted, the heddle raised one set of warp threads, leaving a space, the shed, between these and the remaining warp threads. After the weft spool had passed through, the heddle was dropped, and the other set of threads pulled downwards with a flat-sided stick, which was known as a shed stick. This formed another space, the countershed, through which the weft thread was returned. A comb-like beater or reed held in a batten was then swung against the web of woven cloth to close the weft.

By the end of the seventeenth century the hand loom had become a heavy, rec-tangular, box-like framework with the warp stretched from the warp beam at the back, over the warp roller, forward and over the breast beam, and down to the cloth beam on to which was rolled the finished material. The treadle-operated heddles, up to four in number by then to form both shed and countershed and enable patterned material to be woven, were hung by pulleys from the top of the framework, and the batten for beating the weft was also suspended, and hinged to swing forward. Although there were some wider looms operated by two wea-vers, most were governed in width by the stretch of the weaver's arms as he threw the shuttle containing the weft spool from hand to hand through shed and coun-tershed alternately. Usually this was somewhere between 30in and 40in (0.75–1m). Kay's flying shuttle improved this situation from about 1733, en-abling wider cloth to be woven, and more quickly too.

Apart from this and one or two other minor innovations, hand looms have changed very little right up to the present day. However simple or complicated, most of them function according to the same basic principles. Their purpose is to hold the warp in tension while the weft is interwoven with it to form a web or weave. All have some means of parting the warp threads alternately so that the

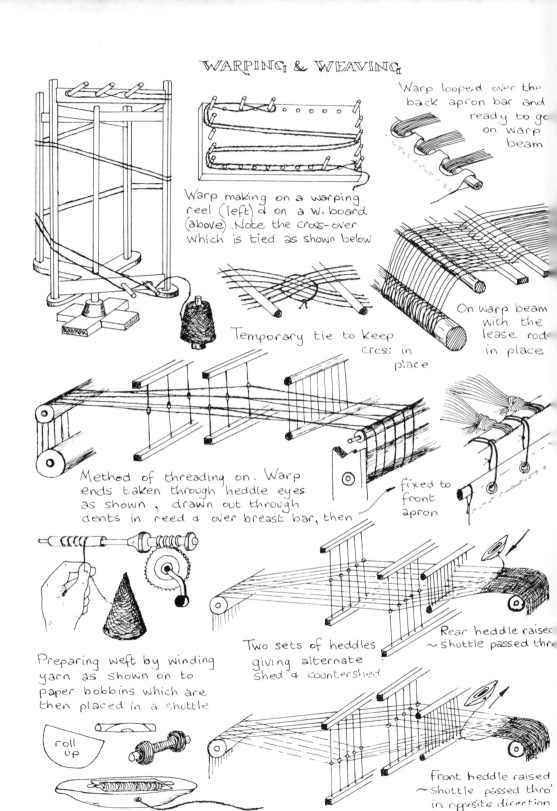

Warp looped over the back apron bar and ready to go on warp beam

Warp making on a warping reel (left) & on a w. board (above). Note the cross-over which is tied as shown below

On warp beam with the lease rods in place

Temporary tie to keep cross in place

Method of threading on. Warp ends taken through heddle eyes as shown, drawn out through dents in reed & over breast bar, then —

fixed to front apron

Preparing weft by winding yarn as shown on to paper bobbins which are then placed in a shuttle

roll up

Two sets of heddles giving alternate shed & countershed

Rear heddle raised ~ shuttle passed thro'

Front heddle raised ~ shuttle passed thro' in opposite direction weft may pass through them unhindered, and all have some means of beating the crossed threads into a firm, even texture.

The weaver's first task is the preparation of the warp. For simple frame looms and some table looms this is a comparatively easy task, as the warp is made directly on to the loom. A warp made in this way can only produce a piece of cloth somewhat less than twice the length of the loom. For larger looms to produce longer pieces of material the warp must be formed off the loom, wound on to the warp beam, and then threaded on to the loom. Winding, beaming and threading on, as this work is called, can take quite a long time where a large loom is concerned.

First the number of threads and their length have to be calculated, and due allowance made for shrinkage and wastage. For large-scale work the required amount is wound off on a warping reel, but for smaller amounts a warping board is used, the purpose of both being to produce a folded length of yarn which can later be cut in such a way that the required number of warp 'ends' are available for weaving. Each folded length is crossed or leased to simplify the threading on, and later, with the aid of lease rods, this helps to keep the ends in order. The cross-over is tied temporarily after winding so that it is not lost.

Methods of beaming and threading on differ according to the type and complexity of the loom. Usually the warp is attached first to the back apron bar, which in turn is fixed to the warp beam by means of a canvas apron. On a simple loom the warp may be attached directly to the beam. Lease rods are inserted, one either side of the cross-over, and these are tied together, the temporary tie now being removed. Then the warp is spread out evenly to the width to which it is to be woven, a comb-like spreader or raddle sometimes being used to aid this process, and the warp is carefully wound on to the beam under even tension. The object here is to ensure that the threads will be parallel as they run through the loom. Beaming is completed when a convenient length remains for threading, and at this stage the folded loops are cut to give the separate warp ends.

Threading is done with a small hook like a crochet hook which is used to draw the warp ends through the heddle loops; for patterned fabric, threading is carried out to a specially prepared sequence set out on a warping plan or draft, but for plain or tabby weave, where two heddles only are needed, the warp ends are simply threaded alternately through back and front heddles. When all the threads are through the heddles they are drawn through a suitable reed which spaces the warp in slots, called dents, to give the correct width and density of finished material. Here the ends are tied loosely in groups of about eight, and when all are through and have been checked to see that they are in the right order and do not cross, they are taken over the breast beam and attached to the cloth beam. This usually has a canvas front apron, and sometimes a separate apron bar, and the groups of ends are secured to this, beginning in the centre and working to left and to right, evening up the tension as they are finally tied off. This tensioning is most important, as threads of varying tension result in a finished cloth which is twisted instead of flat. Getting the warp right is the foundation of good weaving.

Weft preparation, especially for tabby weave and simple patterns, is much more simple. It consists of winding yarn on to small bobbins or spools which are usually held in a boat-shaped shuttle. This enables the weft carrier, as the weft spool is sometimes called, to be passed through the open sheds of a warp with a throwing movement, the shuttle being supported by the lower warp threads. Some shuttles are fitted with rollers which make them glide through the shed more quickly. Various hand-operated mechanical bobbin winders are used for the winding-on process. When mechanisation finally came to the textile industry, people were employed solely as winders, operating machines capable of winding hundreds of bobbins or reels or spools of all kinds, all at the same time.

Weaving on a big loom begins with the formation of a narrow heading which closes any spaces at the beginning of the warp, allowing it to lie in straight lines from the reed to the weaving line. The heddles are lifted in turn by depressing the treadles below – or, in the case of table looms, by the manipulation of levers – and at each lift the weft shuttle is cast through the shed thus formed. After each cast the batten is swung forward so that the reed beats the weave into a firm texture. Weaving continues by the steady rhythmic repetition of these three actions, heddle–shuttle–batten. At regular intervals the finished part of the weave is wound on to the cloth beam below the loom by means of a wheel held in check by a simple ratchet.

In weaving on looms fitted with a flying shuttle, the weaver works the batten with the left hand while the right pulls a cord which causes the shuttle to 'fly' across. Both hands are thus held close together in front of the body, constricting the chest. Champions of the hand-thrown shuttle declared that it was the fly-shuttle which was responsible for the prevalence of consumption among nineteenth-century weavers, because of the working position it demanded and the lack of arm exercise it afforded.

Weaving by hand on a large scale, together with all the other hand processes such as carding and spinning and dyeing, had virtually disappeared by the middle of the nineteenth century. In spite of anti-machine riots among the workers, the factory system, with its 'dark satanic mills', finally superseded the long-established domestic system. In some areas, however, notably the Scottish highlands and islands and the more remote Welsh valleys, the tradition was continued, and today the craftsmen and women in these and other areas are enjoying a healthy resurgence of interest in hand-woven fabrics of many kinds.

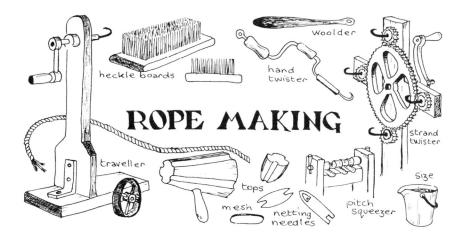

ROPE MAKING

heckle boards — Woolder — hand twister — strand twister — traveller — tops — size — mesh — netting needles — pitch squeezer

Rope making on a commercial scale is now carried out by elaborate machinery in factories, but all ropes were once made by hand – and a few still are – in what were traditionally known as rope yards or rope walks. Narrow and up to 800ft (244m) in length, most of these were just open areas of ground with a few simple pieces of equipment standing around. Rows of trees planted alongside gave shelter from the wind in winter and shade from the sun in summer. Some yards were roofed over but open at the sides, and some later ones were housed inside long, low buildings, while in a certain part of Derbyshire they were to be found inside the limestone caverns of that particular district. It is the earlier, open work spaces that have left a record of their existence, however, in street names such as Old Rope Walk, Rope Yard and Roping or Roper Lane.

Rope making in Britain is a long-established craft, the Corders of the Ropery being one of the earliest craft guilds to be formed in London. During the centuries when Britannia ruled the waves and heavily rigged sailing ships were the very foundation of maritime power, rope making became a vital industry. As the size of the ships increased, so too did the amount and variety of rope used – in 1860 a 13,000-ton vessel carried over twenty different types of rope weighing anything up to 200 tons altogether. Naval rope yards were established in many coastal and riverside towns and villages, and some became world-famous for producing ships' ropes of great strength and durability. Inland rope walks concentrated on the supply of rope and rope products for agricultural purposes, and particularly items for the large horse population of the day.

Rope is made by twisting together suitable fibres to form a strong, continuous length which, when manufactured by hand, has to be pulled out to beyond its final extent – hence the need for the long narrow work space which in naval yards was based upon a standard rope length of 120 fathoms. The fibres, when twisted, form yarn which, after further twisting into strands, is fashioned into rope. Three strands make a rope, and three ropes twisted together make a cable. The twisting creates friction between the fibres, preventing any becoming separated from the rope which, when properly finished, should be firm and compact.

211

Until the introduction of man-made fibres such as nylon, all rope was made from plant fibres of one kind or another. Hemp was the most widely used material, and was once grown in large quantities in Britain specifically for rope making. Colloquially known as gallows grass or neck weed, from the days when death by hanging was a quite common penalty, hemp grows best in rich, damp soil and was formerly harvested when ripe in July, and again in September. The long, grass-like stalks were pulled up by their roots and tied into bundles before being laid out to dry for twenty-four hours. The bundles were then threshed with flails to beat out the seeds, and the remaining stalks either left to the effects of rain and dew or placed in running water for about four days. This process, known as retting, rotted away the softer tissues to leave behind only the strong and more durable fibres of the outer skin. When separated and dried, this fibrous material was ready for use. Flax is treated in a similar way to produce fibres used both in rope making and in making linen. Liquor from the retting process produced an excellent liquid fertiliser once much prized by farmers and market gardeners.

For rope making the fibres must be clean and equal in thickness and initially must lie straight and parallel. To meet these requirements the fibres have to be heckled. Women used to do this work using a coarse comb known as a heckle board. This was a block of wood studded with long steel pins, the size and proximity of the pins varying according to the type of rope being made.

With the heckle board fixed, points upwards, to a bench, the heckler takes a handful of hemp fibres and repeatedly strikes them against the steel points, drawing them through the pins with a combing motion. This sorts out the tangled mass of fibres and lays them parallel. The other end of the handful is similarly treated, a little whale oil or some other oil often being used to moisten and soften the fibres during the process. The short, broken fibres which remain in the heckle pins are made up into tow, which is used as a caulking material and in other forms in a variety of trades, while the heckled streak, as it is now called, is doubled up on itself to prevent tangling and put aside until needed in the next stage.

This involves spinning the fibres into yarn, and is the first job which takes place in the rope walk itself. At one end of the walk, the head end, stands a spinning wheel, 3ft to 4ft (0.9–1.2m) in diameter; when turned, it causes several small rollers, each of which is fitted with a hook, to turn also. The spinner wraps the streak of hemp around his waist, bight to the front and ends crossed over at the back. From the middle he draws out enough of the fibres to produce yarn of the required thickness and, twisting them between finger and thumb, attaches them to one of the hooks on the spinning wheel. While the wheel is turned by a boy the spinner steps backwards down the rope walk, paying out fibres from the bundle at his waist. The turning wheel automatically draws out and twists the fibres, each entangling itself with another, guided by the spinner's hands. His right hand regulates the amount and evenness of the twist, while his left hand, protected by a damp, coarse cloth, lays the fibres flat to produce a smooth-surfaced yarn. Thickness is determined not only by the number of fibres drawn out but also by the speed of hook rotation and the rate at which the spinner walks backwards.

As he walks backwards the yarn is thrown over hooks to keep it off the ground,

ROPEWORK 1

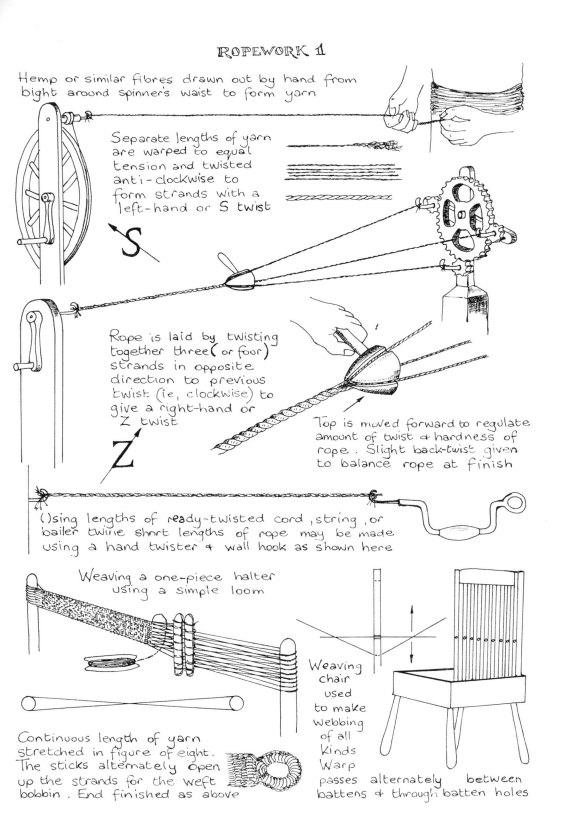

Hemp or similar fibres drawn out by hand from bight around spinner's waist to form yarn

Separate lengths of yarn are warped to equal tension and twisted anti-clockwise to form strands with a left-hand or S twist

S

Rope is laid by twisting together three (or four) strands in opposite direction to previous twist (ie, clockwise) to give a right-hand or Z twist

Z

Top is moved forward to regulate amount of twist & hardness of rope. Slight back-twist given to balance rope at finish

Using lengths of ready-twisted cord, string, or bailer twine short lengths of rope may be made using a hand twister & wall hook as shown here

Weaving a one-piece halter using a simple loom

Continuous length of yarn stretched in figure of eight. The sticks alternately open up the strands for the weft bobbin. End finished as above

Weaving chair used to make webbing of all kinds. Warp passes alternately between battens & through batten holes and when sufficient has been spun the wheel boy detaches his end and fixes it to a winding reel. As he reels in the yarn the spinner walks forward again, holding the far end tightly to prevent the twist unravelling and keeping the yarn taut as it is taken up on the reel. This process is repeated until the reel is full of yarn.

The next process is that of strand making. For some rope makers this represented the first stage of the job, for they bought in ready-spun yarn, as do the few who are still working today. Methods of strand making differ from one walk to the next, particularly between those producing long, heavy ropes and those making shorter lengths and lighter ropes. In the large rope works the yarn, in naval jargon, is first 'warped into a haul' – that is to say, the required lengths are unwound from the reel and stretched out straight and parallel along the rope walk, supported at intervals on T-shaped posts set with teeth, like upturned rakes. The number of lengths of yarn in the haul is determined by the ultimate size of rope to be made, some small ropes requiring only seven or eight yarns to the strand, while a 12in (300mm) ship's cable needs ten times this number.

The required lengths of yarn are drawn together through an iron ring or tube and then, after being knotted together, are attached at one end to a hook on a piece of fixed apparatus known as a tackle board or rope jack, and at the other end to a somewhat similar arrangement mounted on wheels and known as a traveller or sledge. Each has a crank handle and a toothed iron gear-wheel, the one on the tackle board driving three or four revolving hooks, while that on the traveller only drives a single hook. The hook on the sledge revolves in the opposite direction to those on the tackle board. When the crank handles are turned, the opposite but coaxial movement twists the yarns tightly around each other to form a hard, even strand which, shortening as it forms, pulls the traveller closer to the tackle board. In making up, a rope loses about a quarter of the warp length, and an allowance has to be made for this at the start. Strands are twisted anticlockwise, giving them a left-hand lay.

The final process, in which the strands are twisted or laid into a rope, also involves the use of the tackle board and traveller. Three strands, or sometimes four, are laid together to form a rope. These are attached singly to the revolving hooks of the tackle board, while their other ends, all knotted together, go on to the traveller's hook. To control the lay of the rope and to keep it uniform along its whole length the rope maker uses a grooved cone of hardwood known as a top. This is inserted between the strands at the traveller end before the twisting is started, each strand lying in its own groove, the small end of the top towards the traveller. As the tackle board hooks revolve in a clockwise direction, to give a right-hand lay to the rope, the roper walks slowly forward, holding the top in position while the strands form up into a rope behind it. According to the speed at which he moves, the lay of the strands can be made longer or shorter as required, and this is what determines the final hardness of the rope.

In laying heavy ropes for ships' hawsers and cables, winches were used to pull the strands together, and the twisting was done by men using oak levers called woolders. Cables required the use of a large, heavy top which had to be supported on a wheeled carriage. Some ropes, especially those in continual use at sea, were tarred; this process, while reducing their strength by about 30 per cent, preserved

214

47 Laying a small rope by hand

them and lengthened their working life considerably. The loss of strength was overcome by using rope of a greater thickness. Tarring was done before stranding took place, the haul of yarn being drawn slowly through liquid tar, then through a device which squeezed the hot tar into the fibres and removed the surplus at the same time. This was traditionally a thick, upright board with a hole in it, but later adjustable grooved rollers were used. The laying of these tarred ropes was heavy, laborious work often requiring the combined strength of twenty men.

215

48 The wheeled top used in making very large ropes

By contrast, some rope yards specialised in making lightweight ropes and a variety of cords, twines and string. Where ropes are still made by hand it is this type of work which is carried out.

In making these lighter products, slightly different techniques are used, but the basic processes remain the same. Lightweight rope, especially that made in short lengths for special purposes, is technically known as line; clothes line and ships' heaving lines are common examples. Line is made in four stages. First, three groups of yarn are run out between the three hooks on the twisting wheel (similar to the tackle board) and the single hook on the sledge some distance away. Each group makes up a strand, approximately sixteen lengths going into each to make a $\frac{3}{4}$in (19mm) line. This stage is known as warping.

Then the first twist is made, the three groups of yarn being kept separate as the strands form by means of the top which is placed between them at the sledge end. The twist is made in an anti-clockwise direction to give a left-hand lay to the strands. Next the rope is laid, this time in a clockwise direction to give the required right-hand lay, by moving the top forward from the sledge towards the twister. As the top is moved forward the line forms behind it, the speed at which it is moved again determining the hardness of the finished product. Finally, by turning the hook on the sledge (which has of course moved forward as the strands have twisted and become shorter), a small amount of back-twist is put into the line to balance it so that it will not snarl up in use.

Twine and cords of different kinds – rope makers never use the word string – were always made in this way, and a variety of materials were used, just as they are today. Sisal would make a tough, durable line, while cotton, although not as strong, made a smooth lightweight line frequently used for machinery-driving ropes and running rigging on small boats. Jute was used to make filis, a soft type of string once popular with gardeners and nurserymen for tying plants.

Many rural rope yards not only manufactured rope and line, but also made a wide range of rope products. Some spent much of their time making up ropework of all kinds for farm use: plough lines and cow ties, sheep, rick and general purpose nets, and ropes used for horses in all kinds of work – halters, lead reins, cart ropes, belly bands and so on. In addition, rope items were made for a variety of other specialist and local uses.

Some of these products were simply cut and made up from longer lengths of rope made in the yard, but some items were actually made to a particular length and in a special way at the laying-up stage. The best plough lines, for example, which are longish pieces of rope, were graduated or tapered along their length, being lightest at the horse's head. Similar tapered ropes were, and still are, used when breaking in young horses. Church bell ropes were a speciality of some yards, while others made ropes and rope fenders for use on the canals.

Cow ties – short lengths of rope used to tether cows in their stalls – were made with rope which contained horsehair. This made a soft rope less harmful to the animal, but farmers also liked it because it would always 'slip' (untie) easily when required, whereas hemp alone swells when wet, making it difficult to untie, and jute is even worse.

Halters were made in two types – the yoke halter, a simple noosed rope which fitted the animal's neck, and the slip halter, which was not really rope, as it was woven and not twisted. But it was produced from rope materials, and it was made by rope workers. Slip halters were woven in separate lengths on rudimentary 'looms' of various kinds. The simplest of these consisted of one hook low down on a wall and another on a movable upright post similar to a simple rope maker's sledge. Between each hook twine would be stretched in a continuous skein, about thirty strands in all, to form a warp. The twine was crossed over as it was wound out to form a figure of eight. Alternate strands were separated and held in loops

217

of string secured to two short flat sticks known, confusingly, as a harness. A sideways movement of the harness enabled one set of strands to be crossed through the other, thus forming the opening known to weavers as the shed. A bobbin wound with more twine was passed back and forth through alternate sheds to form the weft. A flat wooden batten known as a beater was used to close up and tighten the weave as it formed.

An alternative method used an apparatus known as a bat. This consisted of two upright posts set at the required distance apart, one fixed and one free to move as needed. The warp was again formed from a continuous length, looped at each end so that the problems of fraying were eliminated.

Another simple form of loom associated with this work, and used for making a strong type of webbing employed whenever a wide, flat 'rope' was required, was the weaving chair. The chair 'back' consisted of a framework of narrow, upright wooden battens with very narrow spaces between, each batten having a small hole drilled in it to form a straight line across the back. The chair 'seat' was in fact a shallow box to hold spools of yarn etc., and the whole thing stood on four legs just like a proper chair. It was placed between two hooks, one fixed, on a wall perhaps, the other movable, on a simple sledge. Strands were threaded alternately through the holes and through the spaces in the battens and made fast to the hooks at either side. By means of a stick those threads that passed between the battens could be moved up and down together through those fixed in the holes, thus forming alternate shed and countershed through which was passed a shuttle carrying the weft. Various widths of webbing could be made in this way; it was used to make belly bands for horses and slings for cargo and barrels, and undertakers bought it as coffin webbing 'for lowering purposes'.

Many rope yards made not only cordage but also canvas, weaving the coarse, heavy material and making a variety of goods allied to their main trade and often incorporating rope in their manufacture. Tent making is perhaps the best example of this, the tents ranging from small ones for recreational purposes to giant marquees and circus 'big tops' and including, at one time, large numbers for the army. In coastal yards sail making was an important aspect of the work. Inland, canvas covers of all kinds were made, some rather confusingly called sails but actually used by farmers to cover haystacks. Canvas belting for harvesting and threshing machines was also produced, as were sacks for the grain and for many other purposes.

The making of nets was another important extension of the rope maker's work. Although net-making machinery came into use well over a hundred years ago, hand work continued, as this was considered superior. Some nets still are made by hand, and of course a lot of repair work is done this way. Rope yards in coastal areas had to meet a heavy demand for fishing nets, for although many inshore fishermen bought netting cord from the makers and made up their own nets, the large drift and trawl nets were made entirely in rope yards specialising in such work. At one time large numbers of women were employed as outworkers, making nets, or braiding, as it was known, in their own homes, using materials supplied to them by a local rope yard. Inland roperies made nets mainly for agricultural purposes – stack nets to contain temporary straw stacks or ricks, and

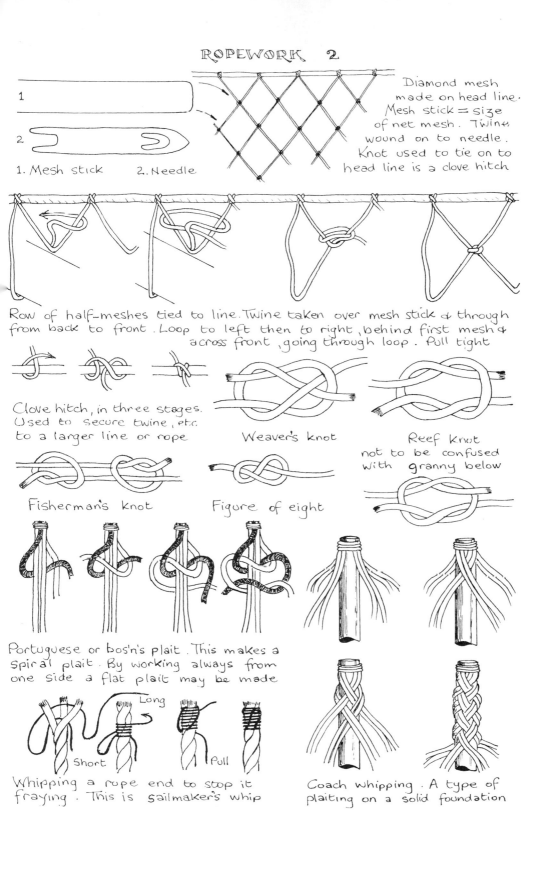

ROPEWORK 2

1

2

1. Mesh stick   2. Needle

Diamond mesh made on head line. Mesh stick = size of net mesh. Twine wound on to needle. Knot used to tie on to head line is a clove hitch

Row of half-meshes tied to line. Twine taken over mesh stick & through from back to front. Loop to left then to right, behind first mesh & across front, going through loop. Pull tight

Clove hitch, in three stages. Used to secure twine, etc. to a larger line or rope

Weaver's knot

Reef Knot not to be confused with granny below

Fisherman's Knot

Figure of eight

Portuguese or bos'n's plait. This makes a spiral plait. By working always from one side a flat plait may be made

Long

Short

Pull

Whipping a rope end to stop it fraying. This is sailmaker's whip

Coach whipping. A type of plaiting on a solid foundation

49 Repairing a diamond-mesh fishing net

animal nets for temporary penning and to cover over open vehicles taking livestock to market. Finer-mesh bird nets were made to protect fruit in orchards and to cover thatch. Netting was also required for tennis courts, cricket practice nets and other sporting purposes, and poachers were good at making nets for their own particular 'sport' – snaring rabbits.

Net making by hand is not difficult; only two tools are required, and both are easily made from flat pieces of wood. The first is a thin gauge equal in width to the net mesh, and the second a netting needle shaped as shown in the diagrams. Some net makers use the fingers of the left hand as a guide instead of a mesh stick or gauge, and for a small amount of work even the needle can be dispensed with.

Plain diamond mesh is the easiest to make, each diamond knotted with a single or common sheetbend. Basically, net making consists of tying a series of these knots. Choose a smooth hemp twine to work with and load the needle tightly with it, making sure that it does not become too bulky to pass easily through the net meshes.

Begin by stretching a light rope tightly between two fixed points to form a head line; for a small net, a length of round wooden dowel can be used and later removed. The first row of what are really half-meshes is worked on this by tying the twine at equal intervals with a clove hitch, working from right to left. The next full row is worked by taking the twine over the mesh stick, up behind it and through the first half-mesh from back to front. Leaving a small loop to the left

220

the needle is taken across to the right, then behind the previous mesh and down through the loop, pulling the whole knot tight. This makes the first sheetbend, and the process is repeated across the width of the net, working always from left to right. At the end of each row the work is turned over so that this procedure can be followed; large nets are hung so that the worker can walk round to the other side. The needle is re-loaded when empty and the ends of twine are joined using the weaver's knot.

Making knots is an art in itself, traditionally nautical but practised by a wide range of people from climbers to crocheters – not forgetting Boy Scouts. Very little of the old sailor's ropework is seen today, in spite of the myriads of small-boat owners. There is, however, a revival of interest in knotting; much of the work now sold as 'macramé' is unfortunately done with coloured string and often incorporates cheap wooden or plastic beads, but work carried out in natural fibres and natural colours can be quite pleasing.

bow cutter

wedging block

turntable

modelling tools

BRICKS & POTTERY

scraper

GLAZE

gauge

potter's kick-wheel

Wooden clay spade

brick mould

Approximately three-fifths, or 60 per cent, of the earth's crust is composed of clay of one kind or another. Fortunately – or unfortunately, depending upon whether you are a potter or a gardener – it is found almost everywhere, usually on or near the surface. The wide availability of clay, and the comparative ease with which it may be shaped, made it suitable for use by even the most primitive civilisations long before the appearance of tools of any kind. Early pots and bricks were crudely pressed out by hand from lumps of clay and simply left out in the sun to bake dry. Later pots were built up from coils of clay, and bricks were made more uniform in size and shape by using moulds.

The clay was worked wherever it was found, and as it is a heavy material and difficult to transport this pattern persisted until quite recently. The emergence of 'the Potteries', that area of midland England, and of other places where the large commercial manufacturers centralised their activities, was due more to the availability of coal to fire their kilns and of a ready market than to the supply of suitable clay. The manufacturers used clay brought from many places, mixed and blended to a uniform, drab colour still to be seen today in the monotonous rows of terraced and semi-detached houses which form the bulk of the dwellings in most industrial towns and cities. By contrast, when brickworks and potteries were as widespread as the clay itself, almost every town and village had its own distinctive ware, due partly to the different clays and partly to the way in which they were worked.

In its simplest form clay is finely powdered rock – decayed volcanic rock, to be geologically precise – representing the product of millions of years of weathering and disintegration. Some clays stayed where they were formed – the white China clay of Cornwall, for example – while others have been carried in suspension in water or by ice, sometimes far from their original sites. These widespread deposits, which may be in either extensive beds or isolated pockets, collected various impurities on their travels, and it is these which produce the different types and colours of clay which are found today. The various colours of clay are due to the presence of certain chemicals – iron in red clays, magnesium in cream-coloured

222

clay, carbon in grey and black clay. Some impurities are not obvious until the clay is fired, while some make the clay quite unsuitable for use. Clay containing a high percentage of sand is more suitable for brick making than for pottery.

The clay may be taken from the ground either by mechanical means or by hand, some large pits employing machines to dig the clay and elaborate conveyor systems to transport it to the works. In small-scale work a spade and a simple trolley or even a wheelbarrow are all that is needed. After being dug, or won, from the ground, the clay generally requires preparation before it can be used. The nature of this preparation depends upon the clay itself and its ultimate purpose, certain clays being ready for use almost as nature made them, while some need certain additives and others require refining. Most need tempering to improve their texture and workability. Clay for bricks can remain coarser than that intended for pottery; the finer pottery clays are usually made by mixing several types of clay with other ingredients to produce a number of different grades of known quality and performance in manufacture. Nowadays the preparation is highly mechanised, but at one time it was all done by hand, and where small amounts are involved this is still quite feasible.

Dug in the autumn, before the diggings became waterlogged, the clay was left in large heaps outdoors to weather during the winter months. During this period it would be cut up and turned several times to expose it to the effects of rain and frost. Special wooden spades tipped with steel were used for this work – clay would stick to an all-metal blade, making the work much more difficult.

After weathering, the clay was sometimes crushed by big rollers and sieved, then passed through a pugging mill or pug mill. This machine, by means of revolving blades inside, mixed the clay into a stiff paste, water being added as and when required. Other ingredients could also be added at this stage, and the finished clay was finally pressed out through an opening ready for use. Pug mills may be mechanically or electrically powered, or turned by hand if they are small enough. Early mills were horse-driven, while earlier still the work was done by barefooted boys who stamped up and down on the wet clay as it lay on the workshop floor. In yet another method the clay and any other ingredients were mixed with a large volume of water to make a kind of thin 'soup' which was 'puddled' in large ponds, or pans, as they were called. There it would be given a stir from time to time, then allowed to settle, after which the surplus water was drained away. When it reached the correct consistency it was cut out and used in the normal way.

Small quantities of locally dug clay may be similarly prepared in the home. The clay is first broken down into small lumps, exposed stones and other visible impurities being removed at the same time. If the clay can then be left outdoors to weather, so much the better. When required for use the lumps are placed in a bucket and completely covered with water. In a few hours the clay will have softened and can then be worked with the hands or by stirring until a thick soup or slurry is obtained. Leave it for a few minutes so that stones drop to the bottom, then sieve the slurry into a second bucket or bowl. A very fine sieve should be used; if none is available, a piece of cloth makes a good substitute. Place a few cupfuls of slurry in the sieve or cloth and work gently with the fingertips to help the flow. Extra water can be used to wash the clay through if necessary.

223

CLAY PREPARATION

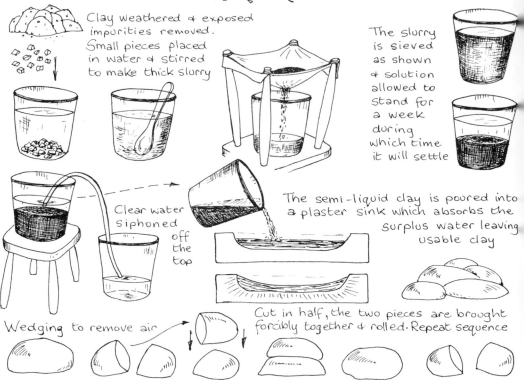

Clay weathered & exposed impurities removed. Small pieces placed in water & stirred to make thick slurry

The slurry is sieved as shown & solution allowed to stand for a week during which time it will settle

Clear water siphoned off the top

The semi-liquid clay is poured into a plaster sink which absorbs the surplus water leaving usable clay

Wedging to remove air

Cut in half, the two pieces are brought forcibly together & rolled. Repeat sequence

The solution collected in the second bucket is then allowed to stand for about a week. Stir it gently two or three times during the first two days to mix the sand (which, being heavier, will have dropped to the bottom in the first few hours) with the finer particles of clay, then leave it undisturbed. At the end of the week the clay and other particles will have settled, leaving the water comparatively clear near the top. Surplus water is siphoned off with a rubber tube to leave behind a very wet mass of suitable but unworkable clay.

The remaining water may be eliminated either by evaporation or by absorption. Evaporation is caused by placing a shallow dish of clay in a warm, dry room, or more quickly by warming it over a stove or gas flame. Squeezing between absorbent cloths is a rather messy job; this can be effective, but it is much better to use a porous 'sink'. One of these can be readily made from ordinary builders' plaster of Paris, using a wooden box as a mould. When the sink has set and is thoroughly dry the semi-liquid clay is stirred well and poured in. After a few hours the plaster will have absorbed the water and a slab of usable clay will be left.

Before the clay is used, any air remaining in it must be removed; this is done by wedging. A lump of clay is cut with a wire and the two halves are brought together with great force on a firm surface. This is repeated many times – the more

224

the better. Essential with locally won clay, this final preparation is advisable with commercially prepared clays as well.

For brick making, clay containing a comparatively high proportion of sand is used, as this helps to reduce shrinkage and warping. In a solid item as large as a brick, pure clay forms a hard outer crust before the inside has had time to dry out properly. The presence of coarse particles in the clay prevents this, allowing the material to dry out more evenly.

Although most bricks are now made by the million by large firms using factory methods, a few country brickyards still produce hand-made bricks to special order. These are usually moulded, and after firing have a certain individual character not seen in the machine-made product. There are two main methods of brick moulding, both very simple. Both use wooden or metal moulds made slightly larger than the finished size of the brick to allow for shrinkage in drying. The actual size of the moulds varies as some clays shrink more than others, the average rate being in the order of 10 per cent.

The moulds have neither top nor bottom and rest on the flat surface of the moulder's bench. In slop moulding the mould is dipped in water and two good handfuls of moist (sloppy) clay are pressed into it. The top is smoothed off with a tool not unlike a carpenter's blunt drawknife, and the filled mould is slid off the bench on to a board. When the board is filled it is taken to the drying room by another workman while the moulder continues to fill more moulds to load up another board. When the bricks in the drying room are firm enough, they are removed from the moulds and stacked honeycomb fashion to dry out properly.

In pallet moulding, sometimes known as sand moulding, the clay used is stiffer and firmer. The mould is placed squarely over a moulding board which often has a raised centre, known as the frog, which forms a depression in one side of the finished brick. This holds the mortar better when the bricks are bonded together and often carries the name or trademark of the yard where the brick was made. Sand is liberally sprinkled inside the mould, and a lump of clay, sometimes first rolled, in sand, is thrown forcefully into it, filling it completely, without air bubbles or spaces, by reason of its own weight and velocity. A piece of wire on a frame, rather like a cheese cutter, removes the surplus clay. A wooden pallet is then placed on top and with a quick movement the brick-shaped mass of clay is turned out of its mould and on to the pallet. The pallets are taken away on a flat wheelbarrow and carefully stacked under cover to be air-dried.

Some bricks are made in a similar manner in moulds filled directly from a pug mill. Here the clay is forced into frames of three or four moulds at a time, the surplus clay being scraped off by hand as before and the frames turned out on to pallets for drying.

The sand used in the moulding process prevents sticking during manufacture, just like flour on a pastry board. It also leaves a rough-cast surface, while chemicals in the sand often combine with those in the clay to produce a variety of pleasing colours after firing. For these reasons sand-moulded bricks are often used as facing bricks – that is, on the façades of buildings – and for decorative features inside.

Another type of brick typical of some country brickyards but lacking the indi-

225

50 A country potter at work

vidual quality of the moulded type is the wire-cut brick. The pug mill used in this work is designed to extrude a rectangular slab of stiff clay a little over the required thickness of the finished brick. This is simply sliced up by a frame-held wire cutter into pieces of the required length, a process which is quite easily mechanised. Some wire-cut bricks are sanded and combed before drying in an effort to imitate their moulded counterparts.

Along with bricks, many yards made roofing tiles and drainpipes, the latter, ironically, often being in great demand where clay was plentiful for the improvement of wet agricultural land. Roof tiles, hardly seen at all where slate is available, varied greatly in design, from ordinary flat tiles to the large, curved pantiles. All were made flat, some rolled out like pastry, the curved types then being placed on moulds to dry out to the required shape. Holes for fixing were made at the moulding stage, either by pegs on the moulds or by means of a simple two-pronged tool.

Brickyards in market-garden areas often had another busy sideline, that of making plant pots. Although clay plant pots, like their plastic counterparts, are all moulded today, they were once individually thrown on the potter's wheel. This was almost always of the kick-wheel type, the design principle little changed from ancient times, the wheel geared to a horizontal wooden flywheel by means

226

of an offset cranked shaft. Either the potter worked his wheel by a sideways movement of his foot against a lever attached to the flywheel or, more often, it would be turned for him by a boy. Although most potters' wheels are now driven by electric motors, many still prefer the kick-wheel, believing it to give them better control of the working speed. Speed of rotation is important in thrown work – a large pot should revolve more slowly than a small one, and while a fast speed is needed to begin a pot, a comparatively slow one is better for finishing.

Clay for a batch of pots was weighed out in bulk, then divided up equally according to the number of pots to be made and rolled into balls. The bulk weight was called a cast, and the number of pots made from it gave the old names to plant pots, which were known as 60s, 32s and so on, meaning that sixty 3in (75mm) or thirty-two 6in (150mm) diameter pots could be made from the cast. Each ball was thrown on to the wheel and quickly shaped into a pot of the correct size, a simple gauge-stick telling the potter when each had reached the right height and diameter. An average potter could make over five hundred medium-sized pots in a working day.

Throwing a pot of any kind looks deceptively easy until one tries it for the first time. Clay can be the most unco-operative of materials for the beginner, especially on a revolving wheel. Only by experience can a measure of success be achieved. Throwing a simple plant pot is good practice, and even some early misfortunes may still be usable.

Take a ball of prepared clay and throw it on to the centre of the stationary wheel, which should be clean and moist. Wet the hands and splash water on to the clay – do this frequently during the work, otherwise the clay will drag – and set the wheel in motion. It should normally rotate anti-clockwise (as seen from above) and at a fairly high speed. Centre the clay by placing the palm of the left hand vertically against it, with the fingers curled round it, and resting the right hand horizontally on top of it, the ball of the hand pressing down, fingers over the left hand, thumb down one side. The arms should be braced against any eccentric movement by resting them firmly on the wheel surround. Firm persuasion is the aim, and practice will tell when the clay is centred.

Next the fingers of the left hand are pressed into the centre of the clay to open it up, pressure from the right hand controlling the clay as it flows out across the wheel to form a thick-sided, shallow dish. Now the clay is drawn up, first by placing both thumbs together inside, fingers pointing down outside, and then with the left hand only inside, the first and middle fingers touching the clay and pressing against the knuckles of the right hand held outside. Both hands are raised slowly, pinching the clay between them to make a cylindrical shape. This shape, which is the basis of most thrown pots, should not be formed too quickly but in about three 'lifts' or stages, and as the cylinder grows the speed of the wheel should decrease.

The plant-pot shape can now be formed, the hands moving slowly upwards from the bottom as in lifting the cylinder. This time the hands allow the pot to flare out at the top, steady pressure between them keeping the wall of the pot uniform in thickness throughout. Beginners are advised to keep the walls fairly thick to begin with.

227

CLAY · THROWING

Opening up the clay

This is the first stage in drawing up

Drawing up, second stage

Shaping the sides

Levelling the rim

Shaping the rim

When completed the pot is removed from the wheel with a cutting wire

The rim is levelled by cutting with a pointed steel tool, which is held in the right hand and pressed against the clay while the first finger of the left hand supports the pot from the inside. The rim can then be shaped by pressing it gently down and rounding it over with the fingertips. Surplus water is removed from inside the pot with a sponge while the wheel is revolving.

The pot is removed from the wheel by cutting it through at the base with a wire and lifting it off with dry hands, using plenty of water to lubricate the wheel surface. It is then placed on a board or shelf to dry out slowly. If the pot is distorted in the lifting it can be patted back into shape, and when the clay is nearly dry – in what is known as the leather-hard state – the pot is turned upside down and the drain hole is cut in the bottom with a pointed knife-blade.

Other thrown shapes call for more precise techniques, and pottery for kitchen, table and decorative purposes has always been the province of more specialised potteries. Most of this work is now in the hands either of large commercial concerns turning out goods of varying quality by mass-production methods or of small 'studio' potteries, many of which lean more towards the 'art pottery' market and the tourist trade than towards the production of simple, functional kitchen- and tableware. Genuine country potteries are now few and far between, in spite of the fact that not too long ago they flourished wherever suitable clay was to be found.

Most of what they produced was earthenware, a basic clay body which remains

228

porous even after firing if left unglazed but can be fired quite satisfactorily in simple kilns of the type used by many country potters. Unglazed earthenware – plant pots are the most familiar example – is known as terracotta. Glazed earthenware owes much of its charm to the practice of glazing the interior but only partially glazing the outside, thus producing a striking contrast between the matt brick colour of the unglazed surface and the rich dark brown of the glaze. Butter dishes, milk jugs and narrow-necked pitchers were glazed in this way. Thick earthenware dishes were popular for pies and puddings, for they could be baked slowly for hours in the old-fashioned ovens, as could casseroles and Lancashire hot-pots.

Those potteries with more efficient kilns produced stoneware, using certain clays which vitrify when fired at a high temperature, the clay particles fusing together to render the article non-porous. A glaze was sometimes added, but either way stoneware is harder and stronger than earthenware. It was used extensively in the manufacture of heavy mixing bowls and storage bins, 'stone' ginger-beer bottles, hot-water bottles and jam pots.

Shapes which cannot be thrown on a wheel are moulded, either in a casting mould or over what is sometimes called a mushroom mould. Both types are made in plaster of Paris, casting moulds consisting sometimes of a single piece, sometimes of two or more. Casting involves the use of slip – a liquid clay of a thick, creamy consistency to which may be added a few drops of a solution of ordinary soda (sodium carbonate) to render it easier to pour, and less likely to leave air bubbles in the moulding process. The solution is made up by dissolving four tablespoonfuls of soda (0.1 l) in half a pint (0.3 l) of warm water; a few drops only should be added to a bucket of slip. Slip is poured into the mould until it is full, and it is kept full for at least five minutes. The plaster absorbs the water in the slip to leave a deposit of clay in the mould. Then the surplus slip is poured out and the mould left to dry for up to an hour, the exact time depending on its size and on the thickness of the clay deposit. Slight shrinkage causes the clay to free itself from the mould, and it can be removed quite easily.

Shallow dishes of oval or rectangular shape are best made on a mushroom mould, which is a mould of the inside shape of the required dish. A slab of clay, rolled out to uniform thickness, is pressed on to this and shaped and smoothed to the contours of the mould. The edge may be trimmed with a knife or a wire and the dish left to dry until it can be easily lifted from the mould. Dishes can also be built up from rolled slabs of clay, the individual parts cut out with a knife and joined together using slip. Pieces to be joined should first be roughened to form a key, and all joints should be rounded over with a suitable modelling tool.

Another useful method of making pots, employed in ancient times before the invention of the potter's wheel, is the method known as coiling. For this, clay is rolled with the outstretched palms of the hands on a smooth hard surface to form coils a little more than the diameter of a pencil in thickness. (A small pug mill which will produce such coils is available.) To begin a pot, a base is first made to the required size, either by coiling a spiral or by shaping a slab. Roughen the outer edge of the base, moisten it with water or slip and start building up the coils on it. Flatten and moisten the top surface of each coil, and weld the coils together

CLAY. SLAB & COIL

SLAB BUILDING

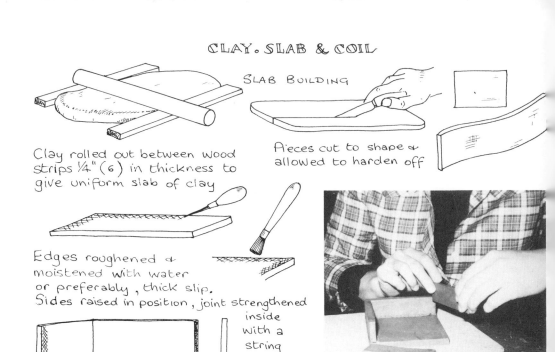

Clay rolled out between wood strips ¼" (6) in thickness to give uniform slab of clay

Pieces cut to shape & allowed to harden off

Edges roughened & moistened with water or preferably, thick slip. Sides raised in position, joint strengthened inside with a string of clay rounded over as shown

COILING

Coils prepared by hand-rolling. Make all coils solid-centred & even

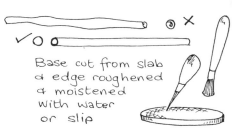

Base cut from slab & edge roughened & moistened with water or slip

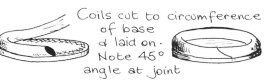

Coils cut to circumference of base & laid on. Note 45° angle at joint

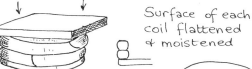

Surface of each coil flattened & moistened

Tall pots built in stages to prevent the clay sagging

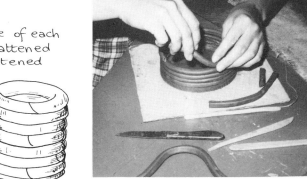

with the fingers as the work progresses. Join in the new lengths of coil with a diagonal splice'. If you are building a tall pot, leave it to dry off and firm up a little after every two or three inches, otherwise it will begin to sag. Inside and outside surfaces can be smoothed off, which helps to seal the joints between individual coils, or the inside only may be smoothed, leaving the outside to show the method of construction, which can be quite decorative.

Mention has already been made of glazing, essential if earthenware is to be made non-porous but much used also for decorative effect. Glazing is a chemical process in which certain substances fuse with the clay when heated to leave a glass-like, waterproof surface. The basis of any glaze is silica; it will also contain lime, lead, soda, borax or potash, to act as a flux, and a binding agent such as alumina, a substance present in clay. Common salt may also be used as a glaze, and salt-glazed stoneware was quite common at one time. Mixed together with colouring agents of all kinds, glazes can be obtained ready-made, needing only to have water added to them before use; for many potters, however, the unpredictable results obtained by using their own glazes are the most exciting thing about pottery. Glazes are applied either by painting on or by dipping when the pot has been fired once and is at what is known as the biscuit stage – bone dry but still porous. The liquid in the glaze is absorbed by the porous pot to leave the fine suspended particles deposited on its surface. When the pot is fired a second time the glaze melts and fuses with the clay.

Firing is carried out in kilns of various kinds which subject the clay – brickyard products and pottery alike – to temperatures which vary between 800°C and 1350°C, depending on the nature of the end product. The earliest bricks and pots, sun-baked to harden them, would soften again when wet, but when heated to high temperatures clay alters structurally, forming what is really an entirely new substance, hard and durable.

Bricks were originally fired in 'clamps' by the process known as burning. Newly dried bricks were stacked criss-cross fashion over channels in a level floor, the channels and the spaces between the layers of brick being filled with 'firing material' – breeze (fine coal), wood or charcoal. The centre of the stack rose stepwise in a dome, and the whole pile was covered with a final layer of old spoilt bricks, known as scovers, left over from previous burnings. The clamp, when lit, burned for a week or more at a temperature around 800°C, controlled, like the charcoal burner's fire, by the careful regulation of the air entering the closely packed mass of bricks and fuel. If the heating was too rapid or the temperature too high the bricks would fuse into a solid lump, and many were spoiled in this way at each burning.

Even in the permanent brick kilns which followed clamps, uneven firing rendered many bricks unsuitable for use or produced 'seconds' of inferior quality. But uneven firing was also partly responsible for the wide variety of colours to be seen in old brickwork, further enhancing the individual character of the different clays.

Modern kilns are much more efficient, but a great deal of skill is required in operating the very large ones. Small-scale kilns of the kind used by specialist or studio potteries are, generally speaking, easier to control. Most resemble ovens, but are lined inside with refractory material to insulate them and are designed to reach much higher temperatures than even the largest domestic oven. They may be heated by solid fuel, gas, oil or electricity, the latter being the most convenient and common. Some potters still fire small outdoor kilns, using wood or, sometimes, bottled gas.

Most potters fire their work twice, the first firing being carried out when the clay is chalk-dry to the touch. If a pot is fired while it is still too damp it will almost certainly shatter as a result of the formation of steam, which expands and blows the pot apart. For the first firing – known as the biscuit firing – the kiln is packed and heat is applied slowly until it reaches about 900°C, after which it is allowed to cool gradually. The total time taken depends upon the design and size of the kiln, but usually it takes several hours to heat up and several more to cool down.

When the pots are cool, glazing can take place as already described, and then they are returned to the kiln when the glaze has dried. More care must be taken this time when packing the kiln; no pots must touch, otherwise the glaze will fuse them together. There is no need to raise the temperature slowly this time, but a higher temperature must be reached to melt the glaze; the precise temperature will depend on the particular glazes being used, but it is normally about 1000°C. Gradual cooling is essential, otherwise the glaze may craze, and this means a wait of several hours before the kiln door can be opened again.

It is the opening of that door that is the potter's moment of truth. Only at that point will he know if his work has been successful or not. The old clay workers with their primitive means had their share of success and failure, and so too does the modern craftsman. The pots may not turn out just as he expected, and there may well be considerable differences between them; it is very difficult to produce a matching set. But then, this is all part of the charm of hand-made pottery.

HEDGING & WALLING

The patchwork pattern of fields and farms, so much a feature of the English countryside, is largely the result of the abandonment of the open field system of agriculture and the final enclosure of land by Act of Parliament in the eighteenth and early nineteenth centuries. Even before this the voluntary enclosure of land had been going on for some time, and some ditches, hedges, walls and earth banks, especially those marking estate and parish boundaries, may well date back to Saxon times. Many of these early boundaries were, and legally still are, ditches, but the growing of hedges along their embanked flanks became common practice throughout much of lowland England and Wales. In upland and moorland areas where the soil is too sparse or too acid and the altitude too great for sturdy growth, walls were built wherever suitable material was available. Elsewhere earth banks or baulks were raised.

Hedges, where planted, were mainly of thorn; two species of hawthorn, *Crataegus monogyna* and *C. oxyacanthoides*, together with hybrids of the two, predominate today. Known mostly as quickthorn or quickset on account of the ease with which it propagates and grows, the first of these – the native May tree, its white and pink blossom a symbol of summer and pagan festivals – was extensively planted under the Enclosure Acts.

Literally millions of seedlings were grown to plant and mark the new boundaries, spaced out usually in a double row and sometimes interplanted with young saplings of elm or ash or other trees. Over the years other plants established themselves by natural means, and the composition of many hedges may have changed, the original planting probably predominant but mixed with oak, holly, elm, hazel, elder and willow, all intertwined with bramble, honeysuckle and clematis and a profusion of wild flowers and grasses growing in the hedge bottom. The number of different species within a hedge is thought to be a reliable indication of its age, each different woody species in a 30yd (27.5m) stretch of hedge indicating a 100-year period of growth.

Hawthorn seedlings are propagated naturally in suitable conditions, often distributed by birds, who eat the bright red berry or haw which surrounds the single

233

seed. To raise young trees, seeds collected in the autumn must be stored in sand for eighteen months, after which time they will germinate readily. Sown in the spring in nursery beds, seedlings are transplanted into new beds in the same nursery two years later. After a further two years' growth they are ready for planting out into permanent positions.

It is the hawthorn's natural prickliness and quick, sturdy growth which make it so effective as a living fence. But left to grow unattended it soon ceases to be stockproof and therefore becomes unsuitable for its purpose. Extended upward growth and the formation of individual vertical trunks, with the crowns touching and intertwining but with spaces in between at ground level, allow easy access for curious sheep and grazing cattle eager to reach the ever-greener grass on the other side of the fence. A hedge in this condition is said to be 'thin in the bottom'. Simply cutting the hedge back to a lower level in no way solves the problem, and so a method of training and trimming known as laying was developed. A laid hedge is one in which the main vertical stems, partly cut through and bent over, are persuaded to grow in a more horizontal position from a point quite close to ground level, thus permanently filling in the gaps. The idea behind the cutting and bending over is to encourage 'tillering' – the growth of young shoots from low down on an original stem. This new growth from near-horizontal stems forms a dense, prickly hedge which is not only stockproof but also forms an effective windbreak. In addition this form of husbandry actually helps prolong the effective life of the hedge and makes it look much neater.

Developed in the Midland county of Leicestershire, the craft of hedge laying owed its existence initially to the requirements of foxhunting rather than to those of good farming practice. The hunting landlords, who, ironically, had caused the hedges to be built in the first place, found their gallops across previously uninterrupted common land barred by obstructions too high and too wide to be jumped with safety. Tenant farmers were instructed to keep their hedges under control, and this they did, effectively, by laying. Their method, along with the fashion for organised hunting, soon spread throughout the rest of England and Wales.

There are now few people left who can lay a hedge well, and although each workman may have his own particular technique, all follow the same basic method and have the same principal aims. The job has always been a winter one, fitting nicely into a quiet time in the farming calendar when the sap is down and there is no foliage to obstruct the work. The hedger – he may be a farm employee or an itinerant worker, working alone or with a mate – uses few tools in his task. A billhook, an axe and perhaps a long-handled slasher if undergrowth has to be cleared are all that is normally required, plus a sharpening stone to keep a good cutting edge on these tools and a heavy mallet for knocking in stakes. Hedging is rough both on the hands and on clothing, and heavy leather gauntlet gloves, an old coat and a leather apron and knee pads are the hedger's usual attire.

The billhooks which are used vary quite considerably from place to place, each locality seeming to have its own preferred type. All were once individually made by local blacksmiths, and so popular were the traditional designs that even when edge tools became a factory product, manufacturers continued to make a wide range in order to meet the demand.

HEDGE LAYING

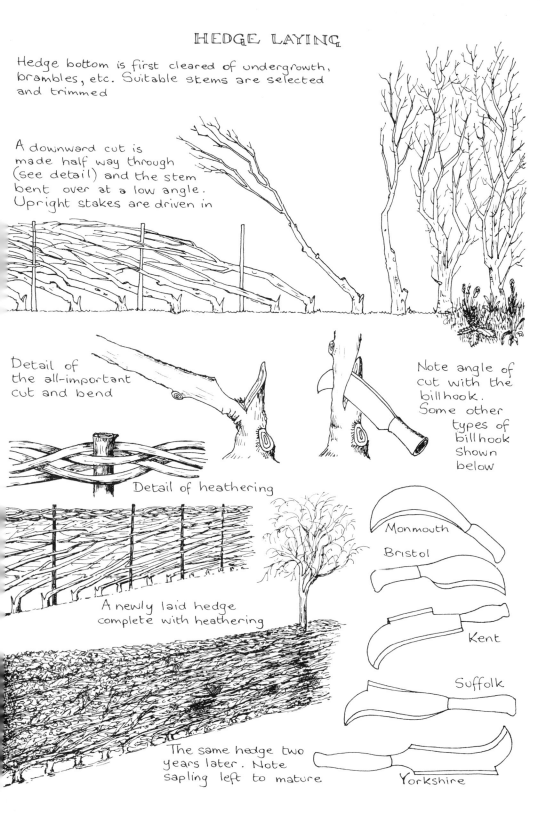

Hedge bottom is first cleared of undergrowth, brambles, etc. Suitable stems are selected and trimmed

A downward cut is made half way through (see detail) and the stem bent over at a low angle. Upright stakes are driven in

Detail of the all-important cut and bend

Note angle of cut with the billhook. Some other types of billhook shown below

Detail of heathering

A newly laid hedge complete with heathering

The same hedge two years later. Note sapling left to mature

Monmouth

Bristol

Kent

Suffolk

Yorkshire

If a hedge has previously been laid, and not too long ago – ideally a hedge is checked over every two years or so – all that is required is a trimming job. This entails the removal of unwanted branches, particularly those growing outwards from the hedge, and the cutting back of long, sappy growth; it is similar in some ways to the gardener's pruning. If there is a ditch, that is cleaned out as the work proceeds to leave everything neat and tidy. Where a hedge has not been laid before, or is considerably overgrown, much more drastic measures are required. First, all scrub and undergrowth is cleared out from the hedge bottom, and unwanted, side-branching stuff is cut back from the main stems, the hedge being roughly trimmed by this means to the required width. Particular attention is paid to the removal of brambles and other sinuous stems which are apt to get caught in the billhook when it is swung, with possible unpleasant consequences for the user. Clearing and trimming are done with upward strokes of the slasher or billhook, which avoids splintering the wood at the cut.

Then, working from left to right along the hedge, the main stems are cut halfway through close to ground level and carefully bent, or laid, to the left at an acute angle. The real skill in hedge laying is in making this cut correctly and in bending over the stem properly. The cut must be made deep enough to allow the stem to be bent without breaking, while leaving sufficient uncut fibres to ensure that the sap, although restricted, is able to rise and support subsequent growth. As a rule the cut is a downward-sloping one from the right (left-handed hedgers work the other way about) made with the billhook. If the stems are thick then the axe may have to be used. Some argue that the cut should be an upward one so that it lies under the bend, the wound thus being protected from the rain and possible rot. The downward cut, however, seems most common. For appearance's sake all the stems are laid over at the same angle, usually about 20°, each overlaying the next to form a close screen.

At intervals of about 3ft (900mm) vertical stakes are required, driven into the ground and interlaced between the near-horizontal stems. These strengthen the hedge until further growth has taken place, and can be of any available wood, cleft or in the round. Some hedgers prefer to use living stems cut to the required height, or sometimes a conveniently placed sapling is utilised, trimmed and cut to the final height of the laid hedge, which may be anywhere between 3ft and 4ft (0.9–1.2m). The whole hedge is then pressed firmly down and the ends of the exposed stakes are bound together, either with the whippy ends of the hawthorn stems themselves or with lengths of bramble, hazel or other pliable material saved purposely from the initial trimming. Plaited in the form of a basket maker's 'rope', the thin stems are intertwined between the stakes to help keep the hedge rigid, this final process being known as heathering or ethering. Where a hedge is thin, or where there is a gap, bent-over stems are pegged into the ground to take root or four-year-old trees may be planted. Temporary 'dead hedges' are made by interweaving cut stems and brushwood between upright stakes until the gap is permanently closed.

It was always customary to allow a single tree to grow to maturity here and there, elm being the species most commonly chosen for this purpose. Certain other trees were allowed to grow on in the same way, and the amount of valuable

51 Laying over the long stems of the hedge between the upright stakes

hardwood timber to be found growing in hedgerows has not always been fully appreciated. Sadly, the ravages of Dutch elm disease have considerably depleted the number of mature hedgerow elms, while some of the operators of tractor-driven hedge cutters, unable or unwilling to discriminate between rampant hawthorn and the stems of hardwood saplings, are killing off any others which might replace them.

In some areas inconvenience and economics have forced farmers into removing hedges entirely in order to make bigger fields more easily managed by mechanical means. Until recently over 2,000 miles (3,200km) of hedge were being grubbed up annually, mainly in those areas where large acreages of cereals are grown by continuous cropping methods. The arguments are that small fields are uneconomic, that each time a tractor or a combine turns it is not doing any work, and that hedges occupy land which could be made more productive and in addition harbour pests which damage crops. While there is some truth in all this, the bare facts are that in some areas hedge grubbing on a large scale has had serious ecological consequences.

For in addition to forming boundaries and restrictive fencing hedges make effective windbreaks, sheltering both stock and growing crops. In some exposed areas a hedge may be the only shelter there is. They are important too in preventing soil erosion, especially in certain areas of light soil, where hedge grubbing has resulted in the soil and its crop being literally blown away by the wind. Fur-

237

thermore, hedgerows form valuable linear wildlife habitats, supporting a wide range of plant and animal life, not all of which is harmful. Neither barbed wire nor the post-and-rail fence has any of these qualities.

Stone walls also make effective wind-breaks, and although most were built originally to mark boundaries, many in addition provide the only shelter on windswept uplands. In the high places where walls can be found meandering for mile after mile across lonely fell and moor, often the only sign of man's existence, one may often find sheep huddled in their lee, and many a shepherd or hill walker struggling through the mist has been grateful for their protection.

As with hedges, there was a spate of wall building during the partition of land in the eighteenth and early nineteenth centuries, but some walls are very much older than this. These early walls probably began as lines of boundary stones used for the demarcation of land rights. Later they were developed into something more substantial, those in exposed places in particular being made capable of enduring year after year of wind, rain, frost and snow. In Tudor times it was the need to confine the all-important sheep on previously unused pastures which played an important part in this development and in the growth of the craft of the dry-stone waller.

The walls which these craftsmen built were, and still are, called dry-stone walls on account of the fact that no mortar is used in their construction. Such walls are held together entirely by their own weight and by the skilful placement of each separate piece of roughly shaped material. Their strength and durability lies in the fact that they are dry and stay dry. A wall of brick or even of dressed stone bonded with mortar would soon succumb to the effects of weathering, mainly owing to the water held in the material, which freezes and expands to cause serious erosion of the surface. By working without mortar, and by arranging his material to be free-draining and well ventilated, the dry-stone waller, or dyker as he is known in some areas, eliminates all the consequences of weather erosion.

Dry-stone walls also represent one of the best examples of good environmental planning, although their builders gave little heed to this at the time. Built of stone taken from the immediate area, and often incorporating outcrops of the same rock into the line of the wall in a most natural way, they harmonise perfectly with their surroundings.

To the casual observer all walls may look alike, but actually they differ both geographically and geologically. Variations relate partly to the temperament of the local sheep – determined Blackface or the more docile Downland breeds – and partly to the nature and structure of the rock found nearby. The northern granites, the gritstone and the hard carboniferous limestone of the Lake District and the Pennine fells form irregular shapes, for there is little horizontal bedding, while the softer stone of the Cotswolds and the easily cleft slate of Wales and the West Country form flat rectangles of varying thickness. The colour changes too – limestone's bleached silver whiteness, the sunlight yellow of Cotswold stone, the darker tones of sandstone and gritstone, those walls high above industrial towns smoke-begrimed and darker still, and finally the grey, green, blue and black of slate.

238

DRY-STONE WALLS

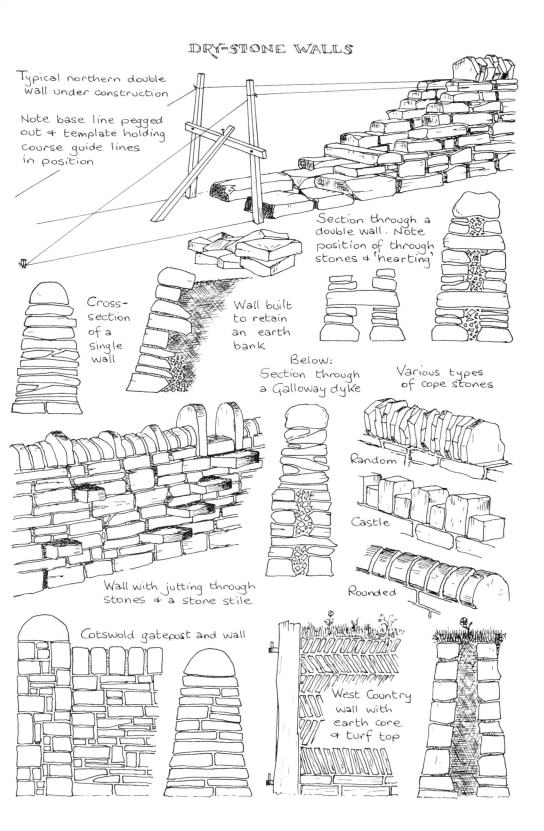

Typical northern double wall under construction

Note base line pegged out & template holding course guide lines in position

Section through a double wall. Note position of through stones & 'hearting'

Cross-section of a single wall

Wall built to retain an earth bank

Below: Section through a Galloway dyke

Various types of cope stones

Random

Castle

Rounded

Wall with jutting through stones & a stone stile

Cotswold gatepost and wall

West Country wall with earth core & turf top

52 A waller at work in Yorkshire. Template and guidelines are used to ensure that the wall is straight and uniform in section

Northern walls, or dykes as they are locally known, are of either single or double thickness, depending upon their height. Walls up to 4ft (1.2m) high are made single-thickness, most of the stone used in their construction being the full width of the wall. Walls which form estate boundaries or border roads are usually higher, perhaps 6ft (1.8m) or so. These are mostly of double thickness, two more or less separate walls with long 'through stones' set in at intervals to tie the two together. The intervening space, known to the waller as the heart, is filled with small pieces of rock to ensure free drainage and good ventilation throughout the entire structure.

The base line of the wall is first fixed with pegs and string and a stretch of foundation firmly levelled. A wooden frame or template corresponding to the profile or cross-section of the wall is set up at one end, and between this and a corresponding frame placed at a convenient distance strings are stretched and levelled to mark the courses of stones to be laid. Loads of stone in random sizes are then brought up – at one time by horse, but nowadays probably by mechanical transport – and placed at intervals close to the line of the wall, and the work can begin.

Foundation stones are selected and laid true in a double row to form a solid base which at this point is generally about 30in (75mm) wide. Smaller stones are then laid on these, selected according to shape and suitability and built up in courses, the builder working roughly to the string lines set out beforehand. Through stones are laid across at intervals, always in the same course but staggered along the length of the wall. These may be trimmed to the wall's thickness,

240

but often, if longer than the wall is wide, they are left protruding, either at the back of the wall only or equally on both sides. Stone step stiles which allow a wall to be climbed easily without dislodging any stones are made in a similar fashion. And as the work progresses the centre of the wall is filled with rock fragments, each as carefully placed as the stones in the rest of the wall. In cross-section the wall becomes narrower as it gets higher, the provision of this slight 'batter', as it is known, adding greatly to the stability of the completed wall.

In the best work two important points emerge. Firstly, as the adhesion of individual stones within the wall, and therefore the solidarity of the structure as a whole, depends upon weight, it is considered poor practice to build a wall with large stones in the lower half supporting progressively smaller ones above. These lighter top stones, unweighted in this type of construction, are easily dislodged, and although one often sees walls built in this way, for appearance's sake perhaps, the reverse procedure is the stronger. In practice most walls are built with stones of different sizes evenly dispersed. Secondly, if the stones are laid so that their top surface is inclined slightly downward and outward, rainwater and melting snow or ice tend to drain away from the heart of the wall and so help maintain its dryness.

A little below the desired height, the top of the wall is brought level and cope or coping stones are added to cap it. These are usually large flat or irregularly shaped stones laid on edge across the width of the wall. Sometimes smaller stones laid on edge have larger pieces wedged in tightly at intervals to give a castellated effect, known to some wallers as ducks and drakes. Often, where there are spaces along a wall, small wedge-shaped pieces of stone may be hammered in to give tension and to help consolidate the whole thing, making it not only sheep-proof but able to withstand the frequent pressure of gale-force winds.

In some areas, the application of a clever bit of animal psychology to this problem of sheep-proofing produced a type of wall known as the Galloway dyke. Noting that sheep, which scramble up and jump down from obstacles rather than jumping right over them, will not attempt anything which appears unsafe, Scottish dykers make their walls quite solid for the first 3ft (900mm) or so, but above this height place stones in such a way that plenty of daylight is visible between them. Apparently the sheep, thinking the wall is about to collapse, decide it is not worth attempting.

Where sheep and the environment are more gentle, walls of a quite different kind are built. Cotswold stone, being more regular in shape and more easily worked, can be placed closely together in a wall, angled turns and gateposts often being formed from pillars of dressed stone expertly fitted together. Walls are rarely more than 3ft or 4ft (0.9–1.2m) high, with a base of 20in (500mm) battered to a 15in (375mm) top. When constructed to a single thickness – that is, without a heart – they may not be built wholly of full-width stones, but rather of overlapping pieces with sufficient through stones to bind the whole together. Higher walls, where necessary, and quite a lot of the low ones, are of double thickness, the heart filled in with stone.

Garden walls may be constructed in a similar manner. Regular-shaped but random-sized stones look best and are easiest to work with. One can often buy stone soft enough and structurally suitable for rough dressing with simple tools, or second-hand material from demolition work, previously dressed professionally but now well weathered, can be used instead. Natural stone should be used in preference to 'reconstructed stone' or coloured concrete blocks. Low double walls filled with good soil and planted out with suitable plants make nice garden features. Similarly, terracing in a garden is effectively done by building suitable retaining walls in stone, embedding each into the soil bank. A batter of 2in to 1ft (50mm to 300mm), or about 10°, is recommended, and the wall should be made free-draining either by backfilling with stones or gravel, or by means of drainage holes, or by a combination of the two.

It is often the practice of Cotswold wallers to bind the coping stones, or combers, as they are known, with mortar. The idea, although hardly in keeping with the 'dry' principle, seems reasonable enough on the milder Downs, but the practice has spread and is now seen more and more frequently throughout the country. It is done mainly to save on maintenance costs, particularly in those areas where damage tends to be caused by human thoughtlessness or sheer vandalism. But it does complicate rebuilding if, as often happens, the stones below collapse.

In south-west Wales and throughout the counties of Devon and Cornwall, walls are built which often look more like grassy embankments. Small granite boulders, or pieces of slate or other rocks which fracture like slate, are used in their construction. Many are built against earth banks, while those built double-thickness as boundary walls have their hearts filled in with earth. Most are topped not with coping stones but with turves of grassy earth, and the whole wall on completion may be given a liberal covering of soil. Before long native grasses and other plants establish themselves along these earth baulks, and small trees and bushes growing from them are not an uncommon sight.

53 A typical West Country wall in herringbone pattern, filled with earth and topped with turf

242

Where the rock used is slate or similar material, it is prepared in pieces about 8in (200mm) square and about 1in (25mm) in thickness. On a firm foundation of larger stones, these are laid side by side, on edge, at an angle of about 30° from the vertical, facing opposite ways in alternate courses to form a herringbone pattern. Laid this way, the courses compress and wedge themselves together into a firm bond. Walls up to 6ft (1.8m) high may be built in this manner. Gateposts are of shaped pieces interlocked and cemented together, or perhaps a single large stone sunk upright into the ground, framing a view of fields and hills, or perhaps the sea.

In parts of Cornwall some of these walls are seen without the usual covering of plants. They are built from the waste material from tin mining, and the arsenic content of the stone inhibits plant growth of any kind so that the walls remain bare, free even of weeds, at all times.

Walling or dyking, wherever it is done, is mainly summer work; some full-time wallers work all the year round, weather permitting, but when the stone is wet or cold it is more difficult to handle, and in upland areas the winter winds and snow make work impossible. Frost is the biggest problem – a wall built with ice-encrusted stones will collapse in the spring when the ice melts and the stones settle.

The men who build these walls use few tools, relying mainly on their eyes and hands, the eyes sharp enough to pick out just the right piece of stone to use next, the hands hard and calloused from continual contact with their material. A 4lb (1.8kg) mason's hammer, and a crowbar for levering, are all they use in the north, where the stone is used largely as it is, with little dressing. Where some shaping does take place, a heavy waller's hammer with one flat face and one cutting edge is the tool most frequently used. In ideal conditions a good waller can build about 1sq yd (900mm²) of double wall in an hour.

The hedges and walls which snake across the countryside are an essential part of the agricultural scene, and over the centuries have become an almost natural feature of the environment. That many are of great antiquity is beyond doubt, while those made as recently as the eighteenth century mark an important phase of social history. Many miles of hedge and wall have gone now, victims of modern economics, but this process is slowing down and may soon cease altogether. The old skills do remain; in some areas competitions are still held at local shows. New hedges are being set and new walls built by caring farmers with an eye to the future and a grant from the government, while enterprising county councils, taking advantage of the same grant, are doing similar work along new and rebuilt roads. Perhaps, in time, we shall see more hand-laid hedges and fewer gaps in dry-stone walls.

Appendix 1:

FURTHER INFORMATION, DISPLAYS, COURSES

Museum of English Rural Life, University of Reading, Berks: agricultural and village social history; collections of tools and craft items; carts and waggons display.

Welsh Folk Museum, St Fagan's Castle, Cardiff: reconstructed buildings and workshops; Welsh crafts and domestic life collections.

Forestry Commission, Maywood Centre, near Warwick: pit sawing; pole lathe turning; woodland work.

West Yorkshire Folk Museum, Shibden Hall, Halifax: craft workshops including those of the wheelwright, cooper, blacksmith, etc; annual 'nineteenth-century crafts' event.

Colne Valley Museum, Golcar, Huddersfield, Yorks: preserved weavers' cottages; hand spinning and weaving; clog making; regular demonstrations.

Museum of Lakeland Life and Industry, Abbothall, Kendal, Cumbria: wheelwright's and painter's workshop; milling, mining and agricultural implements.

Weald and Downland Open Air Museum, Singleton, Chichester, Sussex: reconstructed buildings, coppicing, charcoal burning, saw pit etc.

Chair Museum, High Wycombe, Bucks: tools and representative collection of country chairs.

Many museums have country or folk life displays, as do various National Trust properties and other buildings open to the public.

The Council for Small Industries in Rural Areas (formerly the Rural Industries Bureau), now known as CoSIRA, provides information about country workshops in the *CoSIRA Guide to Country Workshops in Britain* (not all are 'country' crafts). See also their *Select List of Books and Information Sources on Trades, Crafts etc.* Both available from CoSIRA, Queen's House, Fish Row, Salisbury, Wiltshire.

Country crafts workers can sometimes be found at craft demonstrations, competitions and displays at county and agricultural shows, for example the Royal Show, held annually at the National Agricultural Centre, Kenilworth, Warwickshire, or the New Forest Show at Brockenhurst, Hampshire. A list of such shows in England and Wales is published by the Show and Breed Secretaries' Association, The Showground, Winthorpe, Newark, Nottinghamshire. For Scotland, Scottish Farmers' Publications Ltd, 39 York Street, Glasgow, publish a similar list.

Various crafts, including some country crafts, are also demonstrated at the growing number of fairs and festivals held throughout Britain, and at some craft centres. The Abbeydale Craftsman's Fair, organised annually by the Museums Department, Sheffield, Yorkshire, and the regular craft markets held at the Royal Exchange Theatre, Manchester – at both of which the author demonstrates chair making and other wood crafts – are two examples. Others include the Eastern Counties Craft Market, c/o Mrs P. Beswick, Thele, Great Amwell, Ware, Hertfordshire; the Living Crafts Exhibition, held at Hatfield House, Hertfordshire; and the Cheshire Arts Centre, Market Square, Chester.

The National Federation of Women's Institutes, 39 Eccleston Street, London SW1, runs crafts courses and publishes booklets on basketwork, rushwork and corn-dolly making. A list of summer schools where various courses (not all in country crafts) are organised is obtainable from the Educational Development Association, 8 Windmill Gardens, Enfield, Middlesex, while a number of privately-run craft and hobby holidays are advertised in travel and holiday magazines. Short residential and some daily crafts courses are held all the year round at West Dean College, Chichester, West Sussex.

Information of a general nature relating to crafts of all kinds can be obtained from the Crafts Advisory Committee, 12 Waterloo Place, London SW1, or from the Crafts Centre, 43 Earlham Street, London WC2. The Scottish Crafts Centre is at Acheson House, Cannongate, Edinburgh. In America the American Crafts Council, 29 West 53rd Street, New York, NY 10019, provides a similar service; the address of the Crafts Council of Australia is 27 King Street, Sydney 2000.

Appendix 2:

ADDRESSES OF SUPPLIERS

Materials

No one supplies materials specifically for country crafts. Some general suppliers of craft material can provide some items from normal stocks. Generally speaking, however, one must shop around specialist suppliers or utilise materials from local sources. The firms listed below can supply most of the materials required. See also *Guide to Craft Suppliers* by J. Allen (Studio Vista, London, 1974), the yellow pages in the telephone book, and the commercial directory.

BRITAIN
General
Hobby Horse, 15–17 Langton Street, London SW10
Arts and Crafts Unlimited, 49 Shelton Street, London WC2

Timber
Fitchett and Woollacott Ltd, Willow Road, Lenton Lane, Nottingham NG7 2PR
Porters, Station Road, Selby, Yorks

Steel
Tatham and Co, Stanley Road, Cheadle Hulme, Cheshire
Dunlop and Ranken Ltd, Whitehall Road, Leeds, Yorks

Leather
C. & D. Hudson, 3 Roland Way, Higham Ferrers, Northants
W. Jeffrey & Co, 88–90 Western Street, London SE1

Horn
Halesowen Horn Co, PO Box 5, Halesowen, Worcester

Willow, cane and rush
Deben Craftsmen, 9 St Peter's Street, Ipswich, Suffolk
Jacobs, Young and Westbury, Bridge Street, Haywards Heath, Sussex
J. W. Taylor, Basket Works, Ulleskelf, Tadcaster, Yorks

Wheat straw
David Keighley Crafts, 11 Dawley Road, Welwyn Garden City, Herts SG5 1DG

Fleece, rovings and wool yarn
Wool Marketing Board, Oak Mills, Clayton, Bradford, Yorks
Cambrian Factory Ltd, Llanwrtyd Wells, Powys, Wales

Craftsman's Mark Ltd, Trefnant, Denbigh, Wales
Robert Laidlaw & Sons, Seafield House, Keith, Scotland

Hemp and jute yarn
Southwick & Case, 89–91 Prescot Street, Liverpool 7

Rope, cord
Russel and Cheppel, Monmouth Street, London WC2

Clay
The Fulham Pottery, 210 New King's Road, London SW6 4NY
Podmore & Sons Ltd, New Caledonian Mills, Shelton, Stoke-on-Trent, Staffs ST3 7PX
Wengers Ltd, Garner Street, Etruria, Stoke-on-Trent, Staffs

NORTH AMERICA
General
Dick Blick, PO Box 1267, Galesburg, Illinois 61401
Economy Handicrafts, Inc, 50–21 69th Street, Woodside, NY 11377
See also *Where to Get What* from Penland School of Handicrafts, Penland, North Carolina

Steel
Allcraft Tool and Supply Co, 215 Park Avenue, Hicksville, NY 11801

Leather
Tandy Leather Co, 330 Fifth Avenue, New York, NY 10018
The Brown Leather Co, 305 Virginia Avenue, Joplin, Missouri 63042

Willow, cane and rush
Cane & Basket Supply Co, 1283 5th Cochran Avenue, Los Angeles, California 90019
Earth Guild, 149 Putnam Avenue, Cambridge, Massachusetts 02139

Wheat straw
J. L. Hammett Co, Hammet Place, Boston, Massachusetts 02184

Fleece, rovings and wool yarn
Countryside Handweavers, PO Box 1225, Mission, Kansas 66222
Robin & Russ Handweavers, 533 North Adams Street, McMinnville, Oregon 97128
Shuttlecraft, PO Box 6041, Providence, Rhode Island

Hemp and jute yarn
Magnolia Weaving, 2635 29th Avenue, West Seattle, Washington 98199

Rope, cord
Yarn Depot, Inc, 545 Sutter Street, San Francisco, California 94102

Clay
Trinity Ceramic Supply, Inc, 9016 Diplomacy Row, Dallas, Texas 75235
Berkshire Chemicals, 155 East 44th Street, New York City
American Art Clay Co, Inc, 4717 West 16th Street, Indianapolis, Indiana 46222

Tools and Equipment

BRITAIN
For woodwork, general
Joseph Gleave Ltd, Gateway House, Piccadilly Station Approach, Manchester
Buck & Hickman Ltd, PO Box 148, Adair Street, Manchester

Wood carving
Ashley Iles Ltd, Fenside, East Kirby, Spilsby, Lincs

Hand adze
Alex Tiranti Ltd, 70 High Street, Theale, Berks

Rotary plane
Griffin & George, Ledson Road, Wythenshawe, Manchester

For forgework
Buck & Ryan Ltd, 101 Tottenham Court Road, London W1

For leatherwork
Taylor & Co Ltd, 54 Old Street, London EC1V 9AL

For basketwork
Dryad, Northgates, Leicester

For spinning and weaving
The Hand Loom Centre, 59 Crest View Drive, Petts Wood, Kent
The Weaver's Workshop, Monteith House, Royal Mile, Edinburgh
T. Lund & Sons Ltd, Argyll Mills, Bingley, Yorks BD16 4JW

For pottery
Podmore & Sons Ltd, New Caledonian Mills, Shelton, Stoke-on-Trent, Staffs ST3 7PX
Pottery Equipment, 17–18 Progress Way, Croydon, Surrey CR4DH

NORTH AMERICA
For woodwork, general
Craftool Co, Inc, 1421 West 240th Street, Harbor City, California 90710

Wood carving
J. Johnson & Co, 33 Martinecook Avenue, Port Washington, NY 11050

For leatherwork
Tandy Leather Co, 330 Fifth Avenue, New York, NY 10018

For basketwork
Triarco Arts & Crafts, PO Box 106, Northfield, Illinois 60093

For spinning and weaving
Craftools Inc, 1 Industrial Road, Wood Ridge, New Jersey 07075

For pottery
American Art Clay Co, Inc, 4717 West 16th Street, Indianapolis, Indiana 46222

BIBLIOGRAPHY

General

ARNOLD, J., *The Countryman's Workshop* (Phoenix House, London, 1953; reprinted EP Publications, Wakefield, 1977)

——, *Shell Book of Country Crafts* (John Baker, London, 1968; reprinted 1977)

DERRICK, F., *Country Craftsmen* (Chapman & Hall, London, 1945)

EDLIN, H. L., *Woodland Crafts in Britain* (Batsford, London, 1947; reprinted David & Charles, Newton Abbot, 1974)

HARTLEY, D., *Made in England* (Eyre Methuen, London, 1939; reprinted 1977)

HENNELL, T., *The Countryman at Work* (Architectural Press, London, 1947)

HOGG, G., *Country Crafts and Craftsmen* (Hutchinson, London, 1959)

HUGHES, G. B., *Living Crafts* (Lutterworth Press, London, 1953)

JENKINS, J. G., *Traditional Country Craftsmen* (Routledge & Kegan Paul, London, 1965; revised 1978)

RANDOLPH, H. E., HAY, M. D., and JONES, A. M., *The Rural Industries of England and Wales* (4 volumes, Oxford University Press, 1926; reprinted EP Publications, 1977)

STOWE, F. J., *Crafts of the Countryside* (Longmans Green & Co, London, 1948; reprinted EP Publications, Wakefield, 1976)

WOODS, K. S., *Rural Crafts of England* (Oxford University Press, 1952; reprinted EP Publications, Wakefield, 1975)

WYMER, N., *English Country Crafts* (Batsford, London, 1946)

Tools and Devices

BLANDFORD, P., *Country Craft Tools* (David & Charles, Newton Abbot, 1974)

LAMBERT, F., *Tools and Devices for Coppice Crafts* (Evans Bros/Young Farmers Club booklet, 1957)

Sticks and Crooks

EDLIN, *Woodland Crafts in Britain*, pp 49 and 66

GRANT, D., and HART, E., *Shepherds' Crooks and Walking Sticks* (Dalesman Books, Clapham, Lancaster, 1972)

HART, E., *Hill Shepherd* (David & Charles, Newton Abbot, 1976)

HOGG, *Country Crafts and Craftsmen*, p 110

Rakes and Besoms

ARNOLD, *The Countryman's Workshop*, pp 85 and 95

EDLIN, *Woodland Crafts in Britain*, pp 31 and 32

HILL, J., 'Rake Making', *Woodworker* (March 1977), p 84
JENKINS, *Traditional Country Craftsmen*, pp 70 and 83
LAMBERT, *Tools and Devices for Coppice Crafts*, pp 38 and 39

Hurdle Making

ARNOLD, *The Countryman's Workshop*, p 75
JENKINS, *Traditional Country Craftsmen*, p 25
STOWE, *Crafts of the Countryside*, p 22

Clog Making

BAMFORTH, H., *The Clog Maker* (booklet, Colne Valley Museum, Golcar, Huddersfield, Yorks)
EDLIN, *Woodland Crafts in Britain*, pp 24 and 25
JENKINS, *Traditional Country Craftsmen*, pp 22 and 25

Wood Turning

ARNOLD, *The Countryman's Workshop*, p 67
HUGHES, *Living Crafts*, p 90
PAIN, F., *The Practical Wood Turner* (Evans Bros, London, 1957)

Wood Carving

ARNOLD, *Shell Book of Country Crafts*, p 190
JACK, G., *Wood Carving: Design and Workmanship* (Pitman, London, 1950)
MORTON, P., *The Carver's Companion* (A. & C. Black, London, 1950)

Chair Making

ARNOLD, *The Countryman's Workshop*, p 37
EDLIN, *Woodland Crafts of Britain*, pp 151 and 152
GLOAG, J., *The Englishman's Chair* (Allen & Unwin, London, 1964)
SPARKES, I., *The English Country Chair* (Spur Books, Bourne End, Bucks, 1973)

Coopering

HUGHES, *Living Crafts*, p 98
JENKINS, *Traditional Country Craftsmen*, p 89

Carpentry

ARNOLD, *The Countryman's Workshop*, p 117
BAYLISS, R., *Carpentry and Joinery* (Hutchinson, London, 1966)
PINTO, E. H., *The Craftsman in Wood* (Bell, London, 1962)
ROSE, W., *The Village Carpenter* (Cambridge University Press, 1937; reprinted EP Publishing, 1976)

Wheelwrighting

ARNOLD, *Farm Waggons of England and Wales* (Baker, London, 1969)
——, *The Countryman's Workshop*, p 145
DERRICK, *Country Craftsmen*, p 62
JENKINS, *The English Farm Wagon* (David & Charles, Newton Abbot, 1961; new ed 1972)
STURT, G., *The Wheelwright's Shop* (Cambridge University Press, 1930)

Blacksmithing

COSIRA, *The Blacksmith's Craft* (Council for Small Industries in Rural Areas, Queen's House, Fish Row, Salisbury, Wilts, 1952)
——, *Wrought Ironwork* (1957)
——, *Decorative Ironwork* (1962)
HOGG, G., *Hammer and Tongs* (Hutchinson, London, 1964)
LISTER, G. B., *Decorative Wrought Ironwork in Great Britain* (David & Charles, Newton Abbot, 1970)
STOWE, *Crafts of the Countryside*, p 46
WEBBER, R., *The Village Blacksmith* (David & Charles, Newton Abbot, 1971)

Harness Making

ARNOLD, *The Countryman's Workshop*, p 25
EVANS, G. E., *The Horse in the Furrow* (Faber, London, 1960), chapters 16 and 17
HASLUCK, P. N. (ed), *Saddlery and Harness Making* (J. A. Allen, London, 1962)
ROSEMAN, I. R., *Leatherwork* (Dryad, Leicester, 1965)
WOODS, *Rural Crafts of England*, p 82

Hornwork

ABBEY HORN, booklet (Abbey Horn Co, Kendal, Cumbria)
BORGLAND, E. and FLAUENSGAARD, J., *Working in Plastic, Bone, Amber and Horn* (Van Nostrand, Reinhold, New York, 1968)
HUGHES, *Living Crafts*, p 151

Basket Making

ARNOLD, *The Countryman's Workshop*, p 125
EDLIN, *Woodland Crafts*, p 86
HOGG, *Country Crafts and Craftsmen*, pp 23 and 52
KNOCK, A. G., *Willow Basket-work* (Dryad, Leicester, 1970)
WRIGHT, D., *Complete Book of Baskets and Basketry* (David & Charles, Newton Abbot, 1977)

Rushwork

BROWN, M., *Cane and Rush Seating* (Batsford, London, 1976)
FLORENCE, N., *Rushwork* (Bell, London, 1962)
WRIGHT, *Complete Book of Baskets and Basketry*, p 106

Thatch and Straw

COSIRA, *The Thatcher's Craft* (1961)
SANDFORD, L. and DAVIES, P., *Decorative Straw Work* (Batsford, London, 1964)
STOWE, *Crafts of the Countryside*, p 94
WOODS, *Rural Crafts of England*, p 192

Spinning and Weaving

DAVENPORT, E. G., *Your Handspinning* (Sylvan Press, London, 1953)
SIMPSON, L. E. and WEIR, W., *The Weaver's Craft* (Dryad, Leicester, 1932; 9th ed 1963)
SHILLINGLAW, P., *Introducing Weaving* (Batsford, London, 1972)
TOVEY, J., *The Technique of Weaving* (Batsford, London, 1975)

Rope Making

FRY, E. C., *Shell Book of Knots and Ropework* (David & Charles, Newton Abbot, 1978)
HENNELL, *The Countryman at Work*, p 53
HUGHES, *Living Crafts*, p 79
WOODS, *Rural Crafts of England*, p 92

Bricks and Pottery

ARNOLD, *The Countryman's Workshop*, p 107
BILLINGTON, D. and COLBECK, J., *The Technique of Pottery* (Batsford, London, 1964)
WOODS, *Rural Crafts of England*, pp 214 and 227

Hedging and Walling

STOWE, *Crafts of the Countryside*, pp 30 and 38
WOODS, *Rural Crafts of England*, p 182

INDEX

Figures in bold type refer to illustrations